Living with the Active Alert Child

Groundbreaking Strategies for Parents

Third Edition

Linda S. Budd, Ph.D.

Parenting Press, Inc.
Seattle, Washington

**This book is dedicated
to the ones I love:**

Jeff, Heather, and Kimberly

The stories that open each part of this book are actual accounts submitted to me in letter form by parents. I have changed certain identifying features, such as names and professions, to protect the privacy of the parents who so graciously permitted me to use their experiences. In addition, names and various identifying characteristics were changed in the anecdotes and case histories that appear throughout this book.

Copyright © 2003, Third edition, Parenting Press, Inc.
Copyright © 1993, Revised edition, Parenting Press, Inc.
Copyright © 1990, First edition, Prentice Hall Press

Cover design by Magrit Baurecht
Printed in the United States of America

Library of Congress Cataloging-In-Publication Data

Budd, Linda S.
   Living with the active alert child : groundbreaking strategies for parents / Linda S. Budd.-- 3rd ed.
   p. cm
Includes bibliographical references and index.
ISBN 1-884734-77-4 (pbk)
   1. Parenting--United States. 2. Parents and child--United States. I. Title.
HQ755.8.B83 2003
649'.1--dc21

                                                           2003042864

Parenting Press, Inc.
P.O. Box 75267
Seattle, WA 98175
www.ParentingPress.com

Acknowledgments

Many people come together to help in what finally becomes a book. I thank my husband, Jeffrey, who remains one of this work's most ardent advocates. I also remember my daughters Heather and Kimberly who are my teachers in parenting. Lest I should ever become too cocky about parenting or myself as a parent, they have been sent to me as pathways to my own humility. Then, of course there's Lonnie Bell who poetically turns my words into clear, direct reading. I remember my teachers: Dr. Victoria Jacobson, who constantly serves as a guidepost and reminder about how children learn; Dr. Richard Hey, who celebrates in my "reflected" glory as I celebrated his for so many years; and Dr. Richard Fowler, who is a mentor of my spirit.

Then I cannot forget the parents. Anna Fussell and Tom Crane are two of the world's best cheerleaders. I'm glad they are on the team that promoted acceptance and nurturing of children. Patti Spang, Susan Sykes, Anna Fussell, and others share their lives and stories in letters I've used in this book. There are also the hundreds of parents I hear from, both nationally and internationally. They call or write. They come to hear my speeches. I am honored that my work has been useful to so many parents of active alerts.

Of course, I always want to thank the children, both the active alerts and the sure and steady, for they are my teachers.

Personal Message to Readers

Philosophy or Excuse?

As the creator of the term **active alert,** I would like to clarify that active alert is a temperament. It's there at birth. I believe it is a great gift. However, with the gift, as with all gifts, comes a down side—certain weaknesses. Active alerts find it difficult to let go of control, to deal with the intensity of emotions, to admit mistakes, to see a disagreement from another's perspective, and to slow down to gain another's perspective.

The term active alert is not an excuse for a child to continue acting in a way that will not help him or her to belong later in life. It is a philosophy—a philosophy of understanding. When a four-year-old has trouble recognizing his friend's boundaries, or is bossy in a mean way, saying he is active alert is not an excuse for his behavior. The understanding of the source of his behavior is meant to give you patience while you try to teach a much needed social skill to a child who wasn't born knowing it. It is meant to help you understand which areas you as the parent might particularly need to nourish and encourage in your child. When you understand what an active alert is, you also understand his or her own strengths and weaknesses and which coping strategies the child needs to learn.

Contents

Part IV

BEYOND CHILDHOOD	*213*

Part I

LOVING YOUR ACTIVE ALERT CHILD

When we first read Living with the Active Alert Child *three years ago we were astonished at how well you captured life with our daughter. It seems as if you've been a mouse in our house all these years.*

We have an active alert daughter who is now ten years old. We discovered your work through a speech you gave when she was about seven. We had already figured out many of the ways you would have suggested handling her. What we would have paid not to have learned those tricks the hard way! Besides the ones we used that were being affirmed, there were many new ideas which we have subsequently found very useful. All we can say is thank you from the bottom of our hearts.

Let me tell you about Meghan. My husband and I had Meghan in our early 30's. The pregnancy went beautifully. The birth, however, was long and with back labor. Meghan kept slipping back after crowning so after a 24-hour labor with two hours of pushing, she was delivered using outlet forceps. Meghan had no marks from the delivery. She was admired by the nursing staff—a beautiful baby girl with blonde hair. We came home after two nights only to have to readmit Meghan for jaundice a couple of days later. Meghan, except for 24 hours under the lights, was always with me. From the moment of birth she slept very little, crying often as I nursed her every couple of hours all through the day and night.

As Meghan grew, we developed ways of holding her so she could see the world. She accepted my husband as an alternate caregiver, but no one else. Grandmother tried babysitting Meghan when she was between three and nine months of age, but Meghan screamed the whole time. That was the end of grandmother as a sitter. Once when my husband and I went out to dinner, four-month-old Meghan screamed at the woman we left her with (a mother of two herself) for the two hours we were gone. She trained us not to leave her until she was in bed for the night.

When she was a toddler, we developed elaborate strategies to help her sleep. We walked her in order to help her nap; she woke up soon after we finally put her down. All of this occurred while others continued to admire her and say what a beautiful, charming child she was.

Her medical history is incredible. At nine months, while pulling herself up using the couch and turning to reach the coffee table, she fractured her tibia. At two years, she would have small seizures when she fell and hit her head. Her doctors determined these were just two-year-old head traumas. At seven, she fell and broke her wrist while playing in the backyard. At eight, she fractured her thumb, catching it in the car door. At ten, she fell out of a tree. Needless to say, she's a very active child. Given her activity level and the number of risks she takes, we believe the number of fractured bones and other injuries is really quite minimal. Oh, and need I mention the number of times I've had to call the poison control center wondering if this thing she's put in her mouth is poisonous!

Meghan is bossy, precocious, intense, sensitive, bright, and all that you describe. I always thought I was somehow at fault for the difficult aspects of her personality. After all, as a child psychology major, I believed environment was almost everything. When she began preschool, I was relieved and surprised that the teacher found her "delightful," "busy," and clearly a "budding young gymnast." I was interested to observe that Meghan absolutely thrived in the preschool structure and routine. Kindergarten proved to be more of a challenge as her teacher was structured, but lacked warmth. This scared Meghan and, although she was with all her best friends from preschool, she was not excited about going, Luckily for us, she was back with an excellent teacher in the first grade, who was warm and structured. Meghan renewed her faith in school that year. Since then I've dropped discreet hints to the principal about who I think would work best with Meghan. I've sure he thinks I'm just being protective. Since she does very well at school in both her behavior and academics, he doesn't get to see her at her "emotional best." When she was eight and in the school play, he came up to compliment me on what a self-confident child we had. My husband and I loved the complement, but privately we knew she was still too scared to try a hot lunch at school even though sometimes she thought it looked good.

Meghan still has difficulty with transition times. She "falls apart" when she gets home. She still struggles with who the boss is in our house. She's always correcting her little brother. I'm always assuring her that I am here to parent both of them and that she doesn't need to correct him. All subjects excite her at school, but her favorites are math, music, drama, and art. At home she has hundreds of "good ideas" and "projects" galore. She has written neighborhood newspapers, formed an acting club, and created hundreds of wonderful artworks. She loves to write poetry, and I love to read it.

Life with Meghan is easier now, but not easy. She definitely keeps me on my toes. I both fear for her future and believe all things are possible. Thanks for helping us understand her better and for letting us know we are not alone.

1

Do You Live with an Active Alert Child?

I hold you! I love you, I name you . . .
—Madeleine L'Engle
A Wind in the Door

If you put on your running shoes when your child was born and have worn out several pairs watching her grow, this book is for you. If you can't keep the toilet paper on the roll in your house because your child constantly unravels it, this book is for you.

This book is meant for you if you have read other parenting books and think, "They're not talking about my child—it's just not that easy." If you have begun to question what you did to create this little person or to deserve this kind of child, this book is for you.

You have a child some call active, difficult, obstreperous—a child who some see as a problem. You have a child who takes all your energy during the course of the day and then demands more at bedtime. You have a child who gives you a roller coaster ride with high points of incredible joy and low points of anger and frustration.

In a sense, I know and love your child. That's because for thirty years, parents like you have come to me and asked for help. What emerged from my work with those families was an image of a child who doesn't fit the "norm," who slips through the cracks of what "experts" know about child rearing, who has *more* energy, *more* creativity, *more* intensity—*more everything.*

To help you understand your child and because I love him, I have named your child. I call him* *active alert.*

I do not do this lightly. I understand the significance of naming. In biblical times, people believed that a person's self was concentrated in his name. Thus when Jacob was renamed Israel, it signified he had a new self or identity. In her book *The Hero Within,* Carol Pearson defines naming as one way that helps people know who they are. When we name a person, we spotlight his differences as gifts. While labeling suggests that everyone must be similar, naming, in contrast, acknowledges differences, allowing us to value them.

According to Carol Pearson, when we name a thing, we affirm the truth about it. Call your child difficult and you may set up a self-fulfilling prophecy. Your child is not difficult: *parenting* her is. Call a child active alert and you acknowledge the traits that best explain who she is distinct from your experience of parenting her. Both words connote positive traits, and all children are, to some extent, active and alert.

I coined the term "active alert" after studying T. Berry Brazelton's work on the temperaments of infants. Brazelton, a noted Harvard pediatrician, categorized infants as active, average, or quiet. It seemed to me that within the subset of active infants, some were as alert as they were active. The term is also derived from the work of Stella Chess and Alexander Thomas, two psychiatrists who studied temperament in individuals by following them from birth until their early thirties.

The term "active alert" is not, however, a diagnosis. It is not meant to typecast or restrict your child or keep him from fulfilling

---

*Because we are discussing both boys and girls, female and male pronouns are used alternately throughout this book.

his potential. It is simply a way to think about, understand, and affirm your unique child.

■ ■ ■

Hilary Forth, an eight-year-old character from the comic strip "Sally Forth," is one of my favorite examples of an active alert. In one episode, Hilary comes into the room and says, "I'm not going to do it and that's it, no way, final!"

Her mother, Sally, suggests that Hilary sit in her bedroom and reconsider.

"You can make me stay in my room a jillion years and I'm still not going to do it," Hilary declares.

"Now, Hilary, don't make me punish you."

"We seem to be at an impasse here; maybe you should consult the book," Hilary answers.

"The book?"

"The book on parenting. You always read it when you are worried how to handle me."

"You know about the book?"

"Get in the game, Mom; kids know about these things."

"They do?"

Now Hilary suggests, "Here, read the part that says it's bad for my little psyche to crush my budding assertiveness. It's all on page forty-two."

*"First, let me read the chapter about how children manipulate their parents," Sally mutters.**

COULD YOUR CHILD BE AN ACTIVE ALERT?

Does any of this sound familiar? The following assessment should help you decide whether or not you have an active alert child.

---

*Reprinted with special permission of North American Syndicate, Inc.

1. Does your child have seemingly unending energy?
2. Can your child attend to a task, such as being read to or playing a game with a parent?
3. Does (did) your child wake up a lot at night or have difficulty getting to sleep?
4. Does (did) your child seem to need very little sleep as an infant or toddler?
5. Would the last words from your child's mouth be "I'm tired"?
6. Does your child seem to "wind up" over the course of a day; that is, the energy seems to build upon itself?
7. Does your child's memory of details amaze you?
8. Is your child quick or bright in certain areas of learning?
9. Does your child have an unending fount of "good ideas"?
10. Does your child want his way most of the time and have difficulty accepting a "no" answer?
11. Does it seem as if your child tries to be the "boss" of your family or her friends?
12. Did you miss the "terrible twos" in your child's development because you never experienced anything else?
13. In new situations is your child more uncertain or fearful than others?
14. Is your child intensely emotional—very happy or very sad—with little in between?
15. Does your child experience a pattern of moods—from positive to negative and back again—that seem hard for him to control?
16. Is it difficult for your child to play alone, especially up to age six or seven?
17. Is it difficult for your child to determine how to be a good friend, that is, she either sits and watches others or tries to be the boss?
18. Does your child think he is just terrific or totally stupid with little ability to believe that he might be just average or okay?
19. Do other people say they have no difficulty with your child?
20. Do you sometimes wonder if your child has "read your mind"?

If you answered yes to the majority of these questions and feel you will answer yes throughout your child's life, read on.

I know the challenges you face. I also know techniques that will help you in parenting your child. I believe that when parenting an active alert child, you can continue to learn and grow with the challenge.

What follows, then, are some insights that will help you stay with the parenting process and help you become the parent you want to be: one who affirms and delights in your active alert child.

2

The Eleven Traits of an Active Alert Child

You are named! My arms surround you.
You are no longer nothing. You are.

—Madeleine L'Engle
A Wind in the Door

A short time after I began my practice as a therapist specializing in parenting, I noticed some patterns emerging in families who lived with a certain type of child. Often such families arrived with their child's assessment papers in hand. Since various test results, including those for attention deficit, indicated that nothing was "wrong" with these children, frustrated therapists, counselors, and other professionals assumed that something must be "wrong" with the parenting.

As I worked with these families it began to dawn on me that these children, who clearly did not fit any other categories, were, in fact, similar to one another. They seemed to comprise a category in and of themselves. I began to document those similarities. What eventually evolved was the following list of eleven characteristic traits that distinguish the active alert child from other children. Those traits are:

- Active
- Alert
- Bright
- Controlling
- Fearful
- Intense
- Attention-hungry
- Trouble getting along with others
- Fluctuating self-esteem
- Performers
- Empathic ability

TRAIT 1: ACTIVE

What does it mean to be active?

■ ■ ■

When I was little, I used to watch "The Three Stooges." They made me nervous. They were constantly in motion. Frenzied energy seemed to explode from them. Watching the energy of active alerts at their active best reminds me of those three comedians. The best example of a perpetual motion machine can be found in an active alert child at age two, three, or four.

Parents often tell me their child's high activity level was present at birth, if not in utero. In infancy, the activity may exhibit itself as sleeplessness. Many parents come to my office with dark circles under their eyes, telling a tale of physical exhaustion.

Most parenting books describe a newborn who sleeps ten of the twelve daylight hours. These parents say that their child sleeps only two hours a day. Needing relatively little sleep as an infant is a consistent feature of an active alert. Infancy is when the isolation and craziness begin for parents. Instead of finding solace in knowing their child was born "different," they begin to worry.

My friend Francis, who raises dogs, tells me, "Anyone who's ever bred dogs knows each one is different. Each has his own personality. Some are cuddly, some spirited." Although behaviorists know that certain findings about animals can be extended to humans, for some reason they do not address the differences in temperament apparent at birth in children. This is why many parents believe that when their child does not develop "by the book," it is somehow their fault.

My first message to you, then, is: *You didn't create this temperament.* Your child was born with it.

■ ■ ■

Brenda recalls that when her four-month-old Korean baby was carried off the plane, "She was so awake and aware of the world, she had the face of a ten-year-old."

Pediatricians have noted this feature for years. They may even say, "Oh, you have one of the intense ones." The longer you live with your little person, the more you will know that this is true.

Second, *being active is not to be confused with being hyperactive.* Your child can, and will, attend well to things on which he wishes to focus. Perhaps you remember reading several books in a row to your small child while he sat in rapt attention. You know he can watch television and can keep his mind on games. Although they are active—at times frenzied—active alert children do not exhibit the constant motor activity we associate with hyperactivity—the kind that cannot be stopped.

In fact, movement is your child's learning tool. Think about this in relation to a "fussy baby." If you learned best through movement but you could not yet crawl or walk, wouldn't you be "fussy" or colicky too?

Even for older children, this holds true. Does your child move constantly and stay busy with one thing after another?

■ ■ ■

When six-year-old Susan converses with her mother, she uses her hands and feet to shinny up a door frame. Susan is paying attention; it's just that moving allows her to focus better on what her mom is saying.

As a result of his penchant for movement, your active alert child may lose interest in a task more quickly than do other children, especially if the task is not one that he chose. Over the course of the day he may scoot through many different activities, with his productivity nothing short of amazing.

■ ■ ■

When Tommy was five, he told his mother, "My head is busy." Joe said to his dad, "I have music in my head."

Wonderful ideas constantly burst forth from these children! It is truly incredible to observe the "idle" hours of the active alert. The amount of artwork they produce in a day, the number of block buildings they create in an afternoon, boggles the mind.

■ ■ ■

When four-year-old Nathan went to his room for quiet space and decided to work on art, he often produced forty art pieces in about thirty minutes.

But don't let this activity level deceive you. Many parents believe that these children can go forever without getting tired and that, eventually, they simply fall over and go to sleep. Not true.

Young active alert children cannot settle themselves down. If you do not stop your child and provide an environment conducive to unwinding, he will wind himself up like a spinning top and eventually whirl out of control. Overstimulation can lead to trouble for the active alert child who does not know how to block the stimuli he himself creates.

As an attentive parent, you may already know when your child is headed for trouble. Have you spotted that place within your child where normal, high levels of activity suddenly change to a kind of frenzied energy? One of my clients refers to this as "crash and burn." Watch for and monitor it. When your child moves from purposeful activity to a frenzied energy, she is signaling you for external aid. Depending on your child's age, you need, directly or indirectly, to intervene.

It may help to place your child's activity on an energy scale of one to ten. What you want to do is create an environment that allows him to go to eight, then back to three, then up to seven, and so forth. Never let your child get to ten and stay there all day. I find that the best way to relax active alert children is to help them harness physical activity. Stretch them out; relax them through ritualized, controlled movement. As a long-term goal, begin teaching your child how to set and modify his own pace.

TRAIT 2: ALERT

Aren't all children alert?

■ ■ ■

Imagine that "Star Trek" is real and Scotty has beamed you down to the surface of an alien planet. As far as you know, you are the only one of your species there. The sights, sounds, smells, tastes, and textures of the planet are different from anything you've ever encountered. In order to understand as many new stimuli as possible, you keep yourself awake; you observe everything above, below, and around you. You are consumed by new sights, sounds, smells, tastes, and textures. Each second you learn more! You do not want to stop and rest; you must absorb as much as possible about the environment and inhabitants of this planet because, ultimately, it is what you know that will insure your future well-being.

How like an alien planet our world must feel to a newborn child. No longer secure in the tight confines of the womb, his new space must seem limitless, endlessly exciting and dangerous. Think of what he has to learn! How will he move around? What things are a threat? Who can he trust? Just how much control does he have, anyway? Removed from his warm, dark home, he now must cope with cold, wet diaper cloth against tender skin and hunger pangs.

The bright, alert newborn soon finds that crying elicits several responses. So does smiling. He quickly learns that life is more exciting when another person is around, so he develops ways to get attention and stimulation. New tastes, smells, the excitement of human touch—who could sleep with all this going on? Until the alert child, with his sensitive antennae, learns to trust his environment and the people in it, he may be unable to relax.

Alertness has four components, each with its own distinct advantages and disadvantages.

1. Alert children are keen observers.

Advantage.	They notice things that others don't.
Disadvantage.	They may notice things that hurt them, but fearing that they will miss something, they do not turn away.

2. Alert children have no boundaries for self.

Advantage.	They explore everything.
Disadvantage.	They become overstimulated or take in information they aren't ready to understand.

3. Alert children have no boundaries for others.

Advantage.	They get what they want more often when they intrude or violate other people's space.
Disadvantage.	They may not make friends easily. They anger people whose space they violate.

4. Alert children have no sense of boundaries in the form of rules for appropriate behavior.

Advantage.	Their keen observational and advanced language abilities help them to detect inconsistently applied rules.
Disadvantage.	Their lack of knowledge about boundaries makes it difficult for them to determine whether they should or should not try to get their own way.

Let's look at these four aspects of alertness in more detail.

1. Keen Observers

Your active alert misses nothing.

■ ■ ■

Without telling his mother, six-year-old Jeff took off on his bike to Grandma's house. His grandmother lived more than three miles away, and Jeff traveled a route that his parents had not driven the past year because of construction. Upon his return, his mother asked him to show her which roads he had taken. She was amazed at his powers of recollection.

■ ■ ■

In the second grade, Carrie explained to her mother why a certain teacher made her uncomfortable: "Mrs. Jones never smiles at children, only at adults." What an astute observation for a seven-year-old! Carrie not only knew the teacher made her uncomfortable but also could assess and express what caused her discomfort.

■ ■ ■

Terry, age four, ate breakfast one day while the radio was on. Later he asked his mom why someone had beaten a baby. Clearly, he had heard the news segment that was only background noise to the other children in the family.

Evidence of this keen observational ability usually is present at birth. Parents describe how, with wide, penetrating eyes their newborn infants take in the birthing room, absorbing their new world. Their lack of need for sleep often confuses parents. What parents do *not* understand is that although the child does indeed need sleep, his alertness keeps him from letting go.

Clothing preference may be another early indicator of how well your child observes. Many active alert children are sensitive to certain textures. I know of one two-year-old who would wear only silky underwear. Another child insisted on Orlon socks. Each child was very much in touch with physical sensation and could describe in detail how specific fabrics felt.

2. Having No Boundaries for Self

Do you remember a time when you allowed your active alert toddler to stay up too late, only to find he then had trouble settling down and he woke frequently during the night? Did you interpret this as a sign that he was not really sleepy? Or did you realize that the opposite was the case—your child was overstimulated?

Have you let your toddler stay up late thinking it would tire her out and help her sleep better, only to realize that you have started a cycle of overstimulation and tiredness that lasts for several nights?

Active alert children are alert to all sensations. Unable to stop watching and block out the world, they are constantly stimulated—sometimes, bombarded—by all they take in.

Many active alerts rise at dawn. Full of life, they greet the world smiling, eager to learn more. Unfortunately, as the parent of an active alert, you may not feel like smiling back at 5:30 each morning!

Studies indicate that people have different abilities to block out the external world. Some can do it simply by closing their eyes. Others, with their eyes open, can retreat inside themselves for periods of time and simply are not available to the outside world. Psychologists refer to these people as "screeners." The active alert child is a nonscreener.

■ ■ ■

Sasha's parents took their four-month-old to a Thanks- giving gathering where relatives oohed and aahed over her. After about two hours, unable to screen out the relatives' delight, she began screaming. She cried frantically while her parents dressed her in her snowsuit and continued to scream for the first fifteen minutes of the car ride home.

3. Having No Boundaries for Others

Active alert children do not recognize other people's boundaries. They believe that the "other" in their lives—friend, parent—also has no boundaries. They cannot understand why it is not okay to hug and kiss a friend who does not want to be smothered with affection.

■ ■ ■

*Timmy's father described the way his son liked to talk—
nose to nose. "It drives me crazy," he said.*

■ ■ ■

*Sam's mother told me her son climbs all over her "like a
little monkey on my back."*

■ ■ ■

*Judd's mother asked me, "Is it normal that my five-year-old
son touches my breasts when trying to get my attention?"
(Yes, it is. For an active alert, this is not a sexual matter, it's
a matter of sensation.)*

Active alerts need to touch and feel. Since they have no
physical boundaries of their own, they can't understand why
other people set limits. Dealing with this trait is especially
difficult for parents who feel guilty about pushing their intrusive
active alert away from them.

Property boundaries present another problem. Active alert
children do not always understand what belongs to them and
what belongs to other people. Again, this is not a moral failing. It
is a behavior born of your child's limitless exploring.

I know I am dealing with an active alert preschool child when,
during the course of his first visit with me, he explores my entire
office. Such children who come to see me think nothing of
looking inside my cupboards, drawers, and files, under the desk,
and behind the couch. The active alert child does not know that
this is unacceptable social behavior. After all, at home he explores
the whole house—his parents' drawers, the kitchen cupboards,
under the dining room table—every nook and cranny. Why?
Because it's there!

4. Boundaries in the Form of Rules

Your child also does not acknowledge boundaries about
appropriate behavior. Because boundaries do not exist for him, he
believes that all "walls" are made of Jell-O and can be reshaped
to his needs. And you know where that leads—to years of endless
negotiation.

How do you bring social conscience and moral sense to a child who cannot grasp the concept of "limits"? How do you set rules for an active alert?

You help her *learn* how to establish boundaries. Remember that all things are negotiable for your active alert child. Tell her she can play video games for ten more minutes and she'll want twenty until, if you let her, she's negotiated fifteen. She'll negotiate for another ten minutes before bed, two more bites of carrots in exchange for dessert, and on and on and on.

Sound familiar? In chapter 4 we'll discuss how you can and must help your child see the limits, the walls. Life has them. And active alerts need them. My work has shown me time and again that when they are placed in a structured environment, these children feel secure and flourish.

TRAIT 3: BRIGHT

How bright are these children?

■ ■ ■

When Amy was four she was chatting with a family friend while riding in a car. "What is the biggest number in the world?" Amy asked. "Infinity," the friend replied.

"How big is infinity?"

"Nobody really knows; they have never counted that far."

Amy then said, "Well, how do they know it exists?"

Active alert children are bright. Most of them test into their schools' gifted programs. Many come to see me with high IQ and aptitude test scores in hand. Yet active alert children are different from traditionally gifted children. Some gifted programs may actually overstimulate them and raise competition anxiety within them. Active alert children learn differently, as we will discuss in chapter 8.

■ ■ ■

First grader Stephen tested into the high-potential program at his elementary school. After several weeks in the program, however, he told his mother, "I don't like to go to that other room. I can't get my own work done. When I come back to class, I'm so far behind." Stephen's parents decided to withdraw him from the program for a while.

Beyond the intelligence measured by standardized tests, these children possess other unique talents—some of which are not as easily measured.

■ ■ ■

Bobby had a shaky beginning at his preschool screening. The first tester did not introduce herself and simply commanded Bobby to stack the blocks in front of him. He ignored her. Another screener approached, introduced herself, and asked him if he'd like to play some games with her. Bobby whizzed through the screening, completing all tasks well. In fact, he was marked "wrong" for only one response. To the question "What are windows made of?" he answered "squares and rectangles." Now, I ask you, would you have marked him wrong?

The "rights" and "wrongs" of standardized tests are difficult for active alerts to grasp. Often, they have an advanced understanding of spatial relationships (do you recall six-year-old Jeff, who remembered the route to Grandma's house?). I know one active alert five-year-old who can take apart a fan and put it back together again. He doesn't really understand how the fan works, but he has an amazing memory of how things fit together: He actually remembers the pattern in his hands.

Our educational and testing systems don't always recognize or help develop the active alert child's many gifts. As a result, many of my colleagues and I have grave concerns about the validity of how we measure children's abilities.

Can a preschool screening really accurately measure Bobby's extraordinary ability? What would have happened to him if the second tester had not intervened? Would he have been labeled "not ready" for kindergarten? Other active alert children face the problem of "test anxiety" because they find it hard to be in groups.

What can you, as a parent, do about this? You need to become an advocate. You spend more time with your child than anyone else does and are aware of his special gifts. You know how he observes, understands, and uses his knowledge to considerable advantage. Above all, consider these abilities as gifts, not drawbacks, and communicate with your child's teachers from that standpoint. We will say more about this in chapter 8.

TRAIT 4: CONTROLLING

Don't all children try to get their way?

■ ■ ■

Imagine that you have plans to go out with a friend who is not as energetic, verbal, or just plain smart as you are. The bottom line is that you are the one with the fun ideas. Wouldn't you take control and decide what the two of you were going to do that evening?

Active alert children have a high need for control. They are highly verbal and often use those skills to their advantage.

Have you wondered why your active alert child appears to manipulate his playmates—even "boss" them around? It's because he doesn't know he has no "right" to control others. Remember, he does not distinguish boundaries. If allowed, he will continue with such manipulative behavior because he gains a lot from it. How so? Active alerts often have such creative play ideas that peers willingly follow along, even if it means they will surely be dominated.

■ ■ ■

Billy is well known as the boy who organizes neigh-borhood children to write and distribute newspapers, put on plays, operate lemonade stands, and plan bike races. As long as other children have some choice about how they will participate, Billy's events are wonderfully positive.

Your active alert child needs to learn to cooperate and include other people's ideas. She also needs to learn to adjust to her family's needs. It is great to have good ideas, but it is also good to be able to incorporate and build on other people's ideas. You can accomplish all this without squashing her wonderful leadership qualities. We will address this dilemma in detail in chapters 4 and 6.

On a different but related subject are issues of control with regard to siblings that surface in troubling ways for the active alert. It is not uncommon for parents and siblings to tell the active alert child, "You are not the parent."

Often active alerts will decide how a sister or brother should be raised and make their thoughts on the subject known to everyone within earshot.

■ ■ ■

Maria once decided that her sister should not have a sleepover date. "I did not have one at that age, and I won't allow Janey to have one until she's older," she declared.

TRAIT 5: FEARFUL

Isn't everyone afraid of new situations?

■ ■ ■

Rick began a new preschool when he was four. "I'm afraid of school," he told his mom. For an hour each day he stood behind the door and refused to enter. Once in the room, he stood and watched. Finally, he relinquished that behavior, but it took several months before he would join in the group activities.

Active alerts are unable to make transitions and are often fearful in new situations. It's easy to see why. New situations mean new stimuli. To the active alert child, confronting such an onslaught of new stimuli means uncertainty about how much control he will have in his new environment with new adults and peers. The observant active alert always fears that he won't be accepted and won't belong in this new place.

Parents of active alerts know how difficult it is to move to new environments with their child. Whether it be dinner at a new restaurant, a trip to the relatives, or an afternoon at the movies—not to mention major changes such as a new home, new school, or adjustments in the family brought about by divorce or remarriage—transitions are tough for active alerts. The same holds true for encounters with new people.

■ ■ ■

Until she was four, Melissa was terrified of baby-sitters. She asked to be put to bed before sitters arrived so she would not have to see them. Once when she was three, her favorite cousin sat for her. Melissa coped well for twenty minutes and then asked to be put to bed, where she stayed until her mom got home later that afternoon.

■ ■ ■

Five-year-old Chris was invited to a birthday party where he knew everyone but one boy. He refused to go even though the party was going to be held at his favorite restaurant.

Don't be surprised if your introverted active alert child talks openly about her fears. She understands and can articulate how her lack of control in group situations overwhelms her. In the extrovert child, however, this fear of not belonging may simply look like over-excitement. Or, he may behave inappropriately, thinking that it may get the group to accept him.

■ ■ ■

Janie and Charlie, both age four, handled their fears very differently. Janie told her mother in no uncertain terms that she was too afraid to stay at her friend's party without her mom. Charlie, who looked frightened, went in and ran around roaring loudly like a lion.

Any of the following changes may affect your active alert child.

Changing schools
Changing classes at school
Riding in carpools
Riding the school bus
Dealing with student teachers
Having several teachers for different subjects
Making the change from Mom's house to Dad's, or vice versa
Being asked to participate in too many new group activities

Recognize that such things are issues for your child. Indeed, fears about change are intrinsic to her nature. Know also that although you do not create the anxiety your child feels, you can prepare her for the changes and help her make choices that strengthen her ability to cope.

TRAIT 6: INTENSE

How intense are these children?

Your child is intensely active (trait 1), intensely alert (trait 2), intensely controlling (trait 4), and intensely fearful (trait 5).

Doesn't leave much out, does it? Your child's intensity also extends to feelings about himself. One difficulty, one mistake of performance can ruin the whole day for him. And once his rigid standards are not met, he has trouble getting "back on track."

For the active alert, bad days either are made up of one horrible thing after another, or they go well until something upsetting happens. Once something goes wrong, the day will seem like *Alexander and the Terrible, Horrible, No Good, Very Bad Day* to your child.

Life is black and white, happy or sad, for the active alert child. There are no gray areas. And he behaves accordingly: He either cooperates or he doesn't.

Active alerts also perceive themselves as smart or dumb— never average. Extreme in their expectations of themselves, they do not readily accept their own mistakes.

■ ■ ■

Elizabeth often tears up schoolwork that does not meet her standards.

■ ■ ■

When Tommy colored slightly out of the lines, he said, "This is wrong." In his mind, there was no margin for error. Any imperfection meant that he was rotten at coloring and stupid to boot. Only a perfect coloring effort could affirm for Tommy that he was an okay person.

Obviously, such perfectionism presents problems for the active alert child, as well as for her parents. Think of it. You want to help your active alert child get over life's rough spots, but if your child explodes in anger each time, your trying to smooth things over may be reinforcing her attempts to control and unwittingly giving her too much power. In such situations it may be more effective to accept that your child feels really bad. Then ask her to be responsible for those feelings. Encourage her to tell you what she needs from you. In the end, explosive reactions can set the emotional climate for a family, so it is worth it to find other avenues for channeling such behavior.

For example, when your child has a bad day, do you try to point out good things and make him see the light when the day turns dark? This is not always advisable because when you do so, your child may feel you have discounted how bad he feels. First, accept and acknowledge your child's discouragement. Then ask if he experienced any good things that day. Your child needs to realize—and this takes time—that everything does not have to be perfect all the time. In any day there is both light and dark. Accepting that sometimes it's okay to be average or middle-of-the-road is a challenge for the active alert.

It is impossible for anyone to control his environment completely. If active alerts do not learn this at an early age, they use anger inappropriately. In some families, especially those that do not deal directly with anger, frustration, or other "negative" emotions, active alerts get to be powerful, almost tyrannical, people.

■ ■ ■

Eight-year-old Sara wanted to keep the family tape player in her room. When Sara's mother asked her to return it to the family room, Sara, frustrated and angry, replied, "Take it and the next thing you'll want is my bed and then my shelves and finally you'll give all my stuffed animals to my sister."

Generalizing, exaggerating, and making mountains out of molehills are probably familiar behavior at your house. Take comfort. You are not alone. If you learn to sympathize with your child's anger or disappointment at the same time that you aid him to stop escalating emotions, you help both your family and your child. We will discuss this issue further in chapters 4 and 6.

TRAIT 7: ATTENTION-HUNGRY

Don't all children need attention?

■ ■ ■

Mattie runs a business out of her home and uses the phone a lot. Mattie is aware of her daughter Susan's intense need for attention. So, on days when her daughter is not at day care, Mattie limits the time she devotes to telephone calls. Before she even picks up the phone, Mattie first plays with Susan, feeds her a snack, and lays out crayons and coloring books. Still, each and every time, Susan interrupts Mattie's phone conversations by asking her mother questions, hanging on the phone cord, or running screaming through the house. "Mommy, I wanna be up," she says, stamping her feet and trying to crawl in Mattie's lap. ALL the parenting books that Mattie has checked say Susan's behavior could be a sign of insecurity, indicating that the child needs more attention. "But," an anguished Mattie tells me, "I don't think I can give her any more attention."

Is your child a bottomless pit of neediness? Do you give and give and never quite satisfy your child, who takes and begs for more?

There is a reason for this. Active alert infants are stimulus-hungry—they feed on external stimulation. It makes sense, then, that an active alert child has difficulty playing alone, without attention from someone else.

■ ■ ■

"All I need is five or ten minutes for a cup of coffee when I wake up in the morning," a client told me. "But four-and-a-half-year-old Bryan is there right away with, 'Mom, play with me.' If I don't play with him, he heads straight for his sister and starts a fight. One way or the other, he'll get attention; the question is whether it will be positive or negative attention."

How you handle this bid for attention determines your child's positive growth. In some homes, parents become as skilled as a preschool teacher at creating stimulating and interesting environments. Their homes contain many different learning toys and materials for projects. Other parents resent their child's need for attention and find themselves angry with the frequent demands.

One way to solve the problem is to set up quiet times. During those times, provide your child with lots of stimulating things to play with on his own and make sure he knows the rules. Also, remember that the quiet time needs to be "structured" or he will resist separating from you. Structured quiet time should come at the same time each day and last the same length of time. Empower your child by letting him know when this time will end. Say, "Quiet time is over when the timer rings" or "Quiet time is over when the clock says two, zero, zero." As your child becomes accustomed to playing or resting alone, you can gradually increase the length of the quiet time. But don't expect miracles. Although your child eventually will learn to play alone, he may take longer than other children to learn this skill. This kind of play does not come easily to your active alert and is definitely not his preference. Self-play gradually will increase in duration as your child becomes more comfortable by himself.

Does having a sibling solve the problem? Yes. And no. A brother or sister may be a built-in playmate for your active alert, but, rivalry undoubtedly will develop as your active alert competes for your attention.

■ ■ ■

Mary's parents told me, "We could take her brother and bury him in the backyard, and while we were burying him, she'd still complain he was getting too much attention.

TRAIT 8: TROUBLE GETTING ALONG WITH OTHERS

What does all this mean for friendships?

As a friend, the active alert child faces two challenges. The young child has trouble making friends. He seems to ask himself, "Should I stand outside and watch because I am afraid, or should I jump right in and try to control the activity, even if I don't know what's going on?" The older child is concerned with how to keep friends. "Once I get them, how long do I have to know them before they are friends? Can we be friends if we've never had and gotten over a fight?"

Trust in people is a crucial issue for active alerts. It is as if they are learning *how* to trust with each new friend.

■ ■ ■

Nine-year-old Perry summed up the issue: "I know how to make friends, it's just keeping them [that's the problem]. Somehow we can't get through the first fight."

If your child struggles with friendships, it is probably because he has trouble with social graces. He may not recognize those slight nonverbal cues that help him know it's time to let someone else talk, or those territorial cues that help him discern when he is invading another person's space.

Active alerts have such a struggle sorting through stimuli that they can hardly pay attention to the so-called "niceties" of social relationships. Their ideas about what to do in a situation generally spring from within themselves and not from any learned responses or clues from the environment. It follows, then, that your child is probably intrusive or sometimes even a physically aggressive friend.

■ ■ ■

Four-year-old Amber completed a highly structured, sedentary portion of her nursery-school day. As she moved on to the next portion of the program with all of her stored-up physical energy, she poked a finger at one of the boys in her class and boldly challenged him to a game of tag. The boy raced off, bewildered by her aggressiveness. She chased him. Her intensity and energy accelerated, and the frightened boy finally set his boundary: "Don't chase me!" At last, the teacher intervened.

Active alerts tell their friends not only what to play but also how they should play it. Taking turns or relinquishing control does not come easily to them, so they need to be taught social skills. They need to learn what effect they have on others.

Many parents tell me, "I didn't think you had to teach kids how to make friends." Well, you do. Active alert children need to learn, either directly or through well-designed learning environments, along with social-skill lessons, how to interact positively with other children. It is too important to leave to chance. See the discussion in chapters 4 and 6.

TRAIT 9: FLUCTUATING SELF-ESTEEM

How do active alerts feel about themselves?

■ ■ ■

Penny, who reads well for a nine-year-old, tells her mother, "I'm dumb 'cause I can't read as fast as you."

As keen observers, these little people notice when someone does something they want to do well. Whether an older child or a parent performs the task makes no difference to active alerts: They feel they are not good at it if they don't do it equally well.

Self-esteem is a hot commodity today, and all parents want their children to have it. But most psychologists and educators agree that self-esteem is an abstract parenting goal. It is difficult to figure out how to help a person increase self-esteem. Active alert children confuse their parents because they themselves are confused about their worth. Their self-esteem fluctuates from high to low. On any given day, at any given moment, it can change—up or down.

Fluctuations in self-esteem stem from their tendency to base their worth upon feedback received from other people. Because they are perfectionists, active alerts set themselves up for disappointments and negative responses from the environment. We all do this from time to time, but because of their controlling and intrusive traits, active alerts receive more negative messages than do other children. That means they have to work that much harder to keep their self-esteem intact.

Active alert children also tend to internalize what goes on around them. They are vulnerable to their environment, but they are not always good at talking about their feelings. Active alert children have intense feelings and, as we learn in chapters 5 and 6, families differ in their ability to teach children how to express those feelings.

Remember, even if your child doesn't seem to be paying attention, she is absorbing messages. She is aware of all the verbal and nonverbal messages you, her teacher, and other children send. But she may seem especially astute at picking up negative messages.

When your child does something well—not necessarily perfectly—point it out to him. Work to assure that he is accepted and affirmed within the family. (We will discuss how to do this in part II.) As unique and talented as he is, people will give him negative messages. As his parents, you will want to be sure to offset those negatives with positives.

Some active alerts get depressed. Many more become demoralized if no one helps them to monitor their self-esteem. A famous therapist once said that the thought of a trip to Disney World is the key to distinguishing a demoralized child from a depressed one. A demoralized child will ask, excitedly, "When does the plane leave?" The depressed child cannot make that leap of emotion.

Helping children avoid negative self-esteem is a challenging goal for parents and one that you will want to assess constantly. Certainly by the time your child is in the fourth or fifth grade, a mental checklist should reveal that she has more good days than bad. If that is not the case, you may want to assess the cumulative effects of poor self-esteem.

TRAIT 10: PERFORMERS

Why isn't your child like this with everyone?

■ ■ ■

At the piano recital each child hurriedly approached the piano, shoulders slumped and eyes glued to the floor. Susan walked leisurely to the bench and looked directly at the audience before sitting down. She paused, smiled, and played. Her mother knew that Susan was terrified—but she was the only one who did.

Active alert children can be the most charming children around! Teachers say they are delightful, charismatic leaders. Children flock to them.

■ ■ ■

Everyone who knew Philip loved him. He was cute and appealing. His aunt couldn't understand why his parents found the four-year-old so difficult—until he came to stay with her for two weeks when his parents took a long holiday together.

Are you bewildered by how well your child behaves away from home? Do other people fail to notice the behavior that challenges you daily? Did you cause your child's problems? Disparity between what others see in the active alert child and what happens in the family may make you doubt your parenting skills.

I propose two possible answers to this dilemma. Your active alert child behaves better with others because he is unsure of himself. He does not know if he can trust others to react positively to him, so he responds by turning on the charm and performing for them. It is easy for him to fit into this angelic role: He is so alert that he can, when necessary, quickly pick up clues to proper behavior. But he is performing because he does not trust strangers with his real self.

Another possibility—one that parents should consider carefully—is that the home environment doesn't offer enough structure. If that is the case, the school setting may actually make your child feel more secure.

TRAIT 11: EMPATHIC ABILITY

Can your child read your mind?

■ ■ ■

In the classic science fiction series Dune, *Frank Herbert describes a group of people who train throughout their lives to detect nuances of voice, posture, and body movement. With this skill, they then discern through observation other people's emotional states. Active alerts play a similar role in the family, except that, unlike the people in* Dune, *they don't know what to do with the knowledge they acquire.*

Is your child like a barometer of your own or others' emotions? Do you find that when she acts out, you can look back and see that you are or have been upset or stressed? The active alert child has her own stressors, but she is also sensitive to other people's emotions.

An empathic person feels what others feel and sees things from other people's point of view. Active alert children are skilled at doing both. They may respond even before emotions are verbalized. But their response is not always *sympathetic*. Although your child picks up on things, he may not always understand or be able to label and deal with them so he can defuse them.

■ ■ ■

Tip's mother, Maura, dreads visiting her parents. There has always been tension between Maura and her parents. Tip, picking up on the unresolved conflicts, can only perform his angelic act for a brief time. Then he loses control and seems to "bounce off the walls," as his mother says, "better than at any other place."

■ ■ ■

When Sasha's mother was just six weeks pregnant, she was bathing with her three-year-old daughter. Sasha placed her hand on her mother's abdomen and said "Mommy, you have a baby growing in you." Her mother was amazed. Although she knew she was pregnant, she hadn't yet taken a pregnancy test,.

One could say that these children are interpreting nonverbal cues using their superior observational skills. Beyond that, however, I find that many active alerts seem to be connected by an invisible umbilical cord to one parent. Often, that parent proves to be an active alert adult.

Although active alert children share the keen characteristic traits outlined above, they do not all look the same. Which traits are most apparent in any child depends upon many factors, including family life, school environment, age, and physical and emotional development. One active alert child may be more active than another, one may be more intrusive, and another may need to be the center of attention all the time. And just when you think you have her all figured out, she changes!

One thing is universally true for you, the parent of an active alert child: The characteristics that sometimes try your patience and stretch you to the limits of your endurance will at other times intrigue and delight you.

Your active alert child is enchanting, intelligent, and puzzling—but never boring. And parenting her is a challenge. In the next part of this book, we will discuss how to meet that challenge, joyfully and well.

Part II

PARENTING YOUR ACTIVE ALERT CHILD

As first-time parents, we were feeling a great deal of guilt that maybe we were doing things wrong with our son, Colin, because of his intensity, controlling nature, high need for attention, trouble with transition, and frequent blast of "no one likes me!" I have wanted to be very careful not to label him, and though he is very active, I never wanted to consider him as hyperactive. We think Colin is very special and most days we wouldn't change a thing about him. I appreciate your positive focus on active alerts' characteristics even though many times they can be exhausting.

At four, Colin talks continually and is always "in charge" of organizing the day's activities (often to the disgust of neighborhood playmates). It is hard to know how to explain to him that sometimes the kids don't want to play with him because he is so controlling (bossy) and wants to make all the plans—we talk about it and he seems to understand, yet he just can't seem to help himself.

Colin has such a hard time leaving "good times" like favorite aunts/uncles, grandmas, parks, etc. I'm continually searching my inner resources on how to make smooth transitions. He has an incredible memory and often will recall things with complete detail as far back as when he was two and a half. He is very detail oriented and has a hard time playing with a game or toy if pieces are missing.

Lately, whenever he is disciplined in any way, he quickly retorts, "You don't like me; no one likes me; I'm going to move away." I think the fact that he is also adopted makes me feel a bit more sensitive to his verbal responses. I need to learn more about discipline with active alerts. I guess because of how I was raised, I'm not as good at the engage-to-disengage style and need to practice that.

Colin is very sensitive to his environment. We were cutting out tags from his clothing at eighteen months and have continually been fighting the battle of the too-snug underwear, wrinkled socks, scratchy clothes, etc. He prefers to wear mostly sweats. The latest is that he changes underwear about six times a day because if he gets a drop of urine on them he absolutely cannot stand the wetness. He is very intense and can cry at the drop of a hat. We feel certain he could have a very promising acting or political career, as he is never at a loss for words and will talk incessantly even when he has nothing to say! And his negotiating ability has to be a close tie with Henry Kissinger's!

Along with discipline, the other difficult issue right now is, How much attention is enough? Colin can move me from guilt to tears about working part-time and taking him to a baby-sitter (whom he likes quite well once he's there) a day and a half a week. He makes me feel guilty when I need to do housework or attend to his sixteen-month-old brother. He will say, "You never (of course it's never) have time, Mom!" Never enough time to play.

One of the most difficult times comes with trying to socialize. Colin can become very obnoxious until he commands the visitor's total attention, continually inter-rupting, etc. We have had so many discussions regarding these instances that now when we leave, or visitors leave, he immediately asks, "Was I good, Mom?" or "How was I, Mom?" Sometimes he knows my answer ahead of time and says, "I'm going to my room, Mom!"

I think that just knowing that these are innate charac-teristics and that we, as parents, haven't created them some-how—as well as trying to have a sense of humor—has helped us relax and enjoy Colin even more for the unique boy he is.

3

The Three-Part
Process of Understanding
Your Child

You cannot change the music of your soul.

—Katharine Hepburn

While still in the hospital, Martha's mother watched her newborn child. The other infants in the room slept, waking only to eat. Martha, on the other hand, no longer confined by the womb, stretched our her arms and explored her new space. Her mom was enchanted and puzzled by this beautiful child.

Often, parents of active alert children sense early in their child's life that they have embarked on a joyful, challenging journey with an intriguing child. There is little to guide such parents on that journey, however. Much of the previous work on the active alert child focuses on what the child lacks. The goal of such work, it seems, is to eliminate the child's "weaknesses."

In my work with active alert children I focus on each child's individual gifts—on the music of his soul. I believe that by assessing a child's strengths and redefining "weaknesses" as potential gifts, we can create a family system that accommodates and nurtures *all* of its members, parents and children alike.

■■■

A woman called me once to ask what my "success rate" is with active alert children. I was uncomfortable with the question. It implied that once I "changed" the child, the process was over. I responded by saying, "I work with the family system. I don't change the child."

I cannot make an active alert child into a less-active human being. Indeed, that is certainly not how I would define success. I help parents understand and accept their child and figure out how a family system can accommodate, include, and affirm him. In the end, both the child and the parent change, but that change is an outgrowth of understanding.

Think of this part of the book as one in which we develop road maps for your lifelong journey with your child. In it we will explore the exciting task of understanding, accepting, and affirming—in short, parenting—your active alert child.

Parenting the active alert child is a three-part process. It involves understanding your child, assessing your parenting skills, and affirming your child.

UNDERSTANDING YOUR CHILD

Understanding your active alert child's needs and characteristics is the first step in parenting him. As part of that process you will need to examine and perhaps dismantle some societal myths about parenting.

Do expectations get in the way of parenting your active alert child? All of us believe different things about parenthood. If you believe that babies sleep through the night and your child is an active alert, you may be concerned about your alert infant, who by 3:00 A.M. has already been up three times! Your first response may be to wonder what you did to keep your child from sleeping. In fact, your child is just being true to his alert nature.

Babies do not come into the world knowing the rules. No one tells them that crying in the middle of the night is against the rules and that they will be considered "bad babies" if they do so. No one tells them in utero that they will have to sleep ten hours each day.

Given all that, what are you, as parents, supposed to do? Examine the myths you hold dear. Some are hidden deeply in the psyche. You may have to ferret them out. Did you believe that all children were alike? Do you wonder why your second child is not like your first? Let's examine some of the common myths that distort our ability to see our children as the unique people they are.

Myths About Parenting

All children should be happy—all the time. That's a myth I hear frequently. This cause-effect myth is often reinforced by well-meaning people who advise, "Feed him more," "Hold her less," "Just let him cry," "Are you sure she is getting enough milk?" Remember, no one can make anyone else happy. That is especially true of active alert children who have—and seem to need—some negative moods.

Active alerts are often happy, but when they are not, they may seem intensely sad or angry. True to her controlling nature, the active alert child would like to make you responsible for her anger, frustration, or sadness. As an infant your active alert needs more attention. You are constantly trying to soothe and comfort her. As she gets older you stop being responsible for her emotional state. You must help her make the transition and learn that she is the one responsible for her own emotions. Parents who believe a child should always be happy and who try to make her so are in for an arduous parenting journey.

As your child gets older, you'll encounter another myth: There is one best way to teach all children and one methodology works with every child. Now, that's a little like saying there is only one medicine to cure every disease!

■■■

The parents of four children, recognizing the need for a different approach with their second child, came to see me. They were good loving parents, but as the dad put it, "What works with the other three doesn't work well with our second born."

In truth, there are numerous "best" ways to teach children. An active alert challenges parents to be creative teachers. What she may need is not just a stronger dose of the same medicine but an altogether new prescription.

Another quite commonly held belief—that parenting and housekeeping are the same job—is particularly difficult for parents of active alert children. It's also one that is quite prevalent in our society. Cleaning house and rearing children are, in fact, two very distinct tasks. Parents who stay home with an active alert child may find themselves so consumed with parenting that they have little time for homemaking. The active alert child is, by definition, *busy*. Just picking up after his clutter all day can be both discouraging and depressing. Some days, simply making a meal—to say nothing of dusting, doing laundry, running errands, and doing yard work—is a major accomplishment for the active alert child's parent.

What are some other parenting myths?

Spare the rod, spoil the child.
Children hold marriages together.
There is a right or best way to be a parent or family.
All babies are sweet and cute.
All babies sleep a lot.
Parents must always be right.
Children can't be angry.

Little children aren't affected by stress.
Success/failure behavior of children is indicative of
    success/failure of parents.

What did you expect from your little person and how do those
expectations fit with who she is? Is what you believe about children
keeping you from understanding and affirming your own child?

The Enigma of the Active Alert Child

Active alert children are what I like to call enigmas—puzzles to
solve. As such, they are extremely challenging for parents.
Although they appear to want one kind of response, the opposite
approach is often what they need. To understand your child, you
must learn to discern the discrepancy between how he appears
and what he is actually feeling.

Two- or three-years-olds may appear "wound up" and full of
energy when in fact they are really tired and need to be gently held
or helped to settle down. Set limits for an out-of-control active alert
who appears to want no boundaries, and she will calm down.

Take-charge active alerts look most independent when they are
feeling most needy and lost. Help them understand the boundaries
of their independence. And then reassure them that you will always
be there for them—whether they are feeling strong or are in need of
comfort and support.

A child will strike out in anger at parents when she is angriest
at herself. Tell your child you know she is angry at you. At the
same time, acknowledge her embarrassment and frustration with
her own behavior. Let her in on some of your most embarrassing
moments. Telling her that you also struggle with awkwardness
sometimes plants the seeds of self-awareness. Active alerts
demand more attention when they have just received an
abundance of it.

The boisterous, egotistical active alert may be full of self-
doubt. Recognize both parts. Discerning the contradiction
between how your child appears and what he is actually feeling
will help you understand and affirm him. The following chart will
aid in that process.

ENIGMA CHART

Appearance	Reality
Wound up, energetic	Tired
Wants no direction	Seeking boundaries
Independent	Fearful, dependent; needs reassurance
Demands constant attention	Needs closure or help saying good-bye
Extreme self-esteem bordering on egotism	Full of self-doubt
Keen observer	Fails to pick up small nonverbal clues related to other people's boundaries (red light/green light color blind—see below)
Not thorough task workers	Persistent to tasks of interest
Totally out of control	Has too much control—the limited may need to be clarified

Red Light/Green Light

Although active alerts are generally keen observers, in certain circumstances they seem unobservant, almost oblivious to the nonverbal cues signaling that they've made someone uncomfortable. An active alert adult friend helped me reconcile this apparent contradiction by explaining the red light/green light color-blind concept.

"Linda, don't you get it?" said my friend, laughing. "Active alerts are red light/green light color-blind. We simply don't see life's stoplights." It is so simple! Energetic active alerts are so busy moving ahead that they sometimes don't see the intersection, much less the stoplight!

■■■

At age eight, Tasha had finally gotten the idea that she was not allowed to use the makeup and jewelry in her mother's bedroom. When she used the cosmetics that Mom had left in the bathroom, her mother became very angry. In all innocence, Tasha said, "But they were in the bathroom." Suddenly Mom understood: To Tasha, the stoplight was on the bedroom door, not on the concept of using her mother's possessions without permission. Tasha's mom redefined the stoplight for her daughter, saying, "Don't use my cosmetics unless I give them to you for your use."

ASSESSING YOUR PARENTING SKILLS

The second step in understanding how to parent the active alert child is evaluating how you and your family respond to your active alert. Knowing your parenting strengths and recognizing what new skills you need to acquire are not luxuries—they are critical survival tactics! And realizing that you don't already have every parenting skill does not mean that you have been a bad parent. I deal with some wonderful parents who have active alert children. These parents work hard at creatively addressing their children's needs, yet even their skills are taxed by active alert children.

If, as a friend of mine says half-jokingly, parenthood is a series of "traps," parents of an active alert child must be agile! You must learn to avoid or, once in, to get out of those traps. Finely honed parenting skills are the tools for doing so. Among the tools I use when working with families are the following developed by author and family-life educator Jean Illsley Clarke. She defines four different parenting styles: nurturing, structuring, criticizing, and marshmallowing. The following, admittedly simplified, description of Clarke's work sheds light on parenting the active alert child.

Nurturing. Parents who nuture their children offer gentle, caring messages that affirm and support, such as, "I am here to help," "I know you are competent," and "I love you." *Structuring.* Parents who offer structure set limits and ensure the child knows what he needs to know and has what he needs to have to be competent. In effect, these parents say, "I will help you get where you want to go by showing you some paths. Then it is your job to do it. I know you can do it." *Criticizing.* Parents who use a criticizing style attack and negate the child's very being. They attack a child's self rather than his behavior. The message? "You will fail. I will tell you how you will fail." The criticizing parent ridicules, judges, and blames, saying such things as "You never clean your room," "You always fight with your sister," and "You are such a problem."

Sometimes, because it is so difficult to find constructive and consistent ways to respond to their child's traits, parents of active alerts find themselves adopting a criticizing stance. Dismayed, they may begin a pattern, vacillating from criticizing to marshmallowing.

Marshmallowing. Marshmallowing is a little like the proverbial left-handed compliment. Parents who use this style offer support, but at the same time, they judge the child. Buried in the message is the implication that the child will fail. "You poor thing, I'll help you out," "Oh, that's too hard for you to do. I don't think you should even try," and "Let me do that for you."

A combination of nurturing and structuring works best with active alert children. The message from such parenting is "You are competent. I know you can do it, and I will help you when you need help." You'll want to read more about both styles in Clarke's book, *Self-Esteem: A Family Affair.*

I know that it is not always easy to find positive ways to react to your child. I also know that once you do find just the right fit, it all changes.

Each time your child faces new challenges, you must be ready to grow to accommodate him. Learning the different needs of children at different ages is a continuing process; the skills that worked for parenting a two-year-old may not be right for a fifth grader. At each developmental level, your child learns more. She also changes when the family or learning environment changes.

Problems arise when individual family members grow and forget to tell one another. The seams of the family strain, and the system no longer fits the individual who has grown. Given how tremendously fast children develop, it is easy for this to happen within a family—and even easier when the child is an ever-learning, ever-changing active alert.

■■■

Eleven-year-old Martha returned from two weeks at summer camp, where she met new friends and reveled in her independence. On the way home, her family gently teased her about her constantly messy room, and Martha burst into tears. Her mother discovered later that Martha had been the camp leader when it came to keeping her tent clean and had prided herself on her newfound skill. Her family, not knowing this, had resumed old patterns that no longer fit for Martha.

Now, this is nothing new. By their very nature, thriving families must change to meet each member's needs. Sometimes parents accommodate easily; at other times their skills are stretched and they need new insights and options. Reassessment and growth are part and parcel of healthy family life.

Achieving equilibrium is sometimes just a matter of an ever-so-slight shift, such as allowing a child to pour her own juice. So, keep in mind that such striving is not only normal but healthy. You and your active alert child are in a lifelong process during which you will find many ways to be an effective parent. But you will never find the one and only way—because it simply does not exist.

If knowing that you are in a dynamic process leaves you feeling adrift at sea without a compass, don't despair. The eleven traits of an active alert child outlined in chapter 2 can serve as landmarks. Remember, the *traits* remain consistent; the *behavior* changes and seems different at different developmental stages. For instance, it is easier to live with your child's need to control when she is in school and away from home more. Think about it. At school she can exercise more control over choices, such as what friends to play with, how much lunch to eat, and whether or not to wear mittens at recess. Each time she makes a choice, she must live with the consequences of her decision. So much learning takes place in that way!

Used as a consistent reference, these traits help parents respond to behavior that might otherwise baffle them. I find them so helpful that I still refer to them every time I have trouble understanding a child. Placing behavior in the context of the characteristics helps me to find ways to work positively with active alert children.

AFFIRMING YOUR CHILD

Keep in mind that a child—indeed, everyone—thrives best when affirmed. Familiarity with the eleven traits of an active alert child will help you understand what triggers behavior; learning how each characteristic manifests itself will help you to understand and to affirm your child. (I will cover strategies for affirming or giving positive feedback to your child in chapter 7.)

But there is another aspect to this process. To accept and affirm your child, you must accept and affirm yourself. And that is not always as simple as it sounds.

Active alert children constantly push the boundaries you set for them. If you do not feel good about yourself or are not confident in your own beliefs, you may find that living with a child who constantly questions what you do intensifies your struggle.

Your active alert child will routinely test your intelligence and confidence and try your patience. Do you fully understand yourself in relation to your child? Are you angry at your child for pushing your limits or are you angry at yourself because you feel unsure about the limits you set? Psychoanalyst Carl Jung said that if there is anything that you would want to change in a child, examine it and see if it is not something that would be better changed in yourself.

Do you understand what triggers your responses to your child?

■■■

Ashley was almost twelve years old when Mrs. Jones, the next-door neighbor, called to ask her to baby-sit. Ashley's mother, Cathy, was upset for some reason. Without thinking, she said, "You are not old enough to baby-sit yet. You can't go." Ashley was angry.

After she thought it over, Cathy knew she had not been entirely straight with her daughter. There were other issues. For one thing, the thought of having a child old enough to be a baby-sitter was a tangible reminder that she herself was growing older. Moreover, she didn't entirely trust her next-door neighbor, who was the kind of person who "burned up" baby-sitters by overusing them and paying too little for their services.

Cathy reconsidered and reopened the discussion with her daughter. Together they agreed on some rules. Cathy told her daughter, "Sometimes it's hard for me to believe how grown-up and competent you are becoming. I am very proud of you and know you can handle this situation. But I think we need to establish some ground rules." They decided Ashley could sit one weekend night until 11 P.M. and one afternoon each weekend. "You know how tired you get if you stay up later than 11 P.M., so if Mrs. Jones gets home late, you may not sit for her again, but you may continue to sit for other people in the neighborhood." Then Cathy helped Ashley design a flyer advertising her baby-sitting business. Ashley distributed it to nearby neighbors. To counteract feeling too old, Cathy decided to buy tickets to a Rolling Stones concert!

When affirming a child, what you call her and how you describe her are critically important. Be careful to use a positive framework when talking to or about your child. Try to separate the child's behavior from the child's self, so her sense of who she *is* does not get confused with what she *does*. Such labeling could be demoralizing. After all, we cannot change who we are, only how we act.

Below are examples of how people tend to describe active alert children. Following each negative *(N)* or critical example is an alternate way to describe the behavior positively *(P)*.

N. My son is out to get me.
P. My son is capable of recognizing a source of gratification. He knows how to get his needs met.

N. She is so wild.
P. She has lots of energy.

N. He is an attention seeker.
P. He knows how to get his needs met.

N. She is so insecure (anxious, fearful).
P. She knows the limits of her strength.

N. My child is willful (stubborn).
P. My child persists.

N. She is lazy.
P. She takes time to reflect.

N. He is overly sensitive.
P. He notices everything.

N. She is annoying.
P. She is curious about everything.

N. He is easily frustrated.
P. He is eager to succeed.

Reframing how you describe your child's actions helps you to change the way you think about your child. But it may have another effect. By helping your child to see her own traits as being positive, you encourage her to develop her full potential.

How? By affirming a child's behavior you allow him to accept his own self. Once he accepts himself—warts and all—he can stop trying to change who he is and start fine-tuning his own wonderful traits. Think of it. An intrusive or "nosy" child may eventually be perceived as an adult who can empathize and who is interested in others. Refined bossiness may become just the decisiveness we want in our leaders.

■■■

Jennifer, age five, was incredibly "bossy" at the bus stop each morning. Laura was dismayed by her daughter's behavior and talked to her mother-in-law about it. "Laura," said the older woman, "Jennifer's just practicing to be a leader."

Now, think of your own positive parallels for the following phrases.

    N. He is argumentative.
    N. She is rough (tomboyish).
    N. He is exasperating.
    N. She is moody.
    N. He is easily upset.
    N. She is rude to adults.

I will cover more strategies for affirming or giving positive feedback to your child in chapter 7.

The key to understanding yourself in relation to your child is learning more about your child. You began doing that when you started reading this book. Once you begin to understand your child's nature and how you relate to him as a parent, you can expect a number of significant changes to occur.

Now, in light of the three-step parenting process we just discussed—understanding your child, assessing your parenting skills, and affirming your child—let's look in the next chapter at the active alert child's characteristics and discuss the parenting responses to each trait. Keep in mind that these approaches are merely suggestions. There is no right or only way to parent an active alert child; I have simply listed options the parents I work with deem helpful. You will be able to tailor them to your family system and your own active alert child.

4

Parenting Strategies That Fit Your Child's Needs— and Yours

The meeting of two personalities is like the contact of two chemical substances: If there is any reaction, both are transformed.

—Carl Jung
Modern Man in Search of a Soul

Each time a child and parent meet, it is a contact of two distinct personalities. Every one of those contacts has the potential to change life as you know it. The following strategies are ones that the parents with whom I work find effective in dealing with the eleven active alert traits. I think knowing and using them increases the chances that when change does occur it will be a healthy transformation.

TRAIT 1: ACTIVE

Of all the active alert characteristics, this one is the hardest to miss. These children are very active! Yet if they are engrossed, they can sit for hours to read a book, watch television, or build with blocks. They like novel and unusual or interesting things.

Physical in nature, they learn by doing. They have a phenomenal lack of desire to sleep, are easily overstimulated, and do not readily settle themselves down.

Parenting Strategy

Investigate the Physiological Origins of Your Child's Active Behavior. • First of all, try to determine through a physical exam whether or not there are any physiological origins for your child's behavior. A majority of the children whom I call active alert have a history of chronic ear or upper-respiratory infections. Most of them have families with significant allergies.

Scientific data on the link between food and environmental irritants and the activity level of children are controversial. Indeed, such a link is refuted by most of the medical community. I remain perplexed by this common medical history among active alerts, however.

Given the work of pediatric allergist Doris Rapp, in her book *Is This Your Child?*, and the belief on the part of some individuals in the medical community that caffeine, food dyes, and preservatives may irritate an existing condition, I encourage parents to consider whether their child's temperament is irritated by food or environmental allergies. The best way to assess whether or not the child has an allergy is to seek assistance from a pediatric allergist, who assesses environmental allergies and/or uses one of the three diets suggested by Dr. Rapp to determine if there is a food allergy:

1. Single food elimination diet
2. Multiple food elimination diet
3. The rotary diet

The similarities in active alerts' medical histories warrant such investigation.

Many parents of active alert children identify themselves or another relative as active alert. That fact alone may support my belief that there are physiological, genetic origins to being active alert. So, consider the possibility that your child may be sensitive to food or the environment.

Help Your Child Get His Rest   •   Understand that even if
your child does not look tired, he needs sleep—lots of it. It
sounds so simple: "Make sure that your child is well rested." But
you and I know it is not. Active alert children are not easy to put
to bed!

Your active alert child needs consistently structured rest
patterns and bedtime rituals. A young child's bedtime should not
vary more than fifteen to thirty minutes each night. if your active
alert is not well rested, you will have a frenzied child on your
hands, and determining what causes that behavior will be
impossible.

■ ■ ■

*When she is tired, Jennifer does not look it. She behaves
frantically. Her behavior is a cue to her mother that
Jennifer needs rest, including time to wind down before
she goes to sleep.*

Keep in mind that if you put these enigmatic children to bed
later than normal thinking that they will "sleep in" the next
morning, you will get the opposite response. They will rise even
earlier.

Clear rituals help active alert children make the transition
between the world of activity and the world of sleep.

■ ■ ■

*Sam's parents told me he effectively alienated several
evening baby-sitters before his farther figured out what
was going on. Each night Sam liked apple slices and a
drink of water before he brushed his teeth and went to
bed. The baby-sitters did not know the routine and did
not believe Sam when he told them what he wanted. His
sense of justice offended, Sam quit cooperating with the
sitters. Once Sam's father explained the situation, things
went more smoothly.*

Young children or those in certain developmental stages need
extra sleep. When parents tell me their young active alert child
needs only eight or nine hours of sleep each night, I respond by

saying, "Only if he takes a three-hour nap!" This is particularly true of children who have given up their naps or six-year-olds in their first year of all-day school.

Don't wait for your little person to tell you he is tired—something he will seldom admit. Instead, structure a bedtime ritual with pajamas, teeth brushing, and reading to cue his body that it is time to wind down. Such consistency helps children fall asleep fairly quickly.

I'd like to add the following postscript: Today's parents often feel they must provide constant educational stimulation, and they feel guilty if their children go to bed and lie awake for forty-five minutes. I suggest they view this process as coping-skill development. Such patterns help children learn to calm themselves, to make transitions, and to accept change.

Remind your child that it is his job to get a good night's sleep just as it is your job to be a good parent. Tell him that to be a good parent, you need time alone to finish things you can't do during the day.

■ ■ ■

After Jim was tucked in, he was not allowed to get out of bed. If he did, his father reminded him, "You must stay in your room. You may have the night light on. But this is your time to go to bed and my time to be alone. Now, I have some reading to do, and I will sit right outside your room until you go to sleep."

Jim's father made it clear that he was "off duty" once Jim went to bed. He also recognized that Jim needed some quiet reassurances, so he chose to sit outside the child's room. If you use this method of reassuring your child, remember not to speak to him. Rather, let him drift off to sleep on his own. If your child decides to play actively, tell him that if he continues you will have to take away the toy that is keeping him awake. Explain to him that you will return it as soon as he falls asleep so that it will be there if he needs it in the morning.

This nonintrusive support helps your child to learn to settle herself down. Your child doesn't always need to be with you just because she is awake. Rather, she may need a quiet, reflective time away from stimulus. Indeed; this may just be her own style for falling asleep. Transitions are hard for active alert children. So respect this time, however she chooses to structure it, and try not to intrude.

Enjoy and Focus "Monkey Energy" • In my practice, I teach children about "monkey energy." Active alert children, like little monkeys, climb all over the people they are with. They move constantly; they are curious.

I use the *Curious George* books by H. A. Rey to talk with preschoolers about where that energy can lead them. We talk about what happens when George, the little curious monkey, goes to the natural science museum. "Where do monkeys belong?" I ask them. "Where do they not belong?" We discuss where their own "monkey energy" is okay (the playground, the jungle gym) and where it might get them into trouble (at mealtime, at Mommy's or Daddy's office, etc.).

Your child needs to know that she is in charge of her energy and can make choices about what to do with it. Teach your child to stop and think about different ways to use her energy and tell her the consequences of intruding. How? Simply call her to your side and quietly say, "Lauren, your monkey's out. Is this a place for monkeys? If your monkey needs to play, you will need to go outside for a while." Then ask her, "Where do you think you need to be right now? Inside or outside?"

Helping children tune into their own energy and asking them to consider alternatives for using that energy puts them in control of their own bodies and helps them develop coping skills.

Encouraging your child to play by himself is another step in the energy-controlling process. Remember, playing independently does not come naturally to active alert children, but you can nurture it. Set aside quiet time for three- or four-year-olds. Quiet time is a time when you get away from the task of being with your child and he gets away from the stimulation of being with you. Explain that quiet means not loud. Beyond that, there are no other rules. Quiet time may only last thirty minutes and probably should take place in the child's room (you may have to relinquish control at that point; you can take a child to his bedroom, but you cannot make him be still). Over the years, I've heard parents describe some very creative uses of quiet time.

■ ■ ■

Each afternoon during her quiet time, four-year-old Jennifer took the clothing off the closet pole and hung by her legs. She followed the rule: She was quiet—and also got a great gymnastics workout every day. Not a bad use of time for a child who relaxed best through physical activity. And it was great for her mother, who had time to refresh and ready herself to be with her child again.

Younger children need physical space, so pull out an old mattress for jumping. Invest in a child-size trampoline. Hang up a basement swing. Create places where your child can release energy. Especially in cold climates, children need indoor spaces in which to be active. Buy exercise tapes or check them out from the library.

■ ■ ■

Jim's parents deal with his energy by doing stretching exercises with him. When he is especially frantic, they have him run around the house and clock him to see if, competing only with himself, he can better his own time.

An active alert child's need for physical release changes as he gets older. Older children benefit from programmed exercise, including individual sports, such as figure skating, karate, gymnastics, swimming, and skiing. These sports teach skill development, self-limits, self-control, and self-discipline, all of which are useful school skills. Team sports, such as baseball, soccer, and football, are most successful if introduced to a nine- or ten-year-old active alert; younger children often find team sports more difficult. Team sports require social cooperation and attention to the task even while inactive, both of which are harder for the younger active alert.

When dealing with a young active alert child, choose environments and activities carefully. If it is a day when your child lacks a clear sense of her boundaries or seems frantic, consider postponing your shopping trip. Ask yourself, "Is this a grocery store day?" If you think you and your child can successfully survive a shopping trip, by all means go, and offer a reward to reinforce appropriate behavior in the store. The reward may be as simple as a package of sugarless chewing gum or the privilege of picking out a special family treat. Ah, isn't this a bribe, you ask? No, I don't think so. To me, a bribe is something offered for illegal behavior. Cooperating with parents in this way is not illegal.

On the other hand, it's perfectly admissible—sometimes the best choice—to decide to stay home. If your child is having a tough morning and it doesn't seem as if he can tone down his energy, stay home or go to the park.

If you must do the food shopping on a day when your child needs to stay home, look at your options. Hire an afterschool sitter so you can get to the store. If you are a two-parent family, let one parent take the evening off. If you are a single parent, find a relative or friend to offer this type of support.

When she is ready for school, you may need to help your child channel her energy. Inform the teacher about your child's energy level and how it affects her learning. Kinesthetic, or active, learners have the shortest pencils because they get up to sharpen them a lot! And that may be a constructive, wonderfully appropriate use of physical energy in the classroom.

■ ■ ■

One kindergartner told me, "If I get that feeling I raise my hand. I know the teacher will always let me go to the bathroom, and I can run 'cause she thinks I have to go real bad."

Active alert children may learn spelling better at the blackboard, where they can trace or write. Use of learning stations is also an excellent way to give children ample opportunity to move about.

With your advocacy and a teacher's understanding, active alert children are able to develop good coping skills within the classroom.

■ ■ ■

When bright and active five-year-old Adam began kindergarten, his mother taught him that tapping out songs on his leg with his fingers was an unobtrusive way to be physical while the teacher was talking. On his own, he figured out that if he sat in the back of the group, he could move around without distracting anyone. The teacher accepted his choices and Adam learned.

TRAIT 2: ALERT

As discussed in detail in chapter 2, I define an alert child as one who is a keen observer, has no boundaries, does not recognize other people's boundaries, and does not recognize the rules that create boundaries.

Active alert children are open to the world. They are so sensitive, at times, that they seem to be turned inside out, with their nerves on top of their skin. While they are tremendously aware of stimuli, they lack internal blocking or screening mechanisms. As a result, active alert children tend to become overstimulated. An occupational therapist may be able to help with this using sensory integration work.

Because they do not recognize boundaries, they intrude on other people's property and physical space. On the positive side, a lack of boundary awareness yields children who are superb negotiators; however, that skill—highly valued in adults—is extremely trying to parents. The alert characteristic and a high activity level provide the patterns that are most difficult for parents to handle.

Parenting Strategy

Observe Your Keen Observer   •   Your alert child's powers of observation will affect your life in many ways, such as when you turn on the television or radio, and how or what you talk about in his presence.

Here's a simple rule: *If you are not ready to explain, be careful of exposure.*

Information does not slip by an active alert child. She observes your actions and those of other adults. She asks endless questions that may be difficult to answer.

From a young child's wonder at the power of curses to an older child's bewilderment about how to know when adults are joking or serious, you must always affirm your child's capacity to observe. Do this directly by saying, "I really think you're very observant" or "You notice so much about the world around you."

Affirm your child's observation by asking for data. What did your child see or hear that led him to such a conclusion? The conclusion may not be correct, but the observation is most likely astute. Interestingly enough, your child's interpretations of what he observes are usually correct. When incorrect, they are understandable given the data. You then can add to, clarify, or expand on things to insure that accurate conclusions are drawn.

Remember Your Child's Lack of Boundaries for Self

•   Let's begin with infancy. Parents are not always aware of the amount of stimulation bombarding a child. Those of you who have read the work of behaviorist B. F. Skinner may remember his baby tender: an air-conditioned box with shades designed to control the amount of stimulus to the baby.

Now, I am in no way suggesting that parents of active alerts need to build baby tenders. Short of that, there are some creative options you may want to explore when assessing the amount of stimulus your child is receiving.

Take a look at your child's daily routine, his bedroom, and your own family routines. Is there a lot of street noise? Do you often play the radio or CD player for hours at a time? Does the noisy play of other children destroy your child's quiet time or study time? Some parents cover windows with black paper at nap time. Others place a fan or white-noise machine in the bedroom or play a soothing recording of forest or ocean sounds to help a child block out the world.

■ ■ ■

Colin's mother, aware of the impact of color on her son, redecorated his nursery in restful colors so that he could sleep better. She did not choose the primary, stimulating colors that many experts suggest for an infant's room.

■ ■ ■

Before Susan was born, her family listened to the radio during dinner. They discovered early in her infancy that the background music was too stimulating for Susan at day's end. She stayed calmer if the radio was off. Susan is now six, and this is still the case.

Many parents of active alert children notice that their child is overstimulated by events most people assume are fun—indeed, designed—for children: a school carnival, a parade, a birthday party, loud restaurants.

In such places, active alert children may become frantic or, as they lose control, cling to you. Be prepared. These children may actually need you to physically block stimuli. By holding on to your legs or hiding in your skirt, they use you, in essence, to form a physical barrier between them and sensation. Now, that may be a good coping mechanism for them, but if you expected them to enjoy the carnival or parade, you may be baffled and disappointed.

The best offense is a good defense. Learn to anticipate what an environment will be like and talk with your child about what is to come. In effect, try to see how overwhelming the event may look through the observant, seemingly unblinking eyes of an active alert child.

■ ■ ■

*Before taking Katie to the dentist for the first time, her
mother, Julia, called the receptionist and asked what the
procedures were for first-time appointments. She then
scheduled her own appointment right before Katie's.
Julie explained to Katie that going to the dentist was
something only big girls did.*

*"Katie, you and I are going to visit a special doctor
today—a tooth doctor called a dentist," she said. "When
we get there a dentist's helper—a hygienist—will show us
to a special chair that goes up and down and back. The
hygienist will use some special tools to clean our teeth.
Those tools will be a lot like toothbrushes. When our
teeth are sparkly clean, the dentist will come into the
room and with a special mirror look at our teeth to make
sure they are healthy. I will go first so you can watch and
ask questions. Then you can take your turn."*

Teach Your Child About Other People's Boundaries

• Your active alert child does not know where he stops and
others begin, either physically or emotionally. Moreover, your
child does not know the difference between being an adult
and being a child. He does not recognize that some privileges
and activities are appropriate for adults only. Since he is red
light/green light color-blind, you must show him how to
distinguish stoplights.

■ ■ ■

*Lauren's mother told me that when her daugher was
seven, she came to her parents and asked them what sex
was. Her well-educated parents "did a wonderful job of
telling her about sex. We handled the interaction
beautifully." They explained the sexual act and then
Lauren asked, "Do you and Daddy do it?" "Yes, we do,"
Mommy answered. "Can I watch?" Lauren asked.*

*Of course her parents answered, "No. This is
something adults do, but it is not something children
watch." Lauren, in true active alert style, asked, "Are you
doing something you wouldn't want me to see?" and the*

discussion continued with Lauren's parents being exceedingly clear in setting their boundaries. "Lauren, this is a private act between two people," her mother told her. "Only the two people involved share in this special private, loving moment."

Active alert children have a talent for using all they see and know about the world. They are verbally gifted. They debate. Oh, how they love to debate!

Keep in mind the difference between reasoning and action. Otherwise, because your child is wonderfully articulate and entertaining, you may find yourself enmeshed in numerous verbal exchanges that leave you half-amused and half-outraged, wondering how you got trapped into such incredible, time-consuming discussions. A client of mine calls this "analysis paralysis." Active alert children can turn it into an art form.

■ ■ ■

Sondra was always frightened when visiting a new friend's house. Sondra's mother was hoping she could encourage her six-year-old daughter to play at someone else's house once in a while. She told her, "I'm a little tired of always being the mother on duty."

Sondra offered 9 million reasons why it might be a problem for her to play somewhere else: "They might have a dog that bites," "I won't know what to play with there," "I might have to find the light switches in the bathroom. And what if I can't even find the bathroom?"

Each time Sondra raised an objection and her mother suggested a coping strategy, Sondra expressed a new fear. Finally her mom said, "Being at someone else's house will never feel as safe and familiar as being at home, but there will be fun things to do there that you don't do at your own house. You know our phone number and I will be here. If there is a problem you and your friend and her mother cannot solve alone, just call me." Then she added, "Sondra, before you invite another friend over here, you must accept an invitation to play at a friend's house."

I am reminded of a wonderful cartoon in which the father stands over his son, saying. "I've tried effective listening but he won't effectively listen to me." How poignantly accurate. Active alerts do not effectively listen. To them, listening is not the point of discussions. The point to the child is the exchange of words.

What should you do about this? Keep in mind, no matter how cleverly he asks for something, that what your child wants may be totally inappropriate. Trust your instincts. Learn when to stop such discussions with a simple statement: "This is not negotiable: it is inappropriate."

Your task is *to move beyond listening to action and to outline the consequences of the action.* As you do this, remember that *you can actively listen to a child when the child has a problem but not when the child is the problem.*

When you recognize that your child's behavior is the problem, end the listening. Acknowledge the child's thoughts and feelings. Then address the impact of her action on you and on others.

■ ■ ■

Eight-year-old Alice used and broke her mother's lipstick after she had been told not to touch the makeup. Alice's mother told her, "I am angry that you did not listen to me and broke my best lipstick. I know you did not mean to break it, but you will have to buy me another with your allowance."

In this instance, the behavior is the problem and Alice's mother chose not to listen to a round of excuses. If, on the other hand, your child has a problem with, let's say, a friend at school, keep listening.

■ ■ ■

Hilary was upset because Lisa had been mean to her at recess. When her mom picked her up, she got in the car and cried. Hilary's mother said, "You must have had a tough day. Shall we talk about it?"

Here the child *has* a problem and a mother who is willing to listen and help her work through her anguish to a solution.

Establish Rules as Boundaries • Active alert children need absolutely clear and consistent routines. Build them around daily habits such as bedtime, toothbrushing, dressing, and mealtimes. Now, you and I know that being totally consistent is difficult, if not impossible. We are only human. But I also know that by age three, every time you violate a routine, your active alert child will notice it and challenge you when you seek to reinstate it. When you change the order of your child's life, he will try to negotiate it the next time around. Your child will say, in effect, "Toothbrushing? Well, I didn't have to do it on Saturday. Why do I have to do it today?"

In such instances, it's not always easy to discern what your child is thinking. I think that without established routines, she may believe that she is doing a task for you. When that happens, there is a strong likelihood that she will question the need to do it at all. When toothbrushing occurs daily as part of her structure, she clearly can begin to understand that this task is done to prevent cavities in her own teeth. If it occurs at your random prompting, she may get confused and think that she does it just to please you. Consistent routines and structure communicate to your child that she is doing the task for herself. This message will prevent power struggles.

TRAIT 3: BRIGHT

The active alert child is bright. This trait endears her to parents at the same time that it provides all of the difficulties unique to parenting a bright child.

These intelligent children often delve deeply into topics, learning all there is to know about dinosaurs, trains, bats, snakes, dolls, or computers. They glean information like radar scanners. Be prepared! They may know more than you do about a subject. High intellect combined with alertness creates special issues for parents. What should you do?

Parenting Strategy

Learning How Your Child Learns and How to Facilitate That Learning • Young active alerts learn by doing. They create and seek reasons to move. They love action stories, are easily distracted, and often attack problems physically and impulsively before they reason them out. Active alert children love to touch and manipulate their environment. Often, their need to move, combined with awareness and intelligence, yields rather creative behavior.

■ ■ ■

Sally loved to unroll toilet paper so she could count the squares and see where the roll ended.

Rather than trying to stop the flow of curious creative behavior, focus on it, structure it, relocate it, and find appropriate environments for it. Then get away from it when you need a break.

■ ■ ■

Katie's mother was at her wit's end. Her daughter had spent the day using energy inappropriately. Her mother needed to get ready to go to work and wanted to take a bath. She took Katie into the bathroom with her. "After all," she reasoned. "what could she get into in the bathroom?" While in the tub, Katie's mom heard a clinking sound. Katie was stirring a cup of water with her mother's watch. It was the last straw. Her mom admitted with embarrassment, "I blew it! I told her she would go to her room until doomsday."

Ever active alert, Katie asked, "How long is doomsday, Mom?"

Active alert children find creative ways to stay active and to explore. So be prepared to give your explorer what she needs to do that. Active alerts use their skills differently, but all seem to have some rather extraordinary gifts.

■ ■ ■

Megan's passion illustrates this point. Tired of hearing Megan beg for a Barbie doll, Megan's mom bought one for her four-year-old. That same day, Megan spent hours in her room building a doll swing set with string and a portable towel rack. Seven years later, Megan had five Barbie dolls and was still creating "Barbie World" in her bedroom, cutting up old socks to make dresses, building furniture out of toilet paper rolls and swimming pools out of pots and pans. When Megan turned twelve, she and her mother, with some sadness and a great deal of ritual, packed the dolls away "for my daughter," Megan told her mom.

■ ■ ■

Five-year-old Adam could take apart an electric fan and put it back together again. Although his skill boded wonderful things for his future, his parents sometimes overlooked his "gift" in the frustration of seeing a fan in pieces on the living room floor. To appease their child's appetite for mechanical objects and to regain some order in their living room, they began to buy Adam toys with gears that he could take apart. Adam's parents also took him to garage sales where they found mechanical devices that could be disassembled. At the same time, they delineated which items in the house he was not allowed to dismantle.

Accept Your Child and Advocate for Him •   Teaching active alert children is a challenge. They do not fit the mold and thus may not necessarily fit within school systems. You will need to choose carefully not only preschools but also elementary and high schools. (We'll discuss schools in-depth in chapter 8.)

Be challenged by your bright child, but don't forget to enjoy, accept, and appreciate his gift—and never underestimate it. Your child learns by doing, moving, and touching. Help your child understand that his movement is not just a distraction but a way in which he integrates new ideas. Appreciate that new ideas evolve through his movement and active manipulation of his environment.

Lastly, understand the way *you* learn as well as the way your child learns. Some people learn best by watching or seeing; they are visual learners. Auditory learners learn best by hearing or listening. Others are kinesthetic learners; they learn best by moving, touching, and doing. We will discuss learning styles in depth in chapter 8. Your style may be similar to your child's or it may be different. When learning styles differ, expect some conflict.

TRAIT 4: CONTROLLING

Ah! Here we are at last. Is this the trait that drove you to pick up this book in the first place?

Active alert children have a high need to be in control. That need is directly related to their inability to distinguish boundaries or to discern the social order of life. Simply stated, their environment overstimulates them, so they seek to control it. That means you need to constantly teach your intelligent, alert child where the "walls" are.

As the cases of Regan and James show, active alerts can be quite intrusive.

■ ■ ■

Regan, age nine, was in the bathroom yelling at her six-year-old sister, Jan. "Jan took too much toilet paper and she didn't wipe right," Regan explained to Mom. "She was supposed to wipe from front to back, not back to front."

■ ■ ■

Before James, age eight, and his family went out to play soccer, James told his mom, dad, sister, and brother where to stand and how they were to play. Although the family had played together before, James felt compelled to take charge.

Parenting Strategy

Recognizing and Respecting Boundaries • Consistency is an important goal to keep in mind here. Your child remembers well and is smart; each time you fail to follow through he will note it and, rest assured, will remind you of it at some future date.

Many active alert childern seem to keep internal lists. Children I work with tell me that sometimes their parents let them stay up late and sometimes they don't. These same children have learned by experience and observation that such inconsistency is not related to their parents' mood but to how well they, the children, ask, plead, and bargain.

■ ■ ■

Whenever nine-year-old Sam wanted a cookie, he sent his four-year-old sister in to ask their mom for it. Sam waited out in the hall. When mom caught on he explained, "You never say no to her." He was right. Sam's little sister was a real charmer, and Sam had figured out an effective way of getting what he wanted.

Don't use ambivalent no's. No means no!

Build Structure or Routines • Most of us have some basic routines about eating, dressing, and brushing our teeth. Indeed, many childhood tasks have an inherent order. Your child cannot get into his winter clothing without following a routine: snow pants, jacket, boots, and mittens. No one can zip a jacket while wearing mittens. You certainly can't put on snow pants after you put on boots.

Your child needs to learn that by following a prescribed series of steps, she achieves a desired outcome. You can structure such learning with exchanges or barters, that is, exchange a routine for something your child wants. Tell your child, "When you are dressed and have your shoes on, you can eat breakfast." If hunger motivates the child, you do not need to engage in a power struggle. "Brush your hair after you eat breakfast and you can watch 'Sesame Street.'" If a child does not comply, don't turn on the television. That way your child chooses the consequences through his behavior.

Power struggles only teach your child to believe that he has a choice, even when you aren't offering one. Structuring "encouragers" as a reward for accomplishing a task may help you avoid such conflict. Order also is comforting to your child.

Active alert children love patterns, and indeed, they need them. Patterns provide an order to their daily life. Patterns are difficult to establish in some families. Adults who value spontaneity may have trouble meeting this need in their child. (Read more about this in chapter 5.)

Determine Who's in Charge   •   Because active alert children want to be in charge, you may sometimes feel helpless or embattled or that your family life is a war zone.

Remember, you are the adult, and you know more about the world. You know what your child needs to function best. You also know more about your family members' individual needs.

You are not, however, a boss who can forcibly exert your will on your child. That may be what your child is trying to do, but as the adult you must resist that temptation. When your child is exerting control inappropriately over people or places, *do not meet power with power*. Move from that win-lose to a win-win situation. You can set a limit that helps your child learn without creating a "me-against-you" stalemate.

To do that, approach your child as a knowledgeable adult—a *cooperation coordinator*—who values every family member. Assure your child that part of the reason you are there is to insure that, whenever possible, each family member's needs are met. You, the parents, know what individuals as well as the whole family needs. Explain to your child that by giving and taking turns, he will help insure a fair process in which everyone's needs are considered. Help him understand that although this process means that others' needs will sometimes get met before his, eventually he will get his turn.

■ ■ ■

Jeremy's choir concert was the same day as Lisa's skating show. Lisa was angry. "How can you go to both?" she asked her parents. "You'll just have to miss Jeremy's concert." Lisa's parents talked it over and then Dad said, "We love you both and are so proud of you. But we have a bit of a problem. We will all go to the first half of Jeremy's concert. Lisa and Mom will leave during intermission and go to the skating rink. Jeremy and I will come to the rink when the concert is over, and we will get to the rink just as the show starts. It will be a close call, but we can do it if we all work together."

Active alerts are naturally competitive; therefore, you need to take the lead and demonstrate how people cooperate. Teaching that skill aids your child in her interactions with you and with her siblings and peers.

At times, however, you must establish a bottom line. When you find you're getting lost in your child's endless verbal negotiations, use it as a clue. Your child may be signaling that she is having difficulty accepting a no answer or the consequence of a choice she has made.

If this is the case, you can help your child accept the decision. Together, uncover the feeling triggering the child's behavior. Is he sad? Angry? As you talk, make it clear that the decision or consequence stands this time. But when a similar situation arises in the future, use the new knowledge of your child's feelings to help you find a better option.

Keep in mind that understanding your child doesn't mean you are responsible for his behavior. You can understand that some of your child's behavior is temperament-based, however, he is still responsible for his own behavior and choices.

Active learning needs active parenting. Armchair parenting does not work with an active alert child. Don't sit in your chair and expect your child to move away from the crystal vase when you tell her to do so. Get up out of your chair and go to her. Be there, willing to respond to your child.

Engage and then disengage. The active alert child is physical. To get his attention you need to be physically present and make eye contact with him. Then you need to sense when to disengage from such contact. After you have his attention, your child will engage you physically; he may even hit you. Discerning when to be physically engaged with your child and when your presence perpetuates the problem is a vitally important parenting skill.

■ ■ ■

When five-year-old Michael got too wild, his parents told him to go to his room, where he had a trampoline. Michael often refused to go. His father would then pick him up and carry him off, with Michael kicking and screaming. His dad and I discussed the lose-lose nature of this pattern. Michael's father learned to place a hand on his son's shoulder and tell him his monkey was loose. [Note that he disengaged much sooner than when he picked up a screaming child and carried him to his room.] Michael knew if his monkey was out he needed to be in his room because the monkey bothered his dad. If he could not do this, he and the monkey would not be able to wrestle that evening (something Michael loved). As a result of this change, Michael's dad could sit back and let Michael decide to make a positive choice. The first few times they tried this, Michael continued his tantrum behavior, and his dad took his hand and walked him to his room, saying "I am sure you can make a better decision tomorrow."

Because of your child's curiosity and level of activity, childproofing your house when your active alert child is an infant is critical. By doing so, you essentially are engaging the explorer so that you can disengage.

Don't spend time trying to teach your child not to touch a vase. Remove it until your child is no longer interested, or display it well out of reach. You have only so much energy—use it wisely. Choosing the issues with which you will grapple by structuring ways to disengage from certain situations is an appropriate use of your strength and is good, commonsense parenting.

When you do engage your child, remember this tip: Act "as if" she will do what you request. Believe me, your child knows when you are fearful or tentative. If she senses your fear, she will not do what you ask and may attempt to fulfill your worst fears. Children often do what you expect rather than what you ask.

Remember, give your child a choice of what to do or how to do it, but not both. If you offer too many choices, she will get lost in a maze of indecisiveness or begin to think that by manipulating the situation she can have it all.

For example, your child must get dressed each day. He has no choice in the matter. But, within limits, he can choose what to wear. Children, after all, need to feel they are strong and have control over their lives; no one likes to feel powerless.

■ ■ ■

Beth is in charge of who puts what away when cleaning up the playroom. The room gets cleaned up, and Beth has some power in the situation.

Here's a parenting tip. If you and your child are struggling about an issue, try joining forces with your child against "them." Portray yourself as an encouraging advocate rather than the boss.

Choose a particular issue you want to work on with your child. Is it piano practice, bed making, or cooperating with a sibling? Create a chart together and post it on the refrigerator. The chart will help your child to focus on the behavior you want to encourage. Remember to phrase the goals on the chart positively, for example, "I will use a quiet voice" rather than "I won't yell," or "I will talk about my anger" rather than "I won't hit." It's easier for children to remember what you want rather than what you don't want.

Talk respectively with your child about the issue you have identified, explaining that the chart is one way to help her deal with the difficulty. To help focus your child's attention, let her choose a reward to work for, such as a toy or an outing. As your child gets older, this charting process becomes a lesson in goal setting.

After the chart is created and posted, you can back out of the process. The issue is now between the child and the chart on the refrigerator. The child does not have to listen to your reminders, and you get to let go of the issue. The child will not yell at the fridge or make it the focus of a tantrum. When the child does not achieve his goal, reassure him that tomorrow is another day and that he'll have another chance to reach his goal then.

When it comes to a controlling child, *be leery of whimsical servitude.*

■ ■ ■

At breakfast, Carrie asks her mother for cereal. When her mother pours it, Carrie demands an egg. Her mother sighs, boils an egg, and eats the cereal herself. Carrie then says that she doesn't like eggs and wants cinnamon toast.

Okay. Let's examine this issue. Carrie's mother has a choice: She can continue the process of catering to Carrie's whims— forever—or she can stop. Either way, Carrie will yell and scream as she attempts to make the family as miserable as she feels.

In this scenario, Carrie is powerful—too powerful. Healthy families often are tempted to discount a problem such as Carrie's, thinking to themselves, "She's just having a tough morning." First, the truth is that Carrie has a problem, and there is a limit to what her mother can do to help. Second, Carrie's behavior is a problem for her mother. The earlier she learns that her behavior is a problem, the better for her and her family.

Carrie's parents can help her determine who has the problem by helping her understand whose issue this is and what parties are involved. Deciding how to act at breakfast is Carrie's choice. Her parents may need to tell her, "Gee, Carrie, it seems you are having a tough morning. I'm sure you can handle your feelings without making the rest of the family miserable." Or they might joke, "Carrie, you'd better go back to bed. Maybe if you got out on the other side, your day would go better. I'll race you to your bedroom."

If Carrie's mother can help her see that she has a problem, Carrie can address her problem. However, if she cannot, Carrie's behavior will continue to be a problem for her mother.

In which case, her mother may say, "You only get to decide what to eat for breakfast once. Tomorrow you will have another chance to choose."

Set Priorities • What is really important to you? Are you willing to give up something to help smooth out life with your active alert child? On what issues are you going to draw the line? Are you struggling with a child over something that is a low priority to you? You can exercise the choice to let go of some struggles.

■ ■ ■

Jonathan looked forward to the weekly grocery shopping trip. He loved to pick out his own cereal and snacks. Unfortunately, he ran up and down the aisles in the store touching displays and hiding from his mom. Although she was exhausted by his behavior in the store, Jonathan's mother always stayed to finish her shopping. I asked her if she would leave the grocery store to teach Jonathan a different lesson.

I contend that the parent must always be willing to let go. Jonathan's mother decided to change the scenario. The next week when Jonathan acted out in the store, she told him, "If you continue to act that way, you are telling me that you are choosing not to do shopping with me." He continued his behavior, so they left and he did not get to pick out his treats. Subsequently, Jonathan and his mom have had more pleasant shopping trips. He now knows the consequences of his behavior and the boundaries.

TRAIT 5: FEARFUL

Extroverted active alerts seem to fear little except loss of control. Introverted active alerts are fearful and unable to make transitions. Being alert and unable to screen out stimuli, both types spend a great deal of time being afraid.

Parenting Strategy

Prepare Your Child for Change   •   New environments frighten your child, so it's important to help her understand the future. Tell her about changes that you know are upcoming. Outline the agenda. Help her anticipate what might happen by discussing in the evening what the next day will bring. Include in the discussion the events of the day and the feelings that might occur as a result of those events. Talking through what might happen allows your child to verbally role-play things that worry her.

■ ■ ■

Chloe, age ten, decided she wanted to quit piano lessons. Her mother wanted her to continue but chose not to intervene. Instead she said, "You will have to talk with your teacher about this." On the way to her lessons, Chloe asked her mother, "What should I tell Mrs. Peterson?"

"Well," her mother said, "You could say, 'Mrs. Peterson, I'm thinking about quitting piano lessons.' What do you think she will say?"

Chloe and her mother continue to role-play. Chloe came home that afternoon pleased with the compromise she and her teacher had reached. They agreed Chloe would work until the next month's recital and then she would quit.

■ ■ ■

Each evening, four-year-old Paul, trying to articulate his anxiety about his three-day-a-week preschool schedule, asked his parents, "What is the plan? What day is it when I wake up?"

Be clear about when your child will have a choice in events. A child with two employed parents cannot choose to skip day care; however, he can take a favorite stuffed toy to the child-care center for nap time.

Whatever your routine, discussing it with your child reassures her and helps prevent struggles in the morning. Remind an older child about the times she has made successful transitions: "Sometimes it's hard to go, but once you get to places, it seems that you have a pretty good time."

Changes are sometimes unforeseen, and your child needs to know that. Discuss this issue with her and reassure her that you will always be there to support her and that you will never desert her. Because you cannot always be with your child physically, you may want to create a ritual to help her remember your love in times of stress. E.T. gave us a wonderful gesture for doing so: He placed his fingertip on a forehead and in effect said, "I will be with you always." You and your child may want to adopt the gesture as a symbol of support.

Accept Your Child's Fears • It is easy to see why an active alert child can be fearful. A child who is unclear about boundaries and is bombarded by stimuli is certainly going to be anxious in new environments. He won't know how much control he can expect to have over all of the new elements he knows he cannot screen out.

To help your child adjust to new situations, try to preview the day-care center, new school, or friend's house. Explore the building, locate the bathrooms, meet the teacher. When active alert children do not have a concrete picture, they create one, and what they imagine may be worse than anything you or I could picture.

Young active alert children fear such things as not knowing how to read and write before they start school. One preschooler with an older sister worried about doing "desk work" in nursery school because he didn't know how to write. His mother assured him that nursery schools did not require desk work. An older child may be terrified about opening a combination lock on her junior high locker. Think of what a relief it would be to provide her with a "rehearsal" lock to practice with during the summer before she starts junior high.

■ ■ ■

One day at school Joe burst into tears. He was confused about whether he had to take a preschool bus to

*afterschool day care or if it was a day when his mom
would pick him up. He thought he needed to keep track of
his schedule himself, so he did not ask his teacher for
help. Later he told his mom, "Well, I always knew I could
take a cab home."*

*Needless to say, Joe and his mother worked out a
different solution. They created cardboard letters Joe
could carry in his pocket. B stood for bus, M for mom.
Whenever he needed to remind himself what day it was,
he checked the letter. He never once had to call a taxi!*

Taking a child to school a little early may help to ease the
transition between home and school. She can determine, without
the stimulus of other children, what she wants to play with and
where to sit. Often it is easier for active alert children to allow
other children into their play than it is for them to enter other
children's already established activity.

■ ■ ■

*Three-year-old Peter would not visit a new friend unless
his mom stayed with him during the first visit. His
mother learned to deal with this creatively. She
explained the situation to the friend's mother and invited
herself over for coffee.*

Be Careful Not to Push • Because active alert children are
sensitive to all the stimuli around them, they are particularly
vulnerable to "the hurried child phenomenon." Try not to push
your child, even though he may be highly creative and energetic.
Signing him up for too many classes may create too many
transition times for him. Be aware of how your child's scheduling
affects him. Even if all the neighbors have their preschoolers
enrolled in art, gymnastics, swimming, and soccer, those courses
may be too much, too soon for your child.

Enrolling a child in classes before she is developmentally
ready may only result in negative feedback from teachers
about her excessive physical energy. Choosing one class to
attend with your two-and-a-half or three-year-old may set up a

happier situation for both of you. Understand and accept your child—fears and all.

■ ■ ■

Three months into the school year, Lisa's mother, who picks Lisa up each day, was fifteen minutes late. She arrived to find her eight-year-old daughter sobbing, sure her mother had forgotten her. Lisa's mother had never before failed to pick her up. Regardless, Lisa was overcome with fear.

Her brother, four years younger than Lisa, said, "Don't you know Mother will always be here to get you? She loves you." In a nutshell, he described how an active alert's temperament differs from that of other children. Lisa's mother did not teach Lisa to be insecure, nor did she teach Lisa's brother to be secure. Other children just seem to understand that their environment is safe.

TRAIT 6: INTENSE

If active alert children feel lost, they do not feel a little terror but a lot; if their parents are five minutes late, they are sure they are never coming. They are intensely happy or intensely sad, very right or very wrong. Active alert children think of themselves as good or bad, smart or dumb, but never average. They are "all or nothing" kids.

Parenting Strategy

Accept and Affirm Your Child's Intensity • Intensity can be used to control parents unless you learn to accept and affirm your child's feelings by conveying to your child that you believe he is competent to handle his feelings.

■ ■ ■

During Matthew's first week in kindergarten, he cried when he was hit on the playground and again when he had to go to the library. He simply didn't know what would be expected of him in this strange, new place. Each time he cried his teacher told him, rather brusquely, to stop.

Matthew came home and said, "When my teacher says to stop it, I feel scared. It doesn't help me." A reassuring comment from a teacher would have made all the difference to Matthew. The teacher could have said, "I see you are feeling sad right now. I think you can handle the trip to the library to hear a story and pick out a book." When he arrived home, his mother assured him he could handle the library trip. She also told him, "Matthew, it sounds like your teacher can teach you about many things like reading, spelling, and math, but she probably cannot teach you about feelings."

Feelings are facts. You can tell someone not to feel, but it won't work. Instead, labeling the feeling and affirming the child's ability to deal with problems gives him what he needs to be competent.

Although it's important to accept your child's intense feelings, it is not necessary or advisable to cater to or dwell on those feelings. Help him learn that feelings flow and change.

Offer Sympathy While Guiding Your Child   •   If you oversympathize, your child will learn to manipulate you by using these feelings. A better approach is to acknowledge the feelings and help your child identify her alternatives. She can then feel capable rather than victimized.

Help your child determine what action he can take. If your child is young, you may want to brainstorm alternatives for handling emotions. You and your preschooler may want to make a list of all the things he can do when he is angry (for example, stomp his foot, hit a pillow, jump up and down) or when he is lonely (for example, ask for a hug, look at pictures in a book, cuddle a blanket or an animal). For an older child, it may be enough to express confidence in him by saying, "I know you can handle this," and recall previous situations that were handled successfully. Most important, believe in your child's ability to handle himself even in intense moments. Remember, only your child can calm himself, you do not have that power.

Identify "Catastrophizing" with Your Child • When your child is about six or seven, you can help her recognize when she is catastrophizing—making a mountain out of a molehill. Active alert children are experts at catastrophizing. If one thing goes wrong, everything is terrible.

■ ■ ■

Danny and his mother were having a wonderful day at the fair. At the end of their time together, Danny asked if he could go on one more ride. His mother said no, they had to meet Danny's father at the gate in a few minutes and there wasn't time. Danny began to shout that it had been a terrible day and he hadn't had any fun at all.

Intensity often includes loud verbal blasts, behavior that Danny's mother calls "spouting off." For example, let's say your active alert seven-year-old daughter trips and hurts her toe on the way out the door to school. Her parting comment is, "This is going to be a bad day!" Responding to this kind of intense behavior requires steadiness on the part of the parent. It is easy to get caught up in the blast or to treat it as if it has the logic of an adult argument. Model emotional regulation for your child.

Bright, articulate active alert children entangle their parents in their words. Remember, your mission as a parent of an active alert is to determine what really hurts! These youngsters are all-or-nothing children. It sometimes helps if they can rate their hurt on a scale of 1 to 10. This allows both the child and parent to gain perspective. (Read more about turning worst possible scenarios into "most likelies" in chapter 7.)

TRAIT 7: ATTENTION-HUNGRY

Active alert children have what I lovingly refer to as a black hole of attention. They are, in psychological terms, externally referenced. What's going on around them and what other people think are vitally important to them. Parents need to make sure their active alert child has time to be alone with each parent.

Parenting Strategy

Take Time to Be Alone with Your Child   •   Your child needs private time with you to sew a bear, build with blocks, read, and cook. One-on-one time, free of competing tasks or people, says, "You are special to me." Find at least one activity you and your child like to do together. It may be walking, drawing, woodworking, rearranging furniture, or cleaning.

Also, encourage parallel play throughout the day. That means that you work on your projects—cooking dinner, folding laundry, doing yard chores—while your child works on hers—banging pots and pans, doing a puzzle. As she plays, talk to her but encourage parallel play because it is an important form of independence training.

Teach Your Child to Say "Good-bye" to the Good Times   • Even time with you needs some structure. Your child needs to know when he is going to have time with you alone and when that is not an option. If siblings are around, remind him about the time you have reserved for the two of you. Indicate clearly how long that time will last so that your child will know it has not only a beginning but also an end. Do this by setting a timer or show your child where the hand on the clock will be when your time together ends.

■ ■ ■

Nine-year-old Josh and his mother had a wonderful weekend. His older sister had gone to a weekend slumber party, so Josh and Mom spent Saturday and Sunday skiing, reading, and going to the movies.

On Sunday evening at bedtime, Josh got out of bed to tell his mom that he was sad. For the first time in many years, he asked to sleep with a stuffed animal. Twenty minutes later, he came out again and said he had figured out what he needed—some attention.

His mother, who had been extraordinarily attentive to Josh all weekend, thought, "Here's my black hole of attention." *Later, when she spoke to me, we realized it was not attention Josh needed. He was having trouble with a transition; he didn't know how to say "good-bye" to the good times.*

If you believe this is an issue for your child, talk about it directly with him. Anticipating together another good time you have planned will help him let go of the one that has just ended.

For example, Josh's mother could have said to him "We had a good time this weekend and now it's over. Let's choose a date on the calendar when we'll go see another movie, and then you can go back to bed."

Take Time for Yourself • Schedule time away from your child. I cannot stress this too much. For you, as well as for your marriage or relationships, take a break! The commercial "Calgon, take me away!" could have been written for parents of active alerts. Set aside a place in your house where you can shut the door. Let the other parent or a baby-sitter take charge. Teach your child not to violate whatever space you designate as yours.

Structure nap times and do not vary the schedule. If this time is violated, the child will not easily settle back into the routine. As your child grows older and gives up naps, you still will need a break, so insist on a quiet time when your child plays on her own in her room. Such routines are crucial for your child and insure your healthy survival.

Be aware that *once you alter the routine, it is renegotiable*—at least in your child's mind. So stick good-naturedly with the original schedule whenever possible.

TRAIT 8: TROUBLE GETTING ALONG WITH OTHERS

Active alerts tend to be intrusive, trying to control their peers or having trouble interpreting the nonverbal signals.

Parenting Strategy

Teach Them to Make Friends • Extroverted active alert children have trouble making friends. Excited at the prospect of being with other children, they may overwhelm their peers and bowl them over with hugs. In short, they are intrusive.

They are, however, often great fun to be around. They are the children who create new approaches to games or who stir up the ordinary with fresh ideas and are quite attractive playmates. In short, they are the good idea kids.

Tempering their energy is the key. Fortunately, there are ways to help your child learn appropriate behavior. At ages two to four, specify short (one to one-and-a-half hours) playtimes with one other child. Don't expect to get anything done while they are playing, however, because these children need active supervision. Remain in the same room with them while involving yourself in your own activity, or leave a nursery monitor in the room to keep tabs on the play. Encourage cooperation between the children and put out small "fires" before they grow into explosions. This kind of play teaches children what is expected of them when they play with other children.

Helping your child to learn about people's need for personal space is another issue in being a good friend. In addition to the red light/green light idea (see chapter 3), I teach children that each person is surrounded by a protective bubble. That bubble can be large or small, depending on the person and the culture in which he or she grew up. The British, for example, have larger bubbles than people from Saudi Arabia or Italy.

I ask children to picture people inside bubbles. We talk about their mother's, their father's, their brother(s)', sister(s)', and friends' bubbles. I ask them what happens when you touch a bubble. It breaks!

Then I explain that a person whose bubble breaks feels uncomfortable and often angry with the person who broke it. The person who is now without a bubble feels unsafe and may push others away so that he can create another one. By using the bubble analogy, I help children learn to recognize when they are intruding. In this way they become aware of nonverbal distress signals (a scrunched-up, displeased facial expression, a sudden change in the eyes from pleasure to fear or uncertainty). Such an awareness of nonverbal cues is worthwhile to nurture in children.

A similar analogy that I use with school-age children is that of a protective field. This is especially useful with science fiction devotees.

Teach Them to Keep Friends • Some children who have no trouble making friends have trouble keeping them. They seem unable to take a backseat, to take turns, or to handle conflict. Address these issues with your child. Assessing no blame or shame, point out how her behavior affects friendships. Developing a child's capacity to think about how others feel increases her ability to sit back and let others perform.

■ ■ ■

Eight-year-old Alison, the youngest of three children, seldom got to invite children to her home. When she did have a friend over, she played the piano for them the whole time they were together. Now, even though Alison is an excellent pianist, Alison's friends were not enthralled by the "concert." We talked about how Alison's friends might feel when she performed for them all the time. We listed other things that eight-year-olds could do together. Then her mom set aside specific times when Alison could invite friends over. As a result, Alison soon developed good, lasting friendships.

Ask yourself in what ways your child has trouble with friendships. Does he have difficulty making friends? Keeping them? Managing conflict constructively is often a problem in maintaining relationships.

Work on managing conflict starts within the family and spreads to other relationships. My colleague, Dr Richard Bell, says kids have to FACE their anger—Feel it, Accept it, Clarify it, and Express it. Used in the family, this process spreads to friendships. Be there to help your child feel, accept, clarify, and express anger appropriately. Insuring that the feelings of all parties in a dispute get counted is important to developing and keeping friendships.

Begin this process when your child is a preschooler. Simply kneel down and wrap one arm around each angry disputant. Get them to speak to each other. In the beginning, you may have to coach them: "Johnny, tell Fred how you feel about what he did," then, "Fred, tell Johnny how you feel."

This technique allows each child a chance to accept and express his anger while you clarify it for both of them. In this way, they get to decide what to do about their anger, and they also get to resolve their negative feelings. Remember to place your arms around both children or one child will surely run away.

Check the list of wonderful books in the resource section that deal with resolving conflict and read them with your child.

TRAIT 9: FLUCTUATING SELF-ESTEEM

As is true of so many things about them, active alert children have either intensely high or intensely low self-esteem. It seems to change from moment to moment. Because they are such good observers, they are keenly alert to messages about themselves. Among the messages they receive are many "shoulds" about how to behave—expectations they may not always be able to fulfill.

Parenting Strategy

Accept Their Traits and Learning Style   •   Accepting and affirming your child is central to building his self-esteem. It is not easy to do this in our society, which often negatively characterizes an active alert child, as if something were wrong with him or with the parents who created such an anxiety-ridden, fearful, active child.

Respond to such messages by telling yourself, "This child was born into the world with his unique, wonderful disposition." If you "blame" your child or yourself for his temperament, you do two things. First, you discount the good characteristics of your child. Second, you say, in effect, that there is something inherently bad about your child. That destructive message prevents your child from feeling loved.

There are several ways to boost your child's self-esteem. Help her to understand how she learns and how that learning style can work for and against her in school (we'll discuss this further in chapter 8). Then talk about accepting and even rejoicing in what it is that makes her unique. Concentrate on her positive gifts, such as her ability to negotiate, her verbal skills, her knowledge of certain subjects, and her contagious energy.

Point out things your child will be able to do because he learns differently. Use humor to discuss differences. And learn to accept imperfection. After all, perfection implies that there is only one way of being.

Here's the fun part: *You* get to model imperfection! Watching you accept your own mistakes helps your child accept his own— and it takes the onus off you to be perfect!

Always ask yourself, "What do I want my child to learn?" When faced with a fearful child, adults often model competence. Sometimes, it soothes the child more to do just the opposite—to model incompetence.

■ ■ ■

Neal's father wanted his nine-year-old son to feel comfortable asking for help from waitresses, salespeople, teachers, or police. In such situations, however, Neal responded with a timidity that irritated his father. I suggested that Neal's father should mirror his son's fears and work through them to a solution.

The next time they went out to eat, Neal's dad said, "Gee, I have to go to the bathroom. I wonder where it is. I don't want to bother the waitress, but I really have to go. I'm kind of scared to ask for help, but I guess I'd better. After all, she can't hurt me for asking a question." After the waitress answered his questions, Neal's dad smiled and said, "Well, that wasn't so bad!"

It is reassuring for children to know that grown-ups don't know everything. Incompetence, used in that way, affirms that adults as well as children are human beings with both frailties and strengths. Remember, however, that while using a more incompetent role model is useful in demonstrating a skill or in helping your child understand that it's scary to do something the first time, it would not be useful if the situation were a real emergency in which the child needs to rely upon you.

Accept Your Child's Feelings • Active alert children are approach–withdrawal kids. Part of their all-or-nothing approach to life, it dictates behavior in new situations when, rather than "jumping in," your child stands back and assesses what is happening. An angry active alert child may say, "I hate you" or "You never loved me anyway." Being disrespectful of such anger not only creates distance between the two of you but also encourages a child's disrespect for himself.

Identify and accept your child's feelings. Then, rather than asking him to change his feelings, insist that he be responsible for expressing them appropriately. If he continues to act inappropriately, send him to his room or to another area of the house.

Building Internal Referents • Active alert children are externally oriented: They decide whether they are good or bad based on how other people react to them. They need to learn to move from the external referent to an internal one. If your child knows who he is and how he learns, he can make accurate judgments about himself based not on what other people say but on how he intuitively feels.

One way to do this is to encourage your child to close his eyes and "go inside himself." Learning to distinguish his own feelings from the feelings all around him is an important step in moving from an external to an internal referent.

Other suggestions? Read about esteem together. Make a book featuring your child's special qualities: height, weight, number of teeth, color of hair, favorite books and foods. Describe her likes and dislikes so that, in the end, she will get to know herself inside and out.

TRAIT 10: PERFORMERS

Children who gather much of their self-concept from others learn to charm and please. This can be a wonderful gift, but at times it is a sword with which they inflict pain on themselves.

■ ■ ■

Eight-year-old Jennifer's mother was worried about her daughter. Jennifer's teacher said that Jennifer had a normal number of friends, but her mother knew that when it was time to pair up in class, no one ever chose Jennifer as a partner. Her mother and I discussed the situation and discovered that Jennifer was often intrusive and controlling. From the outside, she appeared to have several friends, when in truth she had only admirers because she did everything (she performed) so well.

Parenting Strategy

Enjoy! • Enjoy and appreciate your performer. Active alert children love to take center stage—whether it be piano playing, working math problems on the blackboard, or pitching softball—and they do it well.

Is there a downside to this trait? Yes. Many parents of active alert children feel that the "outside world" gets all the "good stuff"! That's because these children often behave so appropriately, that is, they perform so beautifully, away from home and "unwind" so energetically at home. Enjoy the fact that your child is so esteemed. You may even want to bask in it a little. At the same time, however, remember that your child needs to temper her need to perform because there are some pitfalls to that behavior.

Teach Your Child to Enjoy Other Performers • Be very clear about where and when performing is appropriate. Sometimes children need to sit back and let someone else take a turn leading or performing. Talk with your child about jealousy when someone else is the center of attention. Is your child worried that he will not be loved if he is not always the best?

Most important, love and affirm your child just because he is alive! Catch your child when he is not performing and affirm him for being. That way your child will learn to be gracious on and off stage and understand that he is lovable even when applauding a friend.

TRAIT 11: EMPATHIC ABILITY

Active alert children seem to have antennae! They are exceedingly alert to feelings and emotions that escape other people. They do not always understand the emotions bombarding them, however. Because they have no clear boundaries, they do not always know whose feelings set off their own emotional response.

Their behavior may be triggered by undercurrents of tension, stress, anger, or excitement, long before they even recognize those emotions are present. Most often, they tune into the emotions of one particular parent, with whom they seem to share an invisible umbilical cord.

■ ■ ■

By the time Beth was six months old, her mother was leaving her on a regular basis with baby-sitters. It was not always easy for Beth or her mother. At first Beth cried vociferously for the hour or two her mother was gone; then she learned to cope by sleeping. Each time her mother came home and walked through the door, however, Beth woke and cried.

Parenting Strategy

Accept and Trust Your Child's Instinctual Ability
• Learn to accept your child's empathic abilities and the complexity of his emotions. Astute observers, active alert children are often intuitive. Although their interpretation of what they intuit may not be accurate, you need to honor and respect the gift.

■ ■ ■

Seven-year-old Caitlin did not like to be alone with a particular teacher. She did not mind being with him in a group, but she said that he talked to girls funny when they were alone with him. Caitlin had missed some tests and this particular teacher was scheduled to administer them to her. Her mother was caught in a dilemma. The

*man, after all, had done nothing wrong, but she too
sensed something a little different about the teacher.
Rather than wait for something to happen, she trusted
her child's instincts. Caitlin was too young to label her
feelings, but she could articulate them to an adult who
listened and honored them. The mother talked to Caitlin's
main teacher, who also respected Caitlin's feelings and
asked someone else to monitor the make-up tests.*

Identify Feelings and Label Their Source   •   In some
situations, your child is driven by emotions that do not belong to
her. By naming such feelings, we help the child determine
appropriate actions. Extended family dinners, for example, can
cause havoc for the child who tunes into the unresolved issues
between generations.

Model a path to take through the mire of emotions by expressing your own emotions directly. Remember, your child
learns from what you do—not from what you say.

Take good care of yourself. That invisible umbilical cord may be
linked to you. When you are stressed, so is your child. Don't
count on your active alert to come to you and say, "Let me help
out." More than likely he will react frantically to your unease. It's
up to you to take steps to reduce your stress overload.

With an older child, you may need only to remind her that you
and she are indeed two separate people with different sets of
feelings. Tell her that even if you are angry or upset, she does not
need to take on those emotions. Tell your child that the anger is
yours. You own it and she does not need to feel the way you do or
to be angry at the person with whom you are angry.

This kind of clarification is especially important when parents
are divorced or separating. Because active alerts tend to take on
their parents' emotions, it is vital for parents to let their child
know that their anger at their ex-spouse is their own and not their
child's. The child does not need to be angry for one parent or feel
he must protect the other.

PARENTING STRATEGY SUMMARY

This checklist will help you remember the tips sprinkled throughout this chapter.

1. Active learning needs active parenting.
2. Don't use ambivalent no's.
3. Engage and then disengage.
4. Act "as if" your child will follow through.
5. Be a "cooperation coordinator."
6. Give your child a choice of what to do or how to do it, but not both.
7. Be leery of "whimsical servitude."
8. Know that understanding your child's behavior doesn't mean you are responsible for it.
9. When your child is struggling with a behavior, join with her. Assist her in reaching her goal, and let her know you are on her side and will support her in ways you and she deem appropriate.

For another useful strategy, see "One, Two, Three—You're Out!" on page 143.

5

The Puzzle Known
as the Family

Jigsaw puzzle enthusiasts know that working puzzles is easier when they have the big picture in front of them. Indeed, the more difficult the puzzle, it seems, the more it helps to understand the whole picture. The same holds true when it comes to the family. As parents, all too often we think only of our impact on our children and fail to consider *their* impact on *us*. Knowing about family systems will help us understand how individuals fit into families, but that understanding does not always come easily to families with an active alert child. Such families may have to work diligently to discover how each member fits snugly and comfortably into the puzzle we know as the family.

Still, we all know what happens when we find just the right puzzle piece: The other pieces fall into place, and working the puzzle becomes a joyful, satisfying process. I hope the understanding you gain from this look at family systems may be just the piece you need to help you and your family find the best possible fit for each member.

Don't tell anyone, but in this chapter I'm letting you in on some of my professional secrets. The family theories I present here are the basis of all my work with active alert children. I hope I will explain them in a way that makes sense to you so that you too can use them in your parenting.

First, we'll assess your family style. Then we'll look at the work of Larry Constantine, a family therapist and theorist, on four family paradigms. As we do so, we will uncover how the active alert child fits (or does not fit) in each particular system and how families and individuals can adjust so that all the puzzle pieces fit together clearly.

As you read, keep in mind ways in which you and your family are working well together in addition to looking for ways to adjust your family structure for a more harmonious whole. Ask yourself what happens to the whole system when members are forced to act contrary to their nature. Just as forcing a piece of puzzle into a place it doesn't belong can distort it, forcing a child into a place where he doesn't fit can damage him.

There is no "best" kind of family for active alerts. Indeed, there is no best kind of family for anyone. Each family has a certain combination of characteristics. Your task is to discover how your family works to your child's—indeed, to everyone's—benefit. Let's begin, then, to try to understand the family system in which you and your children are growing.

EXPLORING YOUR FAMILY

All families are unique, but they also have some generic characteristics. Some traits strengthen the active alert child and some present hardships or difficulties for her.

Answer each of the forty statements below according to how you and your family act. Remember, your answers may not always reflect the ideal of how you would like your family to be. They will, however, reveal what your day-to-day family function is really like:

-2   Unlike our family's daily life
-1   Slightly unlike our family's daily life
+1   Slightly like our family's daily life
+2   Like our family's daily life

If you are married, answer each question from your own perspective, not your spouse's. You and your spouse may want to compare responses later.

FAMILY TRAIT ASSESSMENT*

-2 -1 +1 +2	1. We live harmoniously with one another.
-2 -1 +1 +2	2. We use firm and loving control.
-2 -1 +1 +2	3. We are contagiously unconventional.
-2 -1 +1 +2	4. We collaborate to solve problems.
-2 -1 +1 +2	5. Our day-to-day routine is boring.
-2 -1 +1 +2	6. We are warm but strict with our children.
-2 -1 +1 +2	7. We are sometimes playful and freewheeling.
-2 -1 +1 +2	8. When there are problems we discuss and solve them together.
-2 -1 +1 +2	9. We can coordinate well without communicating.
-2 -1 +1 +2	10. Sometimes the punishment we use is more than fits the crime.
-2 -1 +1 +2	11. Our family is lively and unpredictable.
-2 -1 +1 +2	12. We collaborate and negotiate to resolve disagreements.
-2 -1 +1 +2	13. We have a kind of "unspoken agreement" that makes our days go smoothly.
-2 -1 +1 +2	14. Our family members have a stable sense of belonging.
-2 -1 +1 +2	15. Our house is constantly disorganized.

*These items were derived using Sheila Hollern Herbert's doctoral dissertation, "An Empirical Examination of Constantine's Unified Process Theory" (University of Minnesota, 1986).

-2 -1 +1 +2   16.   Our family members are emotionally accessible to one another.

-2 -1 +1 +2   17.   Our family outlook is contentedly uniform.

-2 -1 +1 +2   18.   We are protective of and demonstrate watchful concern for one another.

-2 -1 +1 +2   19.   We live in adventurous disarray.

-2 -1 +1 +2   20.   We must always be honest about our feelings, even when we don't want to be.

-2 -1 +1 +2   21.   Issues and problems that occupy other families don't seem to concern us.

-2 -1 +1 +2   22.   We like a clear order to our lives.

-2 -1 +1 +2   23.   Unplanned enthusiasm is very important to us.

-2 -1 +1 +2   24.   We work hard to have an equal exchange of ideas.

-2 -1 +1 +2   25.   Our family feels emotionally deadened.

-2 -1 +1 +2   26.   There is definite structure in our family life.

-2 -1 +1 +2   27.   The best kind of fun is spur of the moment.

-2 -1 +1 +2   28.   We are thoughtfully inquisitive of one another.

-2 -1 +1 +2   29.   As a unit, we have an implicit, unspoken understanding about our family and where we are going in life.

-2 -1 +1 +2   30.   We have so many rules, they sometimes are burdensome.

-2 -1 +1 +2   31.   We support zany self-expression.

-2 -1 +1 +2   32.   We respect both old and new ideas.

-2 -1 +1 +2   33.   We exercise a kind of timeless tranquility.

-2 -1 +1 +2   34.   We trust our stability.

-2 -1 +1 +2   35.   We are in a constant state of turmoil.

-2 -1 +1 +2   36.   We are attentive and open with one another.

-2 -1 +1 +2   37.   We have within our family a sense of unity, oneness, or calm.

-2 -1 +1 +2   38.   Loyalty, constancy, and steadfastness are our family virtues.

-2 -1 +1 +2   39.   We love our spontaneous energy.

-2 -1 +1 +2   40.   We constantly analyze ourselves and the others around us.

Please add the pluses and subtract the negatives of the following questions:

1, 5, 9, 13, 17, 21, 25, 29, 33, 37   = _____ (S score)
2, 6, 10, 14, 18, 22, 26, 30, 34, 38 = _____ (C score)
3, 7, 11, 15, 19, 23, 27, 31, 35, 39 = _____ (R score)
4, 8, 12, 16, 20, 24, 28, 32, 36, 40 = _____ (O score)

Since the above scale has not been validated through extensive research, your scores are in no way to be used as a diagnosis of your family type. They can, however, serve as a road map that indicates which family type your family most closely resembles.

THE POWER OF FAMILY SYSTEMS

Now, set the survey aside. We'll interpret your results after we look at family systems as defined by Larry Constantine. Then, in chapter 6, you will be able to place the results of the questionnaire in the proper context.

In his work on the four kinds of paradigms—closed, random, open, and synchronous—Constantine noted that although families are different in many ways, all families share three central features:

- who's in charge
- what the family values
- how the family handles emotions

The Closed Family

In the closed family system, someone is clearly in charge, and that person exercises authority about the rules and the discipline. In this type of family the stability of the family is all-important. Traditions and rituals abound to create and affirm this strong sense of family unity. Family members believe that family stability is more important than the individual members in the group. Children in closed family systems grow up with a strong sense of order and feel secure within the structure of their family. Emotions are regulated, prescribed, and formal. A closed family has a difficult time with intensity and emotions that disrupt stability, such as anger, sadness, or fear.

Members of closed families view the child as a blank slate. The parents teach the child what they expect from her and set limits that enable learning. Some closed families do this in a loving and caring way, but at the same time, they make it clear that no one is to question who is in charge or to express too much emotional neediness. The closed family encourages approval-seeking and promotes dependence and obedience. All members are expected to follow the leader—whether the leader is loving and benevolent or distant and authoritarian.

The *Little House* books by Laura Ingalls Wilder and the "Father Knows Best" television series present good examples of closed family systems.

The Random Family

Control in random families is not static; rather, it often changes hands. It is sometimes unpredictable. This type of family esteems personal freedom, choice, competition, challenge, and creative expression. No one person is in charge. The random family values individuals over the family itself. Restricting personal freedom is oppressive to its members. Emotions in this type of family are spontaneous and may be whimsical. People express feelings passionately, intensely, authentically, but sometimes capriciously.

The random family is permissive with children. Parents set few limits and provide limited supervision. They discourage dependence and value individual expression. Someone from a closed family system may think that random families promote disobedience.

The Tuckers in the movie *Tucker* and Grandpa's family in the play *You Can't Take It with You* by George Kaufman and Moss Hart are examples of random families.

The Open Family

In the open family system, members value equality. Control is cooperative, participatory, and persuasive. This type of family uses consensus to make decisions and works to insure that everyone is comfortable with the outcome of those decisions. As a family, members value dialogue, tolerance, and adaptability. The family and the individual carry equal weight in open families; family needs are balanced with individual needs. Members express emotions in a responsive, authentic manner.

In the open family, the child is valued as a partner who needs help in discovering his own limits. Parents and child negotiate limits and collaborate in problem solving. In this way adults promote cooperation and responsibility.

The open family system, touted by much of the therapeutic community as the only healthy system, is not necessarily the answer to all ills. It is simply one viable option. Both Virginia Satir's *Peoplemaking* and Adele Faber and Elaine Mazlish's *How to Talk So Kids Will Listen & Listen So Kids Will Talk* espouse the open family system.

The Synchronous Family

In the synchronous family system, control is understood without one person being its source. It comes from a shared goal or value system, not from any individual. Family members do not talk about this goal; it is indirect and implicit. The members work together in a timeless fashion. They value the correct way they interrelate. This group's members are quite reserved emotionally. They function as a unit, moving toward a greater end, knowing their steps are right.

Limits in the synchronous family may seem invisible to an outsider. Perhaps without even being aware of it, adults assume that children will learn what is correct and what is expected of them simply by watching the parents' example.

Macon Leary, the central male figure in Anne Tyler's book and the movie *The Accidental Tourist*, grew up in a synchronous family. We see this in the way he relates to his brothers and sister when he returns home with a broken leg. They all act as if Macon had never left home when, indeed, he has not only been away for years but married, lost a child, and separated from his wife. Another example of a synchronous system is the central family of the film *Babette's Feast:* The father dies but the sisters continue with the father's ministry and beliefs as if he were still alive.

In the following chart, which summarizes each of the four paradigms, the term "power" refers to the way the family handles who is in charge; "affect" refers to the way a family displays emotions; and "meaning" refers to what the family values most.

Once again, this chart is meant only as a guide or map that indicates which family type your own resembles most closely. Many families do not fit exactly into one type or another. Most families are composites of families that went before them; that is, adults who are still journeying from the families they grew up in carry many attributes of the past system into the new families they create. We will discuss this topic in depth in chapter 6.

CONSTANTINE'S FAMILY PARADIGMS

Open	*Synchronous*
Power: Horizontal or consensual	Power: Above any one person or individual
Affect: Respectful	Affect: No emotions, little talk
Meaning: Adaptation	Meaning: Permanence

Random	*Closed*
Power: Changeable	Power: Vertical or having an identifiable leader
Affect: Spontaneous, intense	Affect: Mostly nondisruptive emotions
Meaning: Creativity and individual expression	Meaning: Stability

---

PARENTING IN DIFFERENT FAMILY SYSTEMS

Still with me? Good. I think the following hypothetical situation clarifies how each family system views the child.

■ ■ ■

Five-year-old Mark runs through the living room.

The closed family reacts. "Mark," says his father, "you are not to run in the living room. You'll have to go to your room until you learn how to behave in here."

The random family reacts. No one notices. Or, depending on how relaxed his parents feel and whether or not Mark interrupted their own activity, his mom or dad may play chase with him.

The open family reacts. "Mark, come here," his mother calls. "When you run like that through the house, you bother your grandma, who's trying to read. You also stepped on the block house your sister is building. We have lots of special things in here that might get broken. It's not okay to run in the living room. Let's think of a place where you might be able to run around without disturbing anyone else."

The synchronous family reacts. "Come sit here beside me while I carve," Uncle Jim says to Mark. Uncle Jim continues to carve, saying nothing to Mark about his behavior. Twenty minutes later, Mark's mother puts items Mark disturbed back in place.

HOW ACTIVE ALERTS FIT
INTO THE FAMILY

The following examples represent families from each of the four paradigms. Although these examples are purely fictional (they are composites, based on many different families), I think they illustrate how different types of families handle an active alert child.

The Matthews: A Closed Family • The Matthews sit down in my office. They have come to discuss Emily, the second of their four children. Mrs. Matthews, a schoolteacher before her childbearing days, is now a full-time mom. She is well dressed and appears confident. Mr. Matthews, a bank officer, speaks first. "We're here to talk about Emily. We love her, but we just don't understand her. What works with the other three just doesn't seem to work with her. We do believe in spanking on occasion. It seems to work with the other three, but it doesn't seem to help with Emily. We don't like to keep punishing her all the time, but she's just plain hard to live with and doesn't take no for an answer."

I think the Matthews are a good example of a closed family. Mr. Matthews is clearly in charge overall, but Mom is the person in charge of "child maintenance." They think that somehow they have done something wrong with their intense, controlling, second-born active alert child. They believe they are supposed to teach her—to manage her. Although they have very clear routines and schedules, which one might think would help a boundary-less active alert child feel secure, life with Emily is a continual power struggle.

The Browns: A Random Family   •   Later that day I see

the Browns. Mr. Brown is an architect. Mrs. Brown is an artist, although she is not currently employed outside the home. The Browns have two lovely children. Their firstborn, Jeannine, is quiet, reserved, and needs little from them. Their second child, Paul, screamed so much during his first year of life that his parents feared the neighbors might report them to the child welfare agency. The Browns love to have fun with their children. Tents and art projects abound throughout the house. Generally, the family seems to move from one crisis to another. The parents, both busy, independent people, struggle with Paul's neediness. The family has no consistent routines for getting up, going to bed, eating, or doing schoolwork. Paul, age five, is constantly acting out. If left alone, he starts fights with his sister, the dog, the cat, anyone in sight. The Browns want help to figure out their puzzling son. They are a classic example of a random family.

The Lowrys: An Open Family   •   Next, I meet with the

Lowrys. Mr. and Mrs. Lowry are both teachers. They adore little Josephine but are quite worried about her. She is their only child, in part because she has been a challenge since birth and they can't decide whether or not they want to have others. The Lowrys have worked hard to meet their bright and demanding daughter's needs. At the same time, they have tried to teach Josie to be respectful of others. And that is the piece of puzzle that gives them the most trouble.

Josie seems to need constant attention. She does well at school but is constantly demanding at home, negotiating anything and everything. Life is a struggle for the Lowrys. Mr. and Mrs. Lowry try to reason with Josephine and consider her needs but, as her mother puts it, "She's so unreasonable." The Lowrys are a good example of how an open family tries to react to an active alert child.

The Moores: A Synchronous Family • Eight-year-old George lives on a farm. His parents work hard from sunrise to sunset. No one in his family talks much. George attends a small school. He doesn't wear the same kinds of clothes the other boys do, but he never would question his parents' authority on the issue.

The Moores' farm has been in the family for three generations. Mr. Moore's great-grandfather built the house, and it hasn't changed much except when they added electricity and running water. There is still an outhouse out back—just in case. George's mother works on the farm with his father. When she isn't baking bread or canning, she helps with the livestock while Dad works in the fields.

George loses his temper once in a while. When he was seven, he smashed a light fixture. Dad fixed it that same night when George was asleep. Neither his mom nor his dad mentioned the incident. The next day, George felt so bad he cleaned out the barn before Dad came in from the fields.

George often feels that he doesn't quite measure up. He feels as if he's different from the rest of the family. Sometimes he just wants to scream. His parents don't always understand George, but they believe he will outgrow his feelings, even though his outbursts of temper are becoming more frequent.

Each of these family paradigms offers something positive to the active alert child. I also think each has patterns of interaction that, if slightly modified, would better suit the needs of the child.

The active alert child, by his very nature, asks parents from each family type to give him something that does not fit with the way they routinely live their own lives. The active alert in an open family sometimes needs her democratic parents to make a hard-and-fast decision. The verbal active alert needs her synchronous family to talk to and with her. An active alert child may feel alienated in a random family and need other family members to include him more in their individual endeavors. And parents in a closed family may need to find ways to affirm the passion and intensity of their active alert child, who is so very different from them.

The following chart outlines what the active alert child receives from each family type. It also delineates what is most difficult for the parents in each family type to give to the child.

WHAT ACTIVE ALERTS GET FROM THE FOUR FAMILY SYSTEMS

Open	*Synchronous*
Feelings acknowledged	Security
Mutual power	Clear order
	Routine

Random	*Closed*
Creativity affirmed	Stability
Intensity affirmed	Structure

WHAT ACTIVE ALERTS MAY *NOT* GET FROM THE FOUR FAMILY SYSTEMS

Open	*Synchronous*
Closure	Verbal road maps
A sense of boundaries	Guidance

Random	*Closed*
Structure	Intensity affirmed
Boundaries	Emotions verified

The challenge for all families is to recognize what is missing for the active alert child—which of his traits the family does not accept and affirm. Then, without trying to change the child's nature, those families must find ways to change their routines and fill the voids. Read on to discover how.

6

Your Active Alert Child and the Family

These fellow mortals,
every one must be accepted as they are.

—George Eliot
Adam Bede

In my work, I strive to make families strong and to acknowledge each system's gifts. To accomplish this, I help the parents with whom I work understand how their family interacts with the child. Often in this process I am reminded of the Mother Superior in *The Sound of Music,* who cherished Maria's energy. It was she who asked the rhetorical question, "How do you keep a wave upon the sand?"

One need only stand at the ocean's edge, watching its powerful ebb and flow, to know that changing the water's natural course is impossible. The same holds true for families who live with an irrepressible active alert child. Families can shift in order to accommodate the child, however. In this chapter, we'll look at ways in which the child fits into the four family types. We'll also see examples of how families adapt to facilitate the active alert child's growth.

THE CLOSED FAMILY:
CHILDREN ARE TO BE SEEN AND
NOT HEARD

The closed system offers stability. In her *Little House* books, Laura Ingalls Wilder is an active alert child in a closed family system. Read the books.

■ ■ ■

Laura and her sister Mary spend a glorious morning sliding down haystacks. Pa comes home, repairs the haystack, and tells them not to slide on it anymore. That afternoon Laura tells Mary, "He said don't slide down, but he didn't say we couldn't run down it."

Laura frequently refers to herself as a child with naughty thoughts and wishes she could be good like her sister Mary. Laura is a passionate, intense child. She is, at first, afraid to go to school, and when the family moves, afraid to live in town. She says nothing about her feelings to her parents. When she has a problem, she waits for her father to bring up the subject before she asks for his advice. What Laura gains from her closed family is a sense of order. The daily household routine is reassuring and secure. Pa, who calls her "Half Pint," is especially affirming of her. And though it remains unspoken, his secret delight in her energy allows her to flourish. In fact, he even helps find outlets for her kinesthetic energy when he allows her to help with the haying and other chores that "ladies just don't do."

The structure and routine of the closed family system provide comfort for people who fear transitions and have trouble setting their own boundaries. Family rituals eliminate the source of many fears and conflicts.

In such families, however, the reality is that someone is in charge. And that someone is not the active alert child—a fact that interferes with the child's need for control.

The challenge for the closed family is not to take the child's need to challenge authority personally. Recognize that although a child cannot be in charge of his family, he can be in charge of himself. Expect a battle when this autonomy is not allowed.

We can see, then, that although the closed family offers security it does not affirm easily the active alert child's intensity. Such families may not appreciate the active alert child's emotionality. Closed families need to understand that their active alert child is not bad or difficult; he is simply operating out of inborn temperament.

THE RANDOM FAMILY: CHILDREN AND PARENTS ARE TO BE SEEN AND HEARD DEPENDING ON THEIR NEEDS

The random family values an active alert's creativity, and that is wonderful, because I'm not sure anyone is quite as continuously creative as an active alert child. A random family also appreciates individual expression. In fact, at its best, this magnanimous system encourages individuals to be all they can be. Family members value passion and intensity.

People in a healthy random system view active alert children as special; these children provide energy, diversity, and an alternative way for family members to engage and connect with one another.

For some reason, most writers portray random systems as unhealthy. I think, therefore, the best examples of healthy random systems are not in literature but in real life. Single-parent households and blended families often function well as random systems.

There is a flip side, however. If a child who lacks the ability to recognize boundaries grows up in a system with few boundaries, isn't she on a collision course with reality? A random system is something of a setup for failure because, ultimately, she may have trouble functioning in systems that set limits, such as school, church, or social groups.

Are there other issues? Yes. Active alert children, if allowed, do become "little dictators." In a family where it is unclear who is in charge, your active alert child more easily usurps that role. Potential for conflict exists between parents and active alert children in such families. When both the child and adult know few boundaries and express intense emotions in spontaneous and capricious ways, passionate arguments may ensue.

One last thing: The active alert child likes to be the center of attention and is externally referenced, so random families must work to include the child. He may feel abandoned because in the random family, on any given day, each member may have a different agenda: One is off skiing, another exercising at the club, and another painting. Inviting the child to take part in what might otherwise be an individual pursuit helps him feel secure and connected to the family. Forming twosomes or threesomes insures that no one feels left out.

THE OPEN FAMILY: CHILDREN AND PARENTS ARE TO BE SEEN AND HEARD EQUALLY

Children in open family systems are asked to cooperate and participate. This process facilitates learning boundaries. Family members express and attend to feelings, and these discussions empower children because adults value their input.

Is all this too good to be true? Perhaps. The danger is that the active alert child with too much power may try to control the family through "analysis paralysis"—endless dialogue. Ending a discussion or declaring that an issue is not negotiable places open family parents in an untenable position. They may feel they are being too authoritarian. Active alert children are able to place parents at odds with their own values. Remember Sally Forth and Hilary in chapter 1?

Open families with an active alert child must ask themselves, Where is the bottom line? Parents need to learn when to end the negotiation that goes on too long and adds no new information to the situation. Such closure respects the child *and* the family.

THE SYNCHRONOUS FAMILY: CHILDREN AND PARENTS ARE TO BE SEEN AND NOT HEARD

The synchronous family offers clear order and routine to the child. Since certainty and stability are the family's chief values, active alert children gain a sense of security in this system. These families need to learn ways to affirm the active alert's spirit, however.

Children in synchronous families learn that because opposition or challenge is not allowed, change is not possible, as all members are equal under the great goal. The active alert child either learns to stifle his creativity or learns to live feeling at odds with his family.

Synchronous families with an active alert child must develop a verbal structure. Children adapt in a family where little is discussed by trying to figure out what's right. Without verbal feedback, they work constantly to better themselves to gain approval. In that way, the system exacerbates the active alert's perfectionist tendencies. When a child always must guess whether or not he measures up, his self-esteem suffers.

Listen to an adult active alert who lived in a synchronous system: "I grew up afraid—afraid of doing something wrong. That fear still affects me. Because I do not believe talking is an option, I seldom check things out verbally and I always guess. As a result, I am constantly afraid of doing something wrong. I tell my wife, "It's not okay to sometimes say you love me and then other times yell at me; you must show me you love me." To rear an active alert child successfully, synchronous families must build a verbal component into their structure. In *Anne of Green Gables,* by Lucy Maud Montgomery, Matthew and Marilla Cuthbert increase their discussion about life by allowing Anne Shirley into their family. Eventually, Marilla even refers to Anne as a "kindred spirit."

Some synchronous families need to look at their denial patterns. These families may all to easily develop unhealthy patterns that discount children with special needs; they dismiss active alerts as "just going through a phase." The child then feels abandoned and may call out for more attention by displaying his behavior more strongly. If the system responds by saying, "There is no need to talk about it. Things will work out. It doesn't do any good to talk about it," the child feels angry and powerless. Even members of a healthy synchronous family, who simply redirect the active alert's energy, need to increase their ability to talk in order to integrate such a child into the family unit.

THE DYSFUNCTIONAL FAMILY SYSTEM

Using Family Paradigms

For each family paradigm there are both healthy and unhealthy versions. More problems arise with the unhealthy or disabled forms: families that are too closed, too random, too open, or too synchronous.

In a too closed or disabled closed family, the punishment may be too severe for the "crime." The rules may be burdensome and excessive.

Too random or disabled random families appear extremely disorganized or in a frantic turmoil. No one knows where the children are. There is no comforting sense of security for children to return to as they face the challenges of growing up.

In the too open or disabled open family a painful forced honesty among members can result in a compulsive analysis of relationships. People in these systems constantly agonize over what is happening and may hurt one another with their insights.

Too synchronous or disabled synchronous families suffer from an emotional deadness. These families no longer live harmonious, parallel lives. They perform daily routines like zombies, feeling nothing as they move, robotic, toward the unwritten goal.

When any of the family systems becomes disabled, the child who lives in it experiences failure and shame. Disabled forms of the family paradigms may create children who seem to be active alert or who exhibit a combination of the eleven active alert traits. Trying to differentiate the cause from the effect—Did the child come into the world and contort the family system, or did the system exacerbate the child's behavior?—creates shame for both parent and child.

In my work, I strive to strengthen families and to acknowledge each system's gifts. I find that judging or blaming is not only unnecessary but prevents people from feeling accepted and seeking the knowledge or help they need.

Addicted Families

Families with a history of addiction share some common issues. Whether dealing with chemical, sexual, work, food, or religious addiction, adults who grew up in an addicted family system or who have conquered their own addiction need to address certain issues. They can do so on their own, in a support group, or with a therapist. This is especially important for those who are parents, because parents with an addiction history face special issues related to denial and boundary setting.

People who are recovering from addiction or who grew up in addicted systems have learned to deny their own awareness of problems and emotions. In Jack Kent's *There's No Such Thing as a Dragon,* a child befriends a dragon. In the book, the mother tells the child there are no such things as dragons. The child then has little recourse but to quit petting the dragon and pretend it is not there. The dragon *is* there, however, and it continues to get bigger and bigger until someone else finally sees it.

Remember, the intuitive and observant active alert child functions best when his insights are acknowledged and affirmed. Parents who have not faced the issue of their own denial cannot do this for their child.

As for boundary setting, addicted families are on–off systems that tend to vacillate between extremes of denial and control. Active alert children, who are intense and prone to all-or-nothing thinking, cannot learn balance from parents who model such behavior. Gaining a sense of boundaries is not easy when parents fluctuate between setting and denying boundaries for children and/or themselves.

HOW THE PIECES FIT— INDIVIDUAL ROLES WITHIN FAMILIES

In their book *Inside the Family,* family therapists David Kantor and William Lehr identify four different roles people assume in their families: movers, followers, opposers, and bystanders. All four roles are healthy ways that individuals relate within the family. When a person is stuck in one position to the exclusion of the others, however, there is cause for concern.

Movers

Movers originate or define an action that the family can take. The mover is the "idea person," but not necessarily a "doer." The mover works by defining moves either openly or covertly. A "stuck mover" may know only how to "define the name of the game" or "run the show." When such a person is unable to get the family to move in his chosen direction, he will start a separate action or engage in a struggle for control of the family. Does this sound like anyone you know and love?

Followers

Followers continue or cooperate with the established action the family is taking. They support or agree with others. Followers select when and whom to follow and thus can be quite powerful. Stuck followers are likely to be weak, dependent, and conforming and to have difficulty deciding what to do.

Opposers

Opposers either change or stop an action the family is taking. They may do this simply by suggesting other moves—constantly. Without opposers, there is little families can do to change. They are a source of creativity and novelty. Stuck opposers are labeled as "bad," "difficulty," "defiant," or "a problem." (Does this also sound familiar?) If less extreme in their opposition, they may be seen as unconventional or eccentric.

Bystanders

Bystanders remain neutral. They watch the action the family is taking. In some ways, bystanders remain outside the family. By offering observations to the family, they may become quite powerful. They help families understand themselves. In the extreme case, a stuck bystander always remains on the outside and is seemingly cold, passive, austere, and detached.

HOW WE FIT IN AND CHANGE AS FAMILIES AND INDIVIDUALS

Here's the final piece of the puzzle: how the four roles defined by Kantor and Lehr fit with Constantine's four family systems. In the diagram on page 113, we see how Constantine combined the two models to show the connection between family systems and the roles of family members. ("↔" means "mutually promotes," that is, movers promote family systems as well as open family systems promoting movers.)

Closed Families

As the diagram shows, closed families generally prefer children to follow. Adults in closed families believe that successful parenting produces children who are good followers.

The closed family will attempt to control opposing members because they threaten stability. Active alerts, who are always moving (and who will oppose if they are not allowed to move), are sometimes scapegoated.

Bystanding is not threatening to closed families.

Movers are carefully monitored in closed families. Only under clearly defined circumstances can someone other than the family head direct the family's movements (for example, while the parents are away the older child is left in charge). The active alert's wish to exert control can be constantly frustrated, leading to exaggerated oppositional behavior.

Random Families

Random families love opposers. In the healthy random family, opposition adds to the family's communal creativity; in the disabled random family, it contributes to chaos. The active alert's movement then becomes opposition.

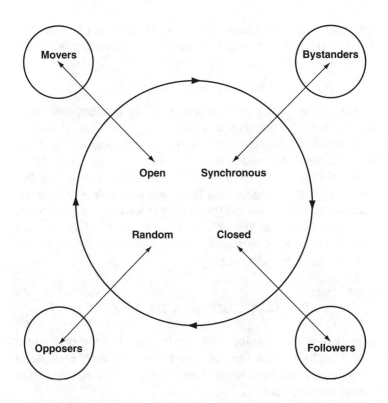

Conversely, moving may be viewed in the random system as an attempt to exert authority or as a bid to dominate. Moving is considered okay only if no one is expected to follow. Because active alerts want to direct others, they are opposed.

Following is not valued at all by random families.

Bystanding, though not considered a problem, may not seem creative to family members.

Open Families

Because open families solve problems consensually, they need movers as well as followers and opposers. Because bystanding promotes watching rather than open communication and involvement, open families are leery of it. When asked to be a bystander in an open family, the active alert child may block everyone else's movement, or she may simply shift into overdrive

leery of bystanders

and react by moving constantly. Obviously, a child who does that never learns how to be still and watch—two necessary skills.

Synchronous Families

The synchronous family is most compatible with bystanders. By definition, its members are watchers.

Movers are acceptable but opposers are not, because there can be no harmony with opposition.

Followers can cause difficulties in synchronous families because behavior implies that there is a leader. In synchronous families, members assume that everyone knows just what to do. Following doesn't fit the bill. Because an active alert does not learn to be a team player easily or early, the child may choose to isolate himself in such a family.

CAN FAMILIES CHANGE?

Just as individuals change and develop, families too evolve over time. Healthy systems flex and grow as each member develops. As a result, families may change from a closed to a more random to a more open system.

Interestingly, Constantine theorizes that closed families cannot evolve into more open families without first going through a random family pattern. I believe that this idea is supported by findings about assertiveness.

Experience in teaching assertiveness shows that nonassertive people cannot move directly into an assertive stance. Now, this comes as no surprise. Many skills, such as ice skating, swimming, and piano playing, are based on a series of prescribed steps that are perfected only through the process of repeatedly doing them incorrectly. The same process holds true for learning to be assertive. Nonassertive people must work through a progression of stages from aggression to assertiveness. Constantine's notion of family development seems to be supported by this process theory. Nonassertiveness is much like following (valued in closed families); aggression is much like opposing (valued in random families); and assertiveness is much like moving (valued in open families).

ACTIVE ALERTS: THE MOVERS

Keep in mind that active alerts are born movers. If they are continually blocked, they learn to be opposers. If they get stuck, they most likely will be stuck opposers or stuck movers. Many of the children with whom I work need to gain release—to get unstuck—and develop the ability to play all four roles. How can they do that?

Stuck opposers must learn to make choices about when, where, and whom to oppose. In this way, opposition comes closer to moving.

Stuck movers need to learn how to stand back and watch other movers. Moving then comes closer to bystanding.

Stuck bystanders need to learn that it is safe to follow or to move. Offering astute observations can facilitate rather than stifle action. In that way they learn to be thoughtful and strong leaders as well as helpful followers.

I do not ask young active alerts to become followers except on very high-priority issues, such as safety. *Following is the most difficult thing active alert children can do.* In my work, rather than expecting children to be followers, I redirect their movement to help them to understand the advantages of certain moves.

Remember, asking an active alert to make a move *for you* means asking them to follow. On the other hand, if you help them to understand the reasons behind certain moves, *they* make the choice and, subsequently, *they* move. For the young active alert these choices may be as simple as saying, "Because it's cool outside you cannot wear short sleeves, but you can wear either your Batman sweatshirt or your red turtleneck." For the older child it might be, "You can play with your friends on Saturday or Sunday. If you choose Saturday you'll have a little longer time, because on Sunday we have to get ready for the school week." At times all children must follow. My advice to you, however, is simple: Force active alerts to follow only on rare occasions.

As parents, you can facilitate your active alert child's natural ability to move. Her ability may need some fine-tuning, but affirming her natural desire takes away the shame and helps her to understand why and how she gets stuck.

Because they are so observant, active alerts can learn to make choices about their movements by bystanding or watching. Who knows, by encouraging and teaching your child to stop and watch before moving you may learn more yourself about stopping and watching before taking action.

You can help an opposer learn how to move, but you cannot teach him to follow first. In other words, you must give him an outlet for his movement before you try to contain it.

■ ■ ■

When Phil asked his active alert son Andrew to turn off the television and do his homework, his son said, "No!" Phil knew that if he responded by saying, "I said turn off the television," a power struggle might ensue.

Instead of offering his child an opportunity to oppose, Phil structured an opportunity for Andrew to move.

"Your choice is not whether the TV is to be turned off, but whether you or I will do it." Since Andrew considered it a privilege to get to turn off the television, Phil had offered an appropriate choice. He had given his son a sense of his own strength, asked him to move, and given him the parameters or boundaries for that movement.

You can help a mover learn to choose movements and watch others' movements, but teaching him to follow remains only a remote possibility.

■ ■ ■

Sarah knew that her son Bill was having difficulty keeping friends. She decided to observe how Bill interacted with his friends. When she went to pick him up at school, she arrived a few minutes early and stood outside the classroom to observe Bill and his friends as they prepared to leave school. She also had him ask friends over to their house to play so that she could keep an eye on their activities. Then she talked with Bill about what she had observed.

"You really seem to like Tim," Sarah told her son, "but I noticed that you pushed him as you were going to the lockers together. Tim got a little angry with you."

"I was mad at him," Bill told his mom. "He told me he didn't like my picture in art."

Another time she said, "When Kelly came to play, you didn't seem to want to share your toys. What was that about?"

"Kelly always wants to run the fastest cars on my track, and I always lose the race," Bill said.

Sarah and Bill discussed each situation and then she asked Bill, "How do you think Kelly felt when you didn't want to share?" Sarah went on to discuss what other options might help both Kelly and Bill feel okay. She did not criticize Bill's behavior; she simply asked him to see the value of observing and thinking about a situation before choosing to move.

UNDERSTANDING YOUR FAMILY TYPE

Let's return to your answers and scores for your family trait assessment in chapter 5. The "S" score is your synchronous score. The "C" score is your closed score. The "R" score is your random score. The "O" score is your open score.

Which one of your scores is the highest? Do you have two scores that are close? Where do your scores place you in Constantine's family circle? If you are married, which score is highest for your spouse? Are there differences between the two of you? Remember, the scores are merely one possible indicator of your family type.

The following examples may offer some perspective on the issues that families must confront when living with an active alert child. (These cases are not of actual families, but they are representative of a clinical population.)

The Sanders

Jane, age thirty-five, was brought up in a disabled random family that was in constant turmoil. The family went from crisis to crisis about money matters, moves, or children. Jane, the oldest girl, became the "responsible one" who tried to steer everyone through the crisis course.

John, age thirty-six, was brought up in what appeared from the outside to be a "Father Knows Best" closed family. Mom stayed home with the two children. Dad worked and clearly made the decisions. Only when John was an adult did he figure out that his dad had a drinking problem.

Over the years, Jane and John had both worked hard to understand their families in which they grew up. Therefore, when they came to see me about their oldest child, it was clear that both had moved farther along the circle. Jane valued the open system but retained elements of the random family in which she grew up. John also valued the open system, but sometimes acted out some opposition. Jane occasionally reacted in a passive aggressive fashion.

Their oldest daughter, a true active alert, was still moving, struggling to get out of opposition. As the family members talked, I realized how much Jane and John helped their child learn about herself and her opposition. Although their daughter was no longer a stuck opposer, John and Jane still had difficulty accepting her tendency to oppose.

After teaching John some communication skills so that he could be more assertive with Jane, we spent time helping Jane and John understand how to allow their daughter to move more and oppose less. We discussed how hard it was to be firm and clear when offering choices to their child. Fortunately, their pain lessened when they noted that their daughter responded well to their clarity in providing boundaries and that she seemed to develop a sense of control over her own life.

The Evans

David and Dana grew up in very different families. Dana was one of four children in a random single-parent family. Dana described her mom, who worked and raised four kids, as a "laissez-faire" parent. Dana's family had no rules; people just did their own thing.

David grew up in a traditional home. Dad was clearly in charge and Mom did not work outside the home. David could not remember much about his childhood, and he seldom saw his parents, who lived 2,000 miles away.

As parents, David and Dana viewed issues differently. David thought Dana was too easy on their two boys. He believed the children's energy level and sassiness resulted from a lack of discipline. Dana said she and the boys were always in shouting matches.

David made it clear that he wanted Dana to be a work-at-home mom whose job was to help the family run smoothly. But the role David prescribed was not something Dana had experienced in her own family, so she had trouble fulfilling her husband's wishes. Life at home, therefore, seemed to mimic Dana's family of origin more than David's. At the end of each day, when David got home, the kids expected him to yell at Dana about the state of the house and kids. Everyone in the family had become great opposers. Dana didn't know who to follow; David was trying to change what Dana was doing; and the oldest son had been born to move and was trying to lead Mom. It almost seemed as if he and David were fighting to see who was in charge of Dana. The younger boy had learned opposing as a coping mechanism in what was an oppositional system. In his case, joining the family meant fighting them.

One of the first problems we addressed in therapy was how David sabotaged Dana's confidence with his outspoken criticism of her leniency with the children. The more he yelled about the lack of discipline, the less structure she imposed, so the parents wound up opposing each other. Clearly, David and Dana needed to learn about their impact on each other.

Additionally, Dana needed a role model for dealing with active alert children. She and I devised a routine for her to use with her children that outlined a clear structure. We also devised a list of support resources that she, in her attempt to be all things to all people, had not been using. That list included day-care assistance, housecleaning services, and friends upon whom she could call for help. When David and Dana felt they were on the same team, they were able to work with their boys, who needed to learn when, where, and how opposing could be useful and productive.

The Millers

Lenny and Phyllis fell in love during college and married the summer after they graduated. Lenny's mother had never worked, and his father, an engineer, had ruled the house. As the second-born son, Lenny grew up idolizing his brother. Even though Lenny's father was a professional, Lenny's family always struggled with money troubles. As we worked together in counseling, it became clear to Lenny that his father had been a compulsive spender.

Phyllis also grew up in a professional family. Dad was a lawyer and Mom stayed at home when the children were young. In later years, she returned to college to become a teacher. Her family was more open than Lenny's. Phyllis fondly remembers the family meetings held during her childhood. The second of three children—she was the only one with red hair and a fiery spirit—she had always felt a little different.

The couple had one little girl, whom Phyllis described as "spirited since birth." Lenny had learned, over the years, to oppose indirectly by being the "man of the house." He was simply not available emotionally and helped out very little around the house. Phyllis and her daughter, when alone together, operated in an open style. As a family unit, however, the combination of a powerful child and a family style that vacillated between the open and closed ends of the spectrum resulted in a system that functioned in the random mode. Lenny had to learn about his own family's history of addiction and his tendency to withdraw from intimacy. Phyllis had to learn about her tendency to shame Lenny when he was being unsupportive. They both had to learn how to set limits for their energetic child. Although they nurtured her, they failed to structure her life in a way that allowed time for their marriage. In fact, each adult had used the child as an excuse to avoid facing their intimacy issues.

If you and your spouse function from different family paradigms, I would bet that adding an active alert child to your family was like adding a high-powered magnifying glass that enlarged each difference. You may have been left baffled, wondering how to handle the magnification.

Your child's demands not only highlight differences between you and your spouse as parents but also any unresolved issues that each of you faces as individuals or that you both face as a couple.

Think about it. Would there be a difference if you were to go back and complete the family trait assessment again, evaluating not how your family is but instead how you want it to be? Do you want to create a more open system but find yourself frequently staging emotional outbursts? Does your child's tendency to be a mover cause you to oppose and block her movements, or can you move and direct her without opposing her?

Some discrepancies will always exist between who we are and who we want to be. The important thing is what we do when we notice them. Keep in mind that when these discrepancies are present, active alert children often use them to further their own ends. Trying to understand the big picture—ourselves, each of our children, and our families—is an important goal, one that is not always easily attained.

Affirm your children and affirm yourself, wherever your family fits in the model I've presented. Affirm your ability to make mistakes and to cope with your own humanity. In this way, you say to your perfectionist active alert, "The goal is not perfection—it is learning to love yourself enough to accept your own whole, if imperfect, self." In that way, we help all members fit within our family.

Part III

DAY BY DAY WITH YOUR ACTIVE ALERT CHILD

Tom and Nancy, a professional couple in their forties, have found dealing with their active alert child to be both challenging and frustrating. Tom is an attorney and Nancy holds a degree in counseling; both have teaching experience, working with junior-high students. It was this very experience with early adolescents—students often described as needing to be "buried and exhumed three years later"—that gave Tom and Nancy a certain confidence about becoming parents. They believed (wrongly, perhaps) that they had seen the worst of the worst, that they could handle any child they were blessed with, and that their child would be different, anyway.

When Tom and Nancy decided to adopt a Korean child, they felt that they wanted to honor her with a name that bespoke what they expected her to bring to their life. They named her Joy. In time, they were glad they hadn't chosen Patience.

Their first inkling that this child was going to be a challenge came as they drove home from the airport, when Nancy attempted to cradle Joy in her arms. At five months, the little girl was remarkably strong and made it quite clear that she expected to be held upright so that she could observe everything. This alertness continued and grew. As Joy's paternal grandfather was fond of saying, "She doesn't miss a trick." She didn't. She not only observed keenly all that was around her, expressing great curiosity about the world, but also demonstrated remarkable recall, especially of conversations.

Joy's quick recall was noted by her day-care provider as well. Never, Janey told Tom and Nancy, had she cared for a child who remembered as much or whose recall was as complete as Joy's. Tom and Nancy felt appropriate parental pride. As Joy approached school age, they decided to have her tested for admission to a private school. Part of the admission procedure included a Stanford-Binet intelligence test. When Nancy called to learn the test results, she was sitting down and her heart was pounding, fearful that the person she and Tom had come to see as their bright little girl would be below the norm in intellectual ability. The verdict: in the very superior range. "Of course," said the admissions counselor, "you're not surprised by that." Nancy could hardly speak.

It all fit. Joy was an extremely verbal child; she demonstrated uncanny insight into people and their feelings; she had what they had jokingly called a "supermemory"; and she believed that everything was negotiable.

In spite of their delight in Joy, Tom and Nancy felt a frustration not experienced by other parents they talked with. These parents may have had very bright children but they were always less intense than Joy.

As Joy entered the "frightful fours," she exhibited what her parents assumed were the normal behavioral traits but with such intensity that Tom and Nancy felt concern. They contacted a child psychologist, who assured them that all they were doing was appropriate and that this, too, would pass. And so, through the next six months, they did their best to remain even keeled, not to let Joy "push their buttons," and to make the limits known, lovingly but firmly. Even so, Joy did push their buttons, particularly Nancy's.

One hot summer day Nancy decided to take Joy swimming. Joy was delighted. They set out for one of the sites operated by the athletic club to which the family belonged; a construction crew was working on the parking lot, requiring a short bus ride from an adjacent building. Because Joy had fallen asleep, Nancy decided to go to a different site and to avoid two conflicts—the "commute," and awakening Joy, who was usually cranky if awakened before she'd "had her sleep out."

After arriving at the second site, Nancy very gently woke Joy, telling her that they were at the club. Joy looked sleepily around the parking lot, said, "This isn't our club," and refused to go in. Nancy attempted to convince her that it was their club and that it had a nice pool. Joy launched into a temper tantrum of such intensity that Nancy felt almost frightened. She explained to Joy that if the tantrum didn't stop, they would return home. At that point, Joy unbuckled her car seat, determined to swim. Nancy held firm and, shaking, insisted they return home. After coming fully awake, Joy was her usual self, cheerful and cooperative. But the transition from sleeping to waking, like all other transitions, was a difficult one.

Other difficulties with transitions had surfaced when Joy was about ten months old; Tom and Nancy had passed it off as age-appropriate stranger shyness. It did, indeed, pass, only to surface with a vengeance a year later. If Joy were taken to the nursery at Sunday school, a place of noisy activity, she became extremely fearful. For the first two weeks of preschool, she clung to her mother at the schoolroom door. Even starting kindergarten in the same school where her mother taught presented separation difficulties.

Now, just prior to the beginning of each school year, Nancy takes Joy to the school. They visited the room she will be in and chat with her new teacher. Nancy lays groundwork by discussing with the school director the "teacher qualities" that will be most supportive and helpful for Joy. Then she follows up with the teacher, explaining Joy's history, personality, and attitude. To date, it has been a very successful approach, one which Nancy regrets not having used when Joy entered kindergarten.

That was a disastrous year for Joy, largely because of the conflict that arose early on with her teacher. Like many active alert children who have difficulty with transitions, Joy attempts to ease that pain by exerting whatever control she can over the situation. When this need to control the environment is coupled with high intelligence, the result can be explosive, especially if the adult involved lacks understanding (learned or intuitive) about the child's needs. This was what happened with Joy. Her teacher undoubtedly saw a smart-aleck kid who was testing authority. Possessing the sensitivity typical of the active alert child, Joy "shut down" and decided that she hated school. Her fragile self-esteem was dealt a nearly fatal blow from which it didn't recover for more than a year. Two years later, she still maintains that she doesn't like school.

As Nancy and Tom become more familiar with the needs of their child, they find it easier to compensate for them and to avoid power conflicts and unnecessary stress. Early on, before they even knew about Joy's trouble with transitions, they adopted the axiom, "Let sleeping children lie." They explained to baby-sitters and teachers that Joy had difficulty with transitions, but that given time and patience, she would adjust.

They allowed Joy to have choices, providing her with a feeling of control over her life. Piano and swimming lessons are non-negotiable (even though Joy tries to make them so); Brownies and church choir are. These efforts have paid off; while Joy will never be an easy child to deal with, life has become easier as she has matured.

Both Tom and Nancy confided in each other during Joy's extended visit with her grandparents that they needed her absence to appreciate the stress she brings to their lives. They noticed that they felt less exhausted and laughed more. An active alert child saps parents' energy. But Tom and Nancy also hope that all the expenditure of energy, all the frustration, and all the accommodation of their child's needs will be well spent. Their hope for Joy is that she has joy in herself. In this matter, they can only make a leap of faith.

7

Special Times: Defusing Land Mines with Love

. . . The actual enemy is the unknown.

—Thomas Mann

Parents of active alert children learn to think quickly and step lightly, because scattered throughout the field of parenting these children are what I call "land mines"—potentially troublesome areas that often take parents totally by surprise.

We already know that many special events that delight other children often overstimulate active alerts. The same holds true for land mines. Some look harmless, but can cause panic in an active alert child.

Land mines can be surprising because if one hasn't gone off for a while, you may forget they are there. Typically, the active alert child's life cycles from smooth, easy times to rocky upsets. When everything is going well and problems seem to have disappeared, parents tend to ignore or deny that land mines exist. When things are rocky, they blame a developmental "phase." What parents forget is that certain events will always overstimulate active alert children.

A bit of foresight helps. With that in mind, I have flagged some mined areas for you. Awareness of the common and not-so-common land mines and how to step lightly around them will help you to safely negotiate the field of parenting and to create a peaceful coexistence within your family.

HOLIDAYS, BIRTHDAYS, AND OTHER FORMS OF CHAOS

Think of the number of holidays we celebrate: Christmas, Hanukkah, Easter, Passover, Halloween, Valentine's Day, Thanksgiving, and more. And children are always attending or throwing birthday parties.

In nostalgic moments, we think of holidays as joyful occasions. More accurately, they are emotion-packed, filled with everything from happiness and excitement to anger, frustration, and loneliness. Holidays can leave even adults overwhelmed and feeling helpless.

What do you do? With any holiday, you must first address your own stress. Ask yourself what your expectations are for holidays. What do you expect from yourself and your family members? What is your role?

In some families, one member prepares the entire event—decorating, cooking, and cleaning. This role of "Christmas Coordinator," for example, traditionally belongs to the wife/mother of the family. If she believes that Christmas must be perfect, complete with freshly baked goodies, children, laughing, and a picture-perfect house, then she may wind up not the coordinator but, as William Doherty refers to her, the "Christmas Martyr," exhausted and anxious before Christmas Eve arrives.

Remember, your observant active alert child doesn't always differentiate your stress from his own; your excitement becomes his excitement, your fears his own. Such a child will feel all his parents' stress in addition to his own excitement and may be unable to cope.

As gift-giving holidays approach, be aware of your active alert child's curiosity. Counter the mounting anxiety by helping your child make a "wish list." Ask her to star the items that are the most important to her. Realize that the list will be very long. Last year, my five-year-old friend Timothy worked from catalogues and wrote a five-page list on the computer! Also, explain that she will not get everything on the list, but that you will use it as a guide for yourself and when friends or relatives ask for gift suggestions.

Recognize your child's nature and deal with your own stress and expectations. Then, let go of the number and length of celebrations around big events. Must you attend all the Hanukkah events? Do you have some choices? Dinner at a different house each night may not be the most stress-free option, but going to Grandma's just for dessert may be.

Evaluate length and quantity. Limit how long and how often your child must behave during seasonal celebrations. It is all right to have standards for her behavior, but remember to make them clear in advance to your child. When you do so, tell her what to do rather than what not to do: "If you don't like the vegetable, just leave it on the side of your plate."

Finally, in a two-parent family, take two cars when possible. That way the parent who is not with his family of origin can leave if the child gets too stimulated. Or arrange with the hostess for a separate place so that you and your child can go there to wind down, if necessary, and determine whether or not he can handle what is left of the occasion. Recognize your child's needs and tend to them.

■ ■ ■

Jeremy's grandparents expected Jeremy's family to spend Christmas Day at their house. For Jeremy, the day began with presents at his own house, a large breakfast at his grandparents', more presents, an even larger midday dinner, followed by an afternoon in which the adults sat around watching ball games and dozing. Before everyone went home around 8 P.M., the family dined on leftover turkey.

Jeremy, who had risen early, missed his nap, had too many new activities and toys to play with, and had eaten food he didn't care for or wasn't used to eating, was in tears before the day ended. When Jeremy turned five, his parents rewrote the rules. The family now spends Christmas morning at home, goes to his grandparents' for presents and a noon meal, and leaves before dinner.

Patterns and Procedures

Alerting a child to the patterns or procedures for special outings and holidays is also important. Knowing when cake will be served or presents opened can mean the difference between celebration and disaster. Telling your child how much longer he has to wait will ward off the "How much longer till" problem. He may even settle down and get involved in an activity that will help pass the time.

In addition, you can make a few changes to accommodate your child's habits, since holidays often change established patterns. If dinner will be served later than your child usually eats, take a small snack or arrive late. If hors d'oeuvres will run late into the evening, maybe your child needs to stay home.

Sometimes adults gather for special occasions and expect children to disappear. Remember that when your child goes to Grandma's or Grandpa's she will want attention: It is a pattern she's come to expect. If you know she will not be nurtured at a family dinner, make arrangements with her special adults to spend time with her some other day and tell your child about those plans. This may help her cope better when Grandma is busy talking only to the adults.

When your child throws a birthday party, let age and staying power determine the length of the party and the number of guests to invite.

■ ■ ■

Marcy's parents planned an afternoon-long party when their daughter turned three. Marcy's friends were invited for the first two hours and then special adults were asked to stop by for an open house in honor of the child. By the time her own friends were ready to leave, Marcy, who had struggled all day with the accelerating level of excitement, finally stripped down to her superheroine underwear, screamed, and began jumping up and down on the couch. Marcy's mother planned a two-hour party for four children the next year.

Step carefully around birthdays. Your child will love to help plan the party. Doing so helps not only her need to control but also her understanding of the transitions during the party. In the midst of the excitement, changing from "clothespin in the bottle" to "duck, duck, goose" can unbalance an active alert.

■ ■ ■

Rebecca's parents breathed a sigh of relief when their daughter was eight and could understand the aspects of planning her own birthdays. That year, she just handed her parents ten pages of party plans, including a guest list and suggestions for a theme, games, and party favors.

Always remember that during holidays and other special occasions, your young active alert needs a stable routine. Keep bedtime and nap times regular. Also, consider dietary changes. For children with sensitivities to foods, this is not the time to forget the effects of diet.

The Game

Over the years, I've developed a "trick" to tap into the active alert child's sensitivity to the negative things in life—their all-or-nothing thinking. I suggest parents use it on vacations or on other occasions that are demanding for their child.

The official name of the trick is "response cost," and it has its origin in the cognitive behavioral school of thought about children. I call it *The Game* because it is a playful way to motivate children. It acknowledges their tendency toward negative thought, but it adds a positive twist.

How do you play? Begin by giving your child ten of something he really likes. Dimes, pennies, keys, erasers, or pencil toppers will do. Tell him about the upcoming event and spell out the behavior you expect of him. Make it clear that the ten trinkets or coins are his unless he behaves inappropriately. Each time he breaks the agreement, he loses one object.

The Game works because it puts the child in control. He is in charge of whether or not he gets to keep the entire treasure. And believe me, he will try to keep as much as he can. It also provides immediate gratification for a job well done and thus works better than the promise of a future reward.

■ ■ ■

Marty, age six, and his family were on vacation. Each day his parents planned special events for the children. They knew from past experience that although Marty had great fun and behaved well during such outings, he did have trouble leaving the hotel room. He often dawdled and fussed over getting dressed, argued about brushing his teeth, could not find his shoes, etc. On this trip, he wanted his own spending money, so his parents decided to let him earn it. Each morning they gave him ten dimes and told him that if he did not get dressed, comb his hair, use the bathroom, and in other ways prepare to leave, he would lose a dime.

The Aftermath

Life does not immediately return to normal for your child after a big event. He may need a transition time to get used to having less attention or excitement. Admittedly, the timing of an active alert child is not optimum! Exhausted adults, anxious to return to the usual routine, often have little patience for arranging a transition time.

■ ■ ■

*Each summer, Christina's family visited Grandma for
two weeks. Grandma doted on Christina and her
brother. And if that weren't enough, all six aunts and
uncles came to visit, so the children had a different
adult to do something fun with every day. For
Christina, a child who loved external stimulation, it
was heaven. Mom and Dad thought it was great, too;
they actually got a break! The first week back home
was always tough, however. The children had to learn
again that at home they did not have a constant stream
of "good times" and that one mom shared by two kids
didn't go as far as six adults. Mom learned to start
talking about this on their way home from Grandma's
and, once home, to start each day by reminding
Christina she has only one mother.*

BABY-SITTERS AND CARE PROVIDERS

Do you believe that no one else will be able to handle your active
alert child given his activity level and fears? Are you reluctant to
subject other people to your child's more trying side? You are not
alone: Such apprehension comes with the territory. Getting a
break from your child is vital, however. Relationships with other
caring adults help your child to grow and develop.

So, given that you must have caregivers and sitters, what
should you look for in them? First of all, look for consistency.
Seek stability for your child, even though it is not always
possible. Finding a baby-sitter who is available most weekends is
not easy.

Use your resources. Ask lots of people—neighbors, friends,
relatives—to recommend someone. Interview sitters when you
find them. Ask them into your home, where you can observe how
they work with your child. The first time you use the sitter, stay
at home and work on a project as you monitor your child's
interaction with the sitter, or tell the sitter to come early while

you bathe and dress. If you allow your child and yourself plenty of time, you may feel more comfortable about leaving her.

Familiarize your sitters with routines and expectations, but allow leeway for flexibility. Although you and your sitters need to share a kindred philosophy and respect for your child, you cannot expect them to do everything exactly as you do. In the end, you must trust your child's feedback about the sitter's effectiveness.

As your child gets older (age four and up) you can help her understand that her cooperative behavior will attract the best sitters. She cannot control whether or not you go out on Saturday night, but she can have some say in whether you get Scribbling Sara, who loves to color, or Mrs. Greenwitz, who doesn't like to play games.

Day Care

When choosing infant day care, search for a calm environment with a low adult-to-child ratio. I am told that active alert infants often pick their own caregivers; they scream at the ones they don't have confidence in and cry less and observe more when content. I do know that active alerts have an uncanny sense of who appreciates, cherishes, and respects their energy and their need to move. Your task is to try to discern such appreciation when choosing a care provider. (We cover other issues related to day care and nursery school in chapter 8.)

TELEVISION AND VIDEO GAME ADDICTIONS

Remember that we are discussing land mines. The question is not whether to permit access to enjoyable pastimes. Television and its concomitant video games are facts of life in most households. Rather than judge the value of this entertainment, let's look at how to manage its use to gain from its good effects and minimize any negative.

Because your active alert child observes everything and is always learning, you have to focus on what he is learning when considering television viewing.

■ ■ ■

When Lindsey was five, she was sitting on an airplane next to her mom. The passenger sitting next to Lindsey ordered an alcoholic beverage with his snack. Lindsey pulled on her mom's sleeve and asked, "Mom, will he beat me?" Mom thought for a minute, realized Lindsey's reference point, and smiled to herself. "No," she answered. A minute later Lindsey pulled again at Mom's sleeve. "Mom, will he get silly?" "No," said her mom.

Lindsey's parents seldom drank. The child's referents were two episodes of "Little House on the Prairie" that had dealt with drinking. In one show, an alcoholic father had beaten his son; in the other, one of the characters, Mr. Olson, had gotten silly after drinking some spiked water from the water barrel.

Your child learns as she watches television, so be ready to explain what she is watching. Is it consistent with your family values? Does she clearly understand the difference between TV magic and real life?

People often view television and video games as passive activities, but recent studies indicate they may not be quite as passive as was first believed. For active alert children, the issue is complicated.

After the television set goes off, there is a universal release of energy in these children. I am uncertain if this is related to repressed kinesthetic energy, the transition between television viewing and the next activity, or the nature of TV programming. I encourage parents to monitor all three aspects. Help your children make the transition from viewing television to another activity. Positively direct them and keep in mind the nature of the medium or the program's aggressiveness.

Research on the link between television and aggression has shown that not all children who watch antisocial television— shoot-'em-up cop shows or superhero cartoons—become more aggressive after viewing them. All children who view antisocial programming, however, do show a decline in rule obedience, persistence to task ability, and frustration tolerance. Since these are already issues for active alert children, you can see that choosing the kinds of programs your child watches is vital.

■ ■ ■

Daniel is not an aggressive child, but after he watches his favorite superhero cartoon on television, his mother says he "flies around the room, goes into overdrive, and bumps into chairs, tables, and siblings. This lasts for abut thirty minutes or until he gets himself into trouble." For Daniel, who already has little sense of boundaries, the program does not help his precarious learning process.

Other relevant research findings reveal how pro-social— positive, helpful—social behavior is affected by TV shows. In one study, children were asked to watch one of two short taped segments. One was an excerpt of the "The Untouchables," the other, a highly active sports sequence.

After viewing the excerpts, the children were told if they pushed a green button they would make a handle easier to turn and help a "supposed" child in the adjoining room. If they pushed a red button, they were told it made the handle feel hot and would hurt the "supposed" child. No matter how short the violent segment was, children who had viewed it made hurting responses more often than those who had watched the sports show.

This finding is one you might want to consider when determining what kinds of programs your child will be allowed to watch.

Watching television with your young child gives you the opportunity to explain what she is seeing. Know that your child views things literally and believes most of what she sees.

■ ■ ■

"Mom, come quick!" four-year-old Paul yelled from the TV
room. "The man says you should call this number. You
have to call them, Mom. He said so."

Explain that people in commercials are actors who are being
paid to say nice things about products. If your child watches a
violent show and sees someone get shot, he may believe that
someone actually got killed. Help your child understand what I
call TV magic—special effects and camera tricks. How can
someone jump out of a twenty-three-story building and live? Is
the car crash real?

Also, consider the other messages she is receiving. Is tough,
violent behavior the way to get what you want? Do all adults
behave that way? You and I know that the world is not really like
the one portrayed on television; your child does not.

Finally, one of the scariest shows on television is the nightly
news. If you have spent time telling your child that most people
don't resort to violence to get their way, but that's all that the
news reports, your explanation may not hold water. News stories
selected for broadcast often paint a gruesome picture of the world.
Your child's limited understanding of the world also limits his
understanding of the stories. After all, the terrorist activities and
war vividly and constantly portrayed on television may be right
next door in your child's literal mind.

Watch television with your child. Discuss alternatives to
violence as problem-solving strategies. Point out stereotypes of
men, women, minorities. By doing so, you use television not as a
baby-sitter but as another form of quiet behavior and possibly as
a learning tool.

Video games, though somewhat addictive, do require fine
motor and hand-eye coordination. Regardless, the same questions
about aggression and repressed kinesthetic energy arise around
this entertainment. When dealing with such games, always
consider balance and timing. Playing an intense video game right
before bedtime may keep an active alert child awake.

Parents who live day-in and day-out with active alerts may administer the TV drug without realizing the price they pay. Even those who realize the consequences of television may feel the temptation to gain half an hour or so of relief. Used this way, television is, indeed, an addiction—for the parents.

Offer other options. Suggest drawing, playing outside, building, cooking, putting on a play, or reading. Keep television and video games as just one of many entertainment options. For a kid who loves external stimuli, the medium is extraordinarily attractive, but active alert children must learn to tap internal resources as well.

SIBLINGS

Is one of your children "born to ask permission and the other born to ask forgiveness"? This quote from a friend of mine may describe the basic difference between active alert children and their more surer and steadier siblings. Though it's not true all the time, it is all too easy to see children in opposing lights.

It's fascinating to watch the patterns flip-flop if the sibling who usually asks permission has an "off day." The other, your active alert, may be truly angelic.

Labeling children is a particularly destructive land mine. Resist the urge to scapegoat or blame the active alert child for family troubles. All the members of a healthy family are good, competent, loving people.

Children need to know that everyone is different, that everyone has good and bad days, and that no one needs to be the family "bad guy."

Interestingly, the sibling issue is, in part, the reason I began looking for a new term to describe the child who is a challenge to parent. We know enough about families now to see that how we think about or what we call a child makes a difference not only to the child but to everyone else in the family.

Four things happen in families when a child is labeled a "problem" child.

1. The child becomes more of a problem as he fulfills the label.
2. The burdened parents make demands on their "normal" children to be "extra good" to compensate for the stress caused by the "problem" child.
3. The needs of the "normal" children get brushed aside as the parents spend more and more time dealing with the "problem" child.
4. The "normal" children begin to resent the "problem" child.

How do you think about your child? How do you picture her in your mind? Do you see the whole child?

Handling Sibling Rivalry

Among all siblings, there is an innate sense of rivalry—the desire to be most loved, to be your favorite. In his book *Sibling Rivalry,* Seymour Reit states, "The real challenge for parents is not to try to eliminate rivalry but instead to keep it within healthy and constructive bounds."

To understand how your children's rivalry works, you might first consider two parts of your family history.

The first part is your rules about conflict, anger, and gender. What do you do when conflict occurs within your family? Is it expressed? How? Is it okay to be angry or is the angry person somehow bad, or shamed? Is anger expressed directly or indirectly? Do you express anger to the person with whom you are angry or to someone else in the family? Are there different rules for the boys and girls in your family?

■ ■ ■

Mary was extremely angry at her husband. She yelled at the dog and sent him outside. Six-year-old Josh said, "Mom, be mad at the person you're mad at!"

The second and equally important question is, What is your history with your own siblings? Do you have siblings you no longer speak with or who are considered on the "outs" with the family in which you grew up? In what ways did your parents contribute to this? Was one sibling catered to? Was one sibling "babied" because of gender? Did someone have to be the "bad guy" in your family? Answers to these questions will give you clues about how you are contributing to an already existing issue.

The most common sibling pattern I find among active alert children and their siblings is a victim–aggressor pattern. Because the active alert does not distinguish boundaries and is experimental and curious, this pattern often begins in the earliest stages of sibling relationships. When you introduce a baby into the family system, the older active alert often may be viewed as dangerous to the infant. At first, this fear may be appropriate given the active alert child's curiosity and energy.

The problems arise when the infant grows and the danger lessens, but parents hang on to their fears. Both children sense this fear.

■ ■ ■

Five-year-old Stephen's parents worried about Stephen's energy around his fourteen-month-old sister, Lisa. One day Dad observed as Stephen walked past Lisa. Although he was not close enough to touch her, Lisa looked at Stephen, fell down, and started crying. Mom ran into the room. "Stephen, be careful of Lisa," she said.

Lisa had learned how to set up her brother as the bad guy to get attention. It is so easy to make the active alert the scapegoat—the one who needs to be watched. It is harder but critically important to remember that when siblings disagree both children share responsibility and both should become participants in working out a solution.

So, when you reprimand the one who hits, spend time talking to the other one about teasing. When parents make negative prejudgments about the active alert child's responsibility for the disruption, siblings learn to bait the active alert child. That is unhealthy for both children. One child gets a message about being bad and aggressive and the other's sneaky, helpless behavior is reinforced. All children need to learn when they are being intrusive or inappropriate. Guide them.

■ ■ ■

Brian's mother resolved problems between brothers by sitting down each child at opposite ends of the kitchen table. Because they were so far away from each other, they could not hit or kick and had to talk about solutions.

■ ■ ■

Libby's mother put arguing children on opposite sides of a window. There they washed the glass until they had resolved their differences without benefit of an audience. When they arrived at a solution, they reported it to Mom, who neither approved nor disapproved of their plan.

Young children sometimes need a facilitator to help them resolve conflict. A parent who kneels down with one arm around each child (as much to prevent escape as to calm them!) can coach them in problem solving.

The second most common sibling pattern is an outgrowth of active alerts' competitive nature. Borrowing a term from Carole and Andrew Calladine's *Raising Brothers and Sisters Without Raising the Roof,* I call it simply, the "competitors."

If you have ever felt like a Ping-Pong ball around your children, you'll know what I am talking about. It is a familiar scenario: One child constantly interrupts the other using "best, better" language. An example would be, "You mean you only did three pull-ups in your fitness test? I did seven!"

Address the pattern by assuring all your children that they are loved. Communicate this through touch—kissing, snuggling, and hugging. Also, verbally accept and affirm your children's differences. One child may be academically skilled, the other may be a wonderful musician or a great athlete. Tell them how much you notice and appreciate their gifts.

Each child is different and cannot be treated equally. Children can be treated "equitably," however. Identify your children's individual talents and needs. Then allocate time on the basis of their special qualities to help to reduce competition.

■ ■ ■

Ramona, whose mother is a quiet, organized woman, often feels jealous of her sister Beezus, who is considered, "Mother's girl." Beezus and her mother enjoy being together sewing quietly and talking. Because of her energy, Ramona does not have a way to connect with her mom. Dad draws and paints with Ramona, so the siblings are treated equitably on the whole, but Ramona misses and seeks a closer connection with her mother. (See Beverly Cleary's Ramona *books)*

Whichever sibling pattern your children fall into—conflict or competition—help them facilitate resolutions by acknowledging negative feelings. Giving voice to negative feelings helps children to identify the problem and to find solutions, and it enables them to become more responsible for and cooperative with one another. Acknowledging such feelings also affirms children. Remember, feelings are facts. Saying that it's okay to sometimes "hate" your sister allows a child to own up to rather than to deny feelings. It thus takes away the frightful power of intense emotions. It also defuses anger. Children whose feelings are acknowledged no longer need to lay blame but are free to work on resolving conflict.

■ ■ ■

I am reminded of Beezus's dilemma in Beezus and Ramona *by Beverly Cleary. On her birthday Beezus admits to her mother that she does not always like her sister Ramona. Her mother and Aunt Beatrice, by confiding that they had similar feelings about each other when they were younger, affirm Beezus and remove the shame she felt about her emotions.*

Acknowledging negative feelings is especially important when dealing with active alert children who, because of their tendency to perform, may be at their most cooperative with people outside their immediate family. Active alert children need to understand that their ability to cooperate, while wonderfully appropriate in the outside world, also belongs in the home among the people who care most about them.

Our society supports the notion that we must be on our best behavior outside the home. As a result, parents sometimes get confused. For example, knowing their children will not argue in front of a neighbor, they tell them to go outside when bickering. Instead, I suggest that they tell their children, "If you don't know how to solve your problems here, in this house, how will I know you can do it with your friends? Until you show me that you can play with each other, you will not be allowed to play with a friend."

"ONE, TWO, THREE—YOU'RE OUT!" GETTING PAST STUCK RECORDS AND POTHOLES

You know the scenario: Day after day, you wake up to find your child is still in a negative mood. On those days your child's presence seems to perpetuate power struggles. It may appear that both of you have forgotten how to have a positive relationship with each other.

Active alert children get stuck in two ways: a repetitive pattern of being stuck like a needle on a record and a brief rough spot like a pothole they must get around. You will recognize this pattern as the one in which your child pursues one behavior or activity that you want him to stop, for example, incessantly bouncing a ball against a wall, or squashing his clay as flat as a pizza on your newly cleaned kitchen floor.

We already know that active alerts experience negative moods. Sometimes parents get in the habit of repeated negative interactions with the child, without noticing how long the mood lasts or asking the child to be responsible for his moods (remember Carrie in chapter 4). The result is a vicious cycle between parent and child in which family life deteriorates steadily. Parents may not even notice the positive aspects creeping out of their relationship.

One, Two, Three—You're Out! is a strategy I developed to help parent and child break the negative cycle in a positive way. As in baseball, once you have three strikes, another inning soon follows. Declare the start of a new inning. Here's how it works. In the one, two, three system, your child gets one bad day. If the second day in a row is bad, look for underlying causes for your child's behavior. For example, make sure he gets enough rest— perhaps he had gotten to bed late two nights before. Check to see if he is feeling physically well or if his diet has changed. On the third day, the child is "out."

When "out" is declared, stop looking for reasons behind the negative behavior and simply flood the relationship with positives. You take the initiative for changing the negative interaction with your child. Take your child out to lunch or to the zoo. Plan a picnic or drop by the child's school for a visit. The point is to do all the positive things you can think of. Tell your child what she is doing well. Flood the relationship with affirming actions.

Same Song, Again and Again

Because behavior is habitual, children, like adults, can get stuck in a response pattern. If you and your child seem to be singing the same song, again and again, a huge dose of positives along with some special activity often moves the needle along the record.

■ ■ ■

Carl's mom and dad had had a terrible three days with their son. At the end of the third day, a friend called to invite Carl and his family out to dinner with him and his grandson. Mom, fearing Carl's behavior would spoil the evening, tried to decline the invitation. The friend, who adored Carl, convinced her to give it a try. Carl's

*mom agreed, took a deep breath, and reminded her son
about restaurant behavior. Sure enough, Carl did so well
that the waitress complimented him on his behavior. The
dinner was enough to turn both Carl and his mom around.*

"It's amazing how this works," said one of my clients. "The
first time you asked me to try One, Two, Three—You're Out! I
wondered how it could possibly work. But I agreed to take Jim to
the zoo. He had been behaving so strangely, I didn't know if he
would run away or jump the railing into the tiger cage. We talked
about appropriate behavior at the zoo. Lo and behold! It was a
wonderful afternoon. We both came back feeling very different
about each other." Explain One, Two, Three—You're Out! to your
child. Tell her that you value her too much to let the two of you
continue in a negative pattern. Tell her that declaring "out" will
help you to learn to be with each other in a joyful, positive way
again.

Like a Pothole in the Road

Active alerts also can get stuck on something they want to do.
Once stuck, it's as if they're caught in a pothole: They seem
unable to change directions. They buzz around like mosquitoes.
Ask them to go to their room and they won't; ask them to get
ready for bed and they refuse. It's a parent's nightmare.

Now is a good time to mention that I do not believe in
physically grappling with an active alert child. The reason is
simple: It seldom works. If you do this, they will oppose you
physically and someone may get hurt. Active alert children seem
to respond in two ways to physical power that is intended to
control them. First, they may say you are hurting them, thus
shifting the attention off their behavior and onto the question of
whether or not you really hurt them. If that tactic does not work,
they try again to make it your fault by implying they don't care
what you do anyway, as nothing you do or say has any effect on
them. By intruding upon their physical space—something you are
trying to teach them not to do—you model inappropriate behavior.

Many times, however, frightened parents believe that the only way to get their stuck child to cooperate is with force. If you are tempted to approach your child in that manner, remember that, given his need to be in charge, everyone will lose. Also, keep in mind that when an active alert's movement is blocked, he opposes. In such situations, I urge parents to out-think the child by using a shortened version of One, Two, Three—You're Out!

Tell the young active alert child, "I will count to three, and then you're out and I will help you." Give her a second to regroup and think about what you have offered her. After slowly counting to three, if she still does not cooperate, take her by the hand and assist her to be a "cooperator." Deep down your child may be looking for a face-saving way out of a "pothole" and welcome your help.

■ ■ ■

Leaving day care was always difficult for four-year-old Aaron. Although his dad tried to get him away, he just wouldn't stop playing. Sometimes it was difficult for Aaron to discern when Dad was ready to go, as his father often chatted with the teachers. The one, two, three method, as well as being a ritual for the transition, cued him when his dad was ready to leave. "I'll count to three and then say goodbye to the teacher" ended the day with fewer frustrations for Aaron and Dad. The verbal cue allowed Aaron to display his positive side. It also allowed his father to affirm his son's appropriate behavior.

By refusing to use force, you, the parent, reject a "win–lose" game and provide your child with a chance to exercise his abilities.

One, Two, Three and the Older Child

When your children are school-age, shift the technique. Because older children understand the importance of mutual cooperation in the family, the meaning of the one, two, three method changes. When you make a request of an older child, she needs to cooperate with you as you cooperate with her. One, Two,

Three—You're Out! now means, "If you cannot cooperate with me, then I will not cooperate with you on something you consider important." The phrase becomes a shorthand way of saying, "If you choose not to help me, then I will also have that choice." Helping the child understand all the ways you meet her needs each day increases the effectiveness of the technique.

A Word of Caution About One, Two, Three—You're Out!

The one, two, three technique is not meant to be used as a punishment, only as a tool that triggers a child to think about choices. Explain that those choices include the ones he makes himself and the ones you make each day about how you will help him. Remind him that you cooperate with him on a daily basis: You drive him to his friends' houses, supervise when friends visit, take him to the store to buy a treat, and allow him to watch television after his homework is completed. Clarify the distinction between what you *feel* for him and what you *do* for him. Never threaten to withhold your love or to abandon him. Tell him that no matter what he does, you will always love him.

■ ■ ■

At ten, David had earned the right to stay home alone for an hour when his mom took his sister to piano lessons. One afternoon he had trouble cooperating. He broke one rule after another. As the afternoon wore on, he continued to push the limits until his mother first warned him and later told him he had lost the privilege of staying home alone that afternoon. David was outraged. His mother listened to his ranting and then said, "David, I've made my decision. I warned you that you would lose the privilege of staying home alone this afternoon if you continued to have trouble. Now you must go with us. I will count to three. If you choose not to go, I will not be able to cooperate with you tomorrow when you want your friends to come over." David chose to accompany his mother and sister, and for a while he did not push the boundaries quite so hard.

FOSTERING THE SELF-ESTEEM PROCESS

■ ■ ■

Mrs. Jones asks me, "Why does Colin look ahead in the book to see what part he'll have to read next, when he's one of our best readers?"

■ ■ ■

Linnea's parents ask, "How do we get her to remember the good things we say to her? She seems to notice only if we ask her to do something differently."

The roller coaster of an active alert's self-esteem is extremely bumpy and it worries parents and teachers alike. As such, it fits well in this discussion of "land mines."

Remember that your child, by nature, is intense. He is 100 percent involved in what is happening in the present moment. Thus, when he is anxious about what he's going to read, Colin is unable to call up past successes to bolster his self-confidence.

As your active alert child grows older, you can help balance her intensity by recalling past peaks and valleys so that she will gain perspective on her present performance. She will recall the day she fell in the skating show as well as the time she played so beautifully during the piano recital. She'll also remember that the outcome of each was okay. Eventually your child will understand that not all performances are or need to be tens. If her average is nine, it means she's had some tens but also some sevens and eights. Perfection is not possible.

A second strategy for shoring up self-esteem is to address the active alert child's tendency to evaluate himself according to what happens in the external world. Because these children judge themselves according to what other people say, moving their referent point along the spectrum from external to internal is a long, gradual process. In fact, I am not sure that these children ever become confident enough to feel good about themselves no matter what other people think. Nonetheless, balancing the two referents is a worthwhile long-term goal. School-age active alerts can learn that how they feel about what they did is as important as any rewards they receive or what other people say.

■ ■ ■

Chelsea, age ten, worked extraordinarily hard on her project for the science fair. When the judges awarded ribbons, Chelsea's project didn't place. "I like my project even though I didn't get a ribbon," she told her parents as they left the school. Later that night, however, she said, "I didn't work hard enough, I'm not smart enough." Chelsea did realize the value of her project, but she didn't fully trust her own evaluation of her good work. Chelsea's mom was pleased that Chelsea could recognize the project's intrinsic value. Such thinking was a departure from the way Chelsea usually thought. But her mom was sad to hear her daughter condemn her work because it hadn't met with the judges' approval.

The two of them talked about what standards the judges used, the standards her mom might have used, and the standards Chelsea herself had used when she did the project. Chelsea's standards and those her mom used were based on hard work and diligence as well as what Chelsea had learned while doing the project. "You know," said her mom, "by our standards you did remarkably well."

"Well, that's true," Chelsea replied. "Still, next year I think I will try to understand what the judges are looking for because that doesn't seem to be the same as what I was trying to do."

Talking Your Way into Self-Esteem

Self-esteem is a process, and you have the role of helping your child to feel good about herself by providing some of the affirmation she needs when she's stuck in a negative slump. To help you, I have compiled, with the aid of Lynne Burmyn, a therapist, a list of affirmations for each active alert trait. Affirmations are a very powerful use of language. They provide a positive way to tell your child what's neat or wonderful about her. I hope these selections will inspire you to create many more ways to tell your little person how wonderful she is!

ACTIVE

It's okay to act, to initiate things.
You can always come back to me; I will be here.
It's okay to do two things at once.
Your energy is beautiful.
It's okay to get excited and enthusiastic.
It's okay to slow down and rest; you don't have to hurry.
You can be proud of your energy.
It's okay to be active and curious.

ALERT

It's okay to try things out.
You can be excited and still go slowly.
You can think before you act; thinking will not spoil actions.
You can be tactful and still be honest.
It's okay to experiment with ideas, it's okay to explore options.
It's okay to want privacy.
You can say no.
It's okay to withdraw for a while.
I will not let you hurt yourself.
I will not let you hurt others.
It's okay to say what you know; it's okay to remain silent.

BRIGHT

It's okay to learn in your own way.
I'm not afraid of your intelligence.

It's okay to be curious; it's okay to ask questions.
It's okay to be unique.
It's okay to be different; you can know who you are.
It's okay to be smart.

CONTROLLING

You can do things your way.
It's okay to choose.
You don't have to act helpless or angry to get your needs met.
Your needs are as important as mine.
We will not forget you; we will include you.
It's okay to take care of yourself, and I will take care of you,
    too.
It's okay to disagree; it's okay to agree.
You can say no.
I am not fragile; I am stronger than you are; you can depend on
    me.
It's okay to do things differently from the way I do them.

FEARFUL

You can be scared; I will comfort you.
You can be powerful and still have needs.
I will not hurt you.
It's okay to want someone to go with you.
You can trust that you'll be protected; I will protect you.
I will not let you get lost.

INTENSE

It's okay to get angry.
I'm not afraid of your anger.
You can understand and still be angry or sad or scared.
You can use the energy from your anger to solve problems.
I am not afraid of your strength.

It's okay to have strong likes and dislikes and to change your
    mind about them.
It's okay to feel sad or disappointed.
It's okay to be angry at someone you love.
I love you when you're angry, too.
It's okay to be realistically "negative."
You don't have to like everything; it doesn't mean you're
    unhappy just because you don't like something.

ATTENTION-HUNGRY

I will not forget you; I will not stop hugging you just because
    you are older.
I can take care of you and pay attention to other family members
    at the same time.
You don't have to wait until you're desperate to get your needs
    met.
We can take turns getting our needs met; I will not neglect you.
There is enough for everyone.
I cannot guess what you want; you must tell me.
Your needs are not too much for me; I like taking care of you.
It's okay to want attention.

GETTING ALONG

It's okay to want to fit in with others.
I enjoy receiving what you have to give.
You can say what you know; you don't have to say what you
    know.
You can choose whom you trust.
You can choose the time and degree of your honesty and how
    you reveal yourself.
It's okay to be generous; it's okay to hang on to things.
You can play and be silly and still be in control.

SELF-ESTEEM

I am proud of you.
I know you love me; I love you, too.
I will not compare you to other children.
Sometimes it's okay to be rude.
It's okay to forgive yourself; I will forgive you.
I like hearing your laugh.
It's okay to be ordinary.
I love you; you don't have to act a certain way to be loved.
You are an important part of my life.
I am glad you are here; you are not a burden.

PERFORMERS

You can be first, but you don't have to be first.
You don't have to pretend not to care.
You can be imperfect and still be loved.
You don't have to act cheerful, responsible, or dramatic to get
   your needs met.
You don't have to be good-looking, charming, or cheerful to get
   your needs met.
You don't have to be perfect; it's okay to make mistakes.
You don't have to act sick, helpless, or supercompetent to get
   your needs met.
You don't have to be superstrong and superperfect.
You don't have to earn my love; I love you no matter what you
   do.
It's okay to be excellent; it's okay not to be excellent.

EMPATHIC

You can take care of yourself; I will not feel hurt if you take care
   of yourself.
You can have all your feelings; you don't have to cheer me up.
I will take your feelings seriously.

It's okay to say what you know.

You can be independent and still have needs.

You are not responsible for my happiness or unhappiness.

You can trust your feelings to help you know what to do.

You don't have to take care of me.

You can trust your intuition.

HANDLING "WHAT IFS"

Among the active alerts' many other gifts is their ability to envision the worst possible scenario (WPS) in any given situation.

■ ■ ■

Nine-year-old Bobby told me he'd had a stiff neck at school all day. He thought his neck might be broken. I asked him if he knew about the "most likelies." "Most likely," I said, "you slept on a pillow that was too high or most likely you pulled a muscle with a quick movement."

Bobby thought it over and said, "Well, I did sleep on my teddy bear last night and it is higher than my pillow, and yesterday I fell playing soccer and jerked my head back."

I told Bobby I thought his ability to write a WPS is one of his gifts. He looked at me askance and said, "I think it's a bad thing I do."

"Bobby," I replied, "envisioning all the possible outcomes is indeed a gift. Think about it. If someone is going to build a bridge I have to cross I hope it's done by someone who's good at imagining the WPS. I want that bridge builder to consider all the bad things that could happen. I want him to figure out what the wind, snow, and river currents might do to the bridge and then build the safest one possible. Do you see how WPS's can work for you? The trick is to use your gift and bring forth the WPS at the right time in the right place."

Active alert children have enough real concerns. They do not need to create additional worries about improbable outcomes. As parents, you can coach your children through the worst possible scenarios by gently reminding them to explore the most likelies in any given situation. When they seem unable to consider the most likelies, begin with the WPS. Envision a plan together for dealing with the worst possible scenario. After they have imagined the worst possibilities, they more easily move into the world of most likelies.

TEACHING YOUR OWN ACTIVE ALERT

Trying to be your active alert child's teacher may be hazardous to your mental health.

■ ■ ■

Christian's mother is a church organist. When Christian was six, he decided to take piano lessons. Although, he loved his teacher, Maria, practicing soon became an issue between Christian and his mother. When Christian did not remember what the teacher had written down for him, his mom showed him how to play the piece. Christian responded by saying, "That's not the way Maria does it." Mom knew that though she was playing correctly, Christian could not listen to advice from her. She learned to disengage by saying, "This is what I believe is right. Do you want to finish by yourself or do you want my help with a different piece?"

If she had asserted her need to be right, most likely a power struggle would have ensued. As it was, she offered Christian an option to use his own strength.

At times you will need to assert your power and set a "bottom line." Try not to create these situations by volunteering to teach things to your child that could be taught to him by others. Whenever possible, use other adults to teach your child. Doing so provides benefits to both you and your child. After all, when your child's intense feelings surface and he feels unloved by you, it helps to know that there are others who love him. Also, when your child does not wish to do an assignment, he will switch the issue from "I am discouraged about the project" to "It's your fault!" If you are not involved, he cannot do this.

You can see the bind. As a parent you are always in a teaching role, so beware of pitfalls. When making suggestions about homework or music practice, consider what your child may be thinking. Ask her how she would solve the problem. If you have to show her how to do a math problem, be careful to label your own approach. For example, say "I was taught this way," instead of "You should do that this way." Using the "I" language steers around your child's control and self-esteem issues.

Your active alert child would like to make you responsible for this happiness. Therefore, rather than tending to a discouraging task, he will "do battle" or oppose you. Remember, his feelings need to stay with him; the responsibility to complete the assignment must be his.

If you invest too much in your child's work, she does not know if she is working for you or herself. If you start getting too involved, your child will push you out, and it won't be a gentle shove. Alternatively, you'll end up taking the blame and holding the bag when she moves on to a new activity.

A QUESTION OF ATTITUDES: THE FEELING CHART

Sometimes the challenges you face as a parent are attitudinal rather than behavioral issues. Certainly, as noted earlier, active alerts can get stuck in habitually negative response patterns. But your school-age child can learn to become aware of those negative slumps and learn how to deal with them.

Present it as a game. Note on a chart how you are feeling and how you perceive other members of your family. Leave room on the chart for other family members to jot down how they perceive you that day. Include a space for each family member to record his own feelings about himself and his other family members.

Place the chart in a common area, where each family member has easy access to it (for example, on the refrigerator). After you do this for a few days, sit down together and discuss what each of you has learned. If family members want to set goals for how they'd like to be perceived, discuss whether they would like your help in that process.

No one really wants to be the grump of the family. Sometimes just making perceptions explicit and public changes the behavior.

YES, MASTER

Young active alert children often display a master–slave theme that parents reinforce almost unwittingly. Parents may fall into a pattern of responding to demands, paying no attention to how rude the child is in making the demands. Although this problem is all too common with most children, the active alert child's need to be in control exacerbates the situation. No one, it seems, is better at issuing orders than active alert children!

Sooner or later, most parents resent being ordered around and address the problem. Sooner is better! Remember, your child will rarely encounter anyone who will respond to her with kindness if she is rude. Why should you? Allowing this pattern to go on sets your child up for painful experiences with other people. She needs to learn how her behavior affects other people, and the best place for her to learn this is with you. After all, you don't want your child to grow up believing she can treat the people she loves badly.

Undo this behavior by saying, "It's difficult for me to get you what you want when you ask that way. If you ask quietly, I'll be glad to help." Of course, you need to be consistent. If you forget and the theme recurs, simply start again with gentle reminders.

I like to teach school-age children about slavery, hoping that the insight gained may help them to be more empathetic. After all, no one wants to be a slave, or, for that matter, a master.

TIME NOW FOR TIME-OUT!

In some parenting circles, time-out—a parenting technique whereby a child is told to sit quietly alone for a specified time—is a heavily used method. Although time-out is one effective way to deal with children, my perspective about how and when this tool is most effectively used differs from that of other professionals. The land mines in time-out are power and overuse. All too often, time-outs can become power struggles.

■ ■ ■

Sam's parents were totally frustrated when they came to see me. For several weeks Sam had averaged ten time-outs a day. Both Sam and his parents knew the time-outs were ineffective, but they didn't know what else to do. His parents were lost in a power-struggle maze. Finally, they recognized that the first step on the pathway out was to stop using time-outs.

Given the active alert child's oppositional nature, this technique, when overused, may worsen an already stuck interaction. Active alerts are born movers and doers. When their movement is blocked, they stand ready to oppose the person who set up the roadblock.

Informed use makes time-outs an effective technique. Time-out is not a method with which to exert power. Rather, it is a way to remove your child from too much stimulation. Sometimes a young active alert child needs to step back from activity and regroup. Choose a place with little stimulation as the time-out place. The steps to your house or a rocking chair in the corner or facing an aquarium will do. The bathroom or the child's bedroom may be too stimulating. Tell the child the energy she is using is not "people" or social energy and that she needs to rock in a rocker (a great kinesthetic energy release) while she watches the fish.

You and your other children are also stimulating to the child, so you should go to another room. Don't talk with a child who is in time-out. Although your child may need to know you are present, speaking with him defeats the purpose of the tool.

When you begin to use time-outs, explain the idea to your child and assist him in being a cooperator. Let the child determine when he is ready to rejoin you. If he makes a poor decision and returns too soon, set a timer for three to five minutes more. Make sure he can see the timer and hear the bell when it rings. Also, make his choices clear by discussing them before you implement the plan. That way he has more control and responsibility when he decides how to act.

Always act "as if" your child will cooperate. If she does not, reset the timer. For every minute she refuses to go to time-out, tack on another minute to the time she will be expected to spend there. Even young children learn quickly that the time-out is shorter when they cooperate.

The time-out method is one of many at your disposal. Use it to help your child to learn about himself and his responsibilities as a social being. But be careful: If you find yourself using it exclusively, you may be using it more to control than to teach.

Time-out is a method of last resort and usually feels punishing to both child and parents. After each use, reconcile with your child by hugging her and telling her you're glad she's back. The goal, after all, is not to shame your child but to teach her more effective ways to relate to others after she has had time away from the stimulation of those people.

PLAYING UPROAR

Picture an angry active alert child. Does he calmly release his anger in appropriate ways? Is he articulate about why he is angry? Does he distinguish his own feelings from someone else's? Or, in an attempt to release the tension, does he try to involve you and make you responsible for his struggle?

The advent of the microwave oven has made the pressure cooker an anachronism, but bear with me. The image of that old-fashioned pot is a great one to use when describing the game I call Uproar. Pressure cookers release steam gradually during the cooking process. If the steam valve is faulty or not set correctly, however, the lid blows off and food winds up on the kitchen ceiling.

The game of Uproar is like that malfunctioning cooker. It involves a child irritating the parent until she blows up. The person who explodes is left feeling foolish and is logically to blame for the results of the explosion. Uproar begins when your child digs in her heels around an issue and refuses to budge. Often the issue is so innocuous that parents fail to understand how it could bother the child in the first place. (Keep in mind that the pressure has been building and the defined issue may not be the real or only one. It is just the trigger.)

Parents play Uproar in two ways. They either ignore the negative behavior or try to reason with the child. A child playing Uproar refuses to be reasonable, however, and will persist in his behavior even when ignored. Escalating emotions ensue. Parents become increasingly irritated and the child more determined until at last the adults "blow their top." In the end, the angry parents, feeling sheepish about their lack of control, are particularly vulnerable when their child says, "It was all your fault."

When dealing with an active alert child, you need to be direct and acknowledge problems up front before they build a head of steam. Model appropriate ways to release tension. Talk with our child as problems arise. Is your child being too loud, aggressive, or rude? Explain the problem, how it affects you, and what your child must do to change the situation. Then engage to disengage. Offer choices, affirm his ability to handle the situation, and then back away so that he can decide (that is, has control over) what to do.

In the back of his mind, your child may believe that Uproar is an effective way to get what he wants. One of the children with whom I work told me, "If I get my mom angry enough, she'll give in." The reality was that in his family, when the child set off such intense anger, the mother never relented. Maybe he had had past success with the game. In any case, he believed in the power of Uproar even when it no longer worked for him.

■ ■ ■

When Terry's family visited Grandma's, he slept in a sleeping bag in his parents' bedroom. He set the bag right in his mother's path to the bathroom. When his mother moved it and explained why that arrangement wouldn't work, Terry was angry. At bedtime he lay in his bag making noises; no one could get to sleep.

There are two possible endings for this scenario. Let's play them both out.

Terry's mom could say, "If you sleep in our room, you need to get out of the path we use to get to the bathroom. So, here's your choice: Either sleep in the living room or move your bag. Now, you know Grandma gets up early, so she might wake you if you decide to move to the other room. But I'm sure you can make a comfortable choice for yourself." Then his mom could back off and let Terry decide.

The second scenario is what actually occurred. Terry continued to make noises. His parents ignored them as best they could, but finally they were so irritated they blew up. Everyone in the house woke up and Terry was blamed for disturbing their sleep. He, in turn, took out his anger on his mom. "It's your fault. If you hadn't moved my bag, this never would have happened."

When it comes to Uproar, I have one suggestion: Don't play.

8

How Your Child Learns

I learn by going where I have to go.

−Theodore Roethke
"The Waking"

A ctive alerts are active. They learn by going where they have to go! At the core of all active alerts is a kinesthetic learner—a mover.

It is important for parents and teachers to understand how all children go about the task of learning. But for those of us who live with or teach active alert children, it is a vital matter.

Although most active alerts behave fine in school, some problems may arise because they are "different." Active alerts are bright, but not in a traditionally "gifted" sense. They are, rather, wonderful alternative thinkers. Remember the four-year-old at preschool screening who responded to the question, "What are windows made of?" by saying, "Squares and rectangles"? His answer was not wrong, but it is not the most common one. How about the adult who remembers using a ruler to try to answer the question, "Which is larger, five, seven, or nine?"

Understanding your own learning style as well as that of your child will prepare you to face the issues that arise when you have to choose and work with a teacher and a school.

Later in this chapter, we will assess the way both you and your child learn. First, let's look at the learning styles defined by psychologists Walter B. Barbe, Ph.D., and Raymond H. Swassing, Ed.D.

Barbe and Swassing describe three basic learning modalities: kinesthetic, auditory, and visual. Most people eventually develop a mixed-modal learning style, combining elements of two or three. Knowing about all three styles will enable you to help your child to strengthen his auditory and visual skills so that he gains other pathways to information.

As you read, you will probably pick up on how our society is biased in favor of the visual learner. It's important to remember that one learning style is not better than another. When you know about learning styles, you can work with your child and help her to understand why certain things come easily to her and why other things may be difficult.

■ ■ ■

Ten-year-old Lynn and I were swimming one day when she asked me, "Linda, Mom's going to get a special computer program to help me learn to spell. I'm really dumb in spelling and she says this is a good program. What do you think?"

I'd known Lynn for a long time. She takes piano lessons and plays in competitions with much older children. I asked her some questions about how she spelled words. In our conversation it became clear to me that here was a talented auditory learner who spelled words the way they sounded, which doesn't always work in the English language.

I responded by saying, "Lynn, you have a special gift. You learn through sounds, which means that spelling is going to be hard for you. Using your gift, there are two ways to spell cat: K-A-T or C-A-T. It's not that you're dumb. Your gift helps you in your music; it just gets in the way a little in spelling. You know, the national spelling bees are often won by auditory learners. That's because those tests use words few people have ever seen, so in order to win you have to be a keen listener." Lynn looked at me with relief and said, "Would you tell my mom that?"

Let's take a look, now, at the three learning styles as defined by Barbe and Swassing.

THE KINESTHETIC LEARNER

All children seem as if they are learning by doing, by touching. But some infants watch more; some are more attuned to sound; and some really do touch everything. Some begin to practice another modality as they reach school age. By age seven or eight, active alerts may mix kinesthetic and auditory or kinesthetic and visual styles, but they do retain a very strong kinesthetic response. There is no way around it: The kinesthetic approach is basic to their learning.

What are kinesthetic learners like? Children who learn kinesthetically prefer action stories. They probably will not be avid readers because reading is a sedentary activity. When kinesthetic learners do read, they take a lot of breaks, and frequently change body position.

Listen to them and talk. Even as they speak you hear the emphasis on action and doing. An adult kinesthetic learner may say, "Let's run with that idea" or "We really need to get a jump on this concept." As children, kinesthetic learners "jump for joy" or "bounce off the walls." They may be "poor spellers" who need to write words down to see if they "feel" right. Because such learners move around a lot, people tend to think of them as "distractable" children or, later, as "nervous" adults.

For kinesthetic learners, moving into action is their first response. Therefore, they appear to be impulsive. They gesture with their hands when they speak, attack problems physically, and "fidget" when they have to sit still. In groups, they are the ones who always have their hands up. Kinesthetic learners express emotions physically, "stomping off" or developing tummy aches when nervous.

According to Barbe and Swassing, approximately 15 percent of school-age children are kinesthetic learners.

If you recognize your child as a kinesthetic learner, then you need to ask yourself: Does my child's teacher arrange the school environment so that my kinesthetic learner can move? Are there active, manipulative learning tools, such as cards, beads, or movable alphabet letters in the classroom?

The Auditory Learner

Auditory learners learn through listening—through listening they take in information and instructions. People who learn this way enjoy conversations but may have a difficult time waiting for their turn to talk. They love to read dialogue but avoid lengthy written descriptions of scenery.

As they speak they emphasize sound: "That sounds like you . . ." or "I hear what you are saying . . ." Young auditory learners hum a lot, sing a lot, and make a lot of different sounds. They talk through their problems in order to reach a solution. Sounds may distract them. Because they are sensitive to noise, they express emotion by changing the volume and pitch of their voice. A phonics approach to reading is a useful tool for young auditory learners.

According to Barbe and Swassing, approximately 25 percent of school-age children are auditory learners.

The Visual Learner

Visual learners learn by seeing—by watching a demonstration or reading directions. They learn to read by recognizing words by sight or through the whole-word recognition approach, which

Swassing-Barbe Checklist of Observable Modality Strength Characteristics

AREA OBSERVED	VISUAL	AUDITORY	KINESTHETIC
Learning style	• Learns by seeing; watching demonstrations	• Learns through verbal instructions from others or self	• Learns by doing; direct involvement
Reading	• Likes description; sometimes stops reading to stare into space and imagine scene; intense concentration	• Enjoys dialogue, plays; avoids lengthy description, unaware of illustrations; moves lips or subvocalizes	• Prefers stories where action occurs early; fidgets when reading, handles books, not an avid reader
Spelling	• Recognizes words by sight; relies on configuration of words	• Uses a phonics approach; has auditory word-attack skills	• Often is a poor speller; writes words to determine if they "feel" right
Handwriting	• Tends to be good, particularly when young; spacing and size are good; appearance is important	• Has more difficulty learning in initial stages; tends to write lightly; says strokes when writing	• Good initially, deteriorates when space becomes smaller; pushes harder on writing instrument

	Visual	Auditory	Kinesthetic
Memory	Remembers faces, forgets names; writes things down, takes notes	Remembers names, forgets faces; remembers by auditory repetition	Remembers best what was done, not what was seen or talked about
Imagery	Vivid imagination; thinks in pictures, visualizes in detail	Subvocalizes, thinks in sounds; details less important	Imagery not important; images that do occur are accompanied by movement
Distractibility	Generally unaware of sounds; distracted by visual disorder of movement	Easily distracted by sounds	Not attentive to visual, auditory presentation so seems distractible
Problem solving	Deliberate; plans in advance; organizes thoughts by writing them; lists problems	Talks problems out, tries solutions, verbally, subvocally; talks self through problem	Attacks problems physically; impulsive; often selects solution involving greatest activity
Response to periods of inactivity	Stares; doodles; finds something to watch	Hums; talks to self or to others	Fidgets; finds reasons to move; holds up hand
Response to new situations	Looks around; examines structure	Talks about situation, pros and cons, what to do	Tries things out; touches, feels; manipulates

AREA OBSERVED	VISUAL	AUDITORY	KINESTHETIC
Emotionality	• Somewhat repressed; stares when angry; cries easily, beams when happy; facial expression is good index of emotion	• Shouts with joy or anger; blows up verbally but soon calms down; expresses emotion verbally and through changes in tone, volume, pitch of voice	• Jumps for joy; hugs, tugs, and pulls when happy; stamps, jumps, and pounds when angry, stomps off; general body tone is a good index of emotion
Communication	• Quiet; does not talk at length; becomes impatient when extensive listening is required; may use words clumsily; describes without embellishment; uses words such as see, look	• Enjoys listening, but cannot wait to talk; descriptions are long but repetitive; likes hearing self and others talk; uses words such as listen, hear	• Gestures when speaking; does not listen well; stands close when speaking or listening; quickly loses interest in detailed verbal discourse; uses words such as get, take
General appearance	• Neat, meticulous, likes order; may choose not to vary appearance	• Matching clothes not so important, can explain choices of clothes	• Neat but soon becomes wrinkled through activity

| *Response to the arts* | • Not particularly responsive to music; prefers the visual arts; tends not to voice appreciation of art of any kind, but can be deeply affected by visual displays; focuses on details and components rather than the work as a whole | • Favors music; finds less appeal in visual art, but is readily able to discuss it; misses significant detail but appreciates the work as a whole; is able to develop verbal association for all art forms; spends more time talking about pieces than looking at them | • Responds to music by physical movement; prefers sculpture; touches statues and paintings; at exhibits stops only at those in which he or she can become physically involved; comments very little on any art form |

Excerpted from *Teaching Through Modality Strengths: Concepts and Practices*, by Walter B. Barbe, Ph.D., and Raymond H. Swassing, Ed.D., with Michael N. Milone, Jr., Ph.D., published by Zaner-Bloser, Inc., 2300 W. Fifth Ave., P. O. Box 16764, Columbus, OH 43216.

relies on the way a word looks—its configuration. Appearance and order are important to them. Disorder or movement distracts them. Visual learners think in pictures or detailed images.

Visual learners are deliberate and make plans in advance. Frequently they even jot notes to themselves. Their language reflects the preferred visual-learning modality: "I see what you mean" or "Let's look at the problem from another point of view."

According to Barbe and Swassing, 30 percent of school-age children prefer a visual-learning modality.

Whom does that leave? *Approximately 30 percent of all children learn through a mixed-modal learning style,* for example, both kinesthetic and auditory, auditory and visual, kinesthetic and visual. Successful adults develop ways to transfer from one mode to another, but many retain a distinct preference for one style, especially when they encounter new or difficult material.

The excerpt from Barbe and Swassing's *Teaching Through Modality Strengths* will give you some sense of how your child learns and help you to understand your child's perceptual strength. Although the chart is geared to a seven- or eight-year-old, I believe that it is helpful in explaining the perceptual ability of younger children as well. It also might be useful for you in determining your own learning style.

To help you determine your own learning style, I have included a second chart oriented toward adults, titled "Find Your Modality Strengths" by Walter B. Barbe, Ph.D., and Michael N. Milone, Jr., Ph.D. This survey points out the similarities and differences in how you, your spouse (if married), and your child learn. Identifying differences in learning styles within your family may help you to identify potential conflict areas between you and your child. First, complete the survey and then read the section in this chapter that addresses the issue of learning-style differences.

FIND YOUR MODALITY STRENGTHS

Listed below are ten incomplete sentences and three ways of completing each sentence. Check the statement that is most typical of you. Then count the number of checks in each column. This will give you a rough idea of the relative strength of each of your modalities.

1. My emotions can often be interpreted from my:
   - ☐ Facial expressions
   - ☐ Voice quality
   - ☐ General body tone

2. I keep up with current events by:
   - ☐ Reading the newspaper thoroughly when I have time
   - ☐ Listening to the radio or watching the television news
   - ☐ Quickly reading the paper or spending a few minutes watching television news

3. If I have business to conduct with another person, I prefer:
   - ☐ Face-to-face meetings or writing letters
   - ☐ The telephone, since it saves time
   - ☐ Conversing while walking, jogging, or doing something else physical

4. When I'm angry, I usually:
   - ☐ Clam up and give others the "silent treatment"
   - ☐ Am quick to let others know why I'm angry
   - ☐ Clench my fists, grasp something tightly, or storm off

5. When driving I:
   - ☐ Frequently check the rearview mirrors and watch the road carefully
   - ☐ Turn on the radio as soon as I enter the car
   - ☐ Can't get comfortable in the seat and continually shift position

6. I consider myself:

☐ a neat dresser

☐ a sensible dresser

☐ a comfortable dresser

7. At a meeting I:

☐ come prepared with notes and displays

☐ enjoy discussing issues and hearing other points of view

☐ would rather be somewhere else and so spend my time doodling

8. In my spare time I would rather:

☐ watch television, go to a movie, attend the theater, or read

☐ listen to the radio or records, attend a concert, or play an instrument

☐ engage in a physical activity of some kind

9. The best approach to discipline is to:

☐ isolate the child by separating him or her from the group

☐ reason with the child and discuss the situation

☐ use acceptable forms of corporal punishment

10. The most effective way of rewarding students is through:

☐ positive comments written on their paper, stick-ons, or posting good work for others to see

☐ oral praise to the student and to the rest of the class

☐ a pat on the back, a hug, or some other appropriate physical action

Total number of boxes checked

_____ visual   _____ auditory   _____ kinesthetic

WHAT ARE THE OTHER FACTORS IN LEARNING?

Besides the issue of a person's chief learning style, children have other distinct learning preferences. Drs. Kenneth and Rita Dunn along with Dr. Gary Price have designed the Learning Style Inventory. It is used by schools to assess learning styles as well as other factors—environmental, emotional, sociological, physical, and psychological preferences—that affect learning. Although it is not feasible to reproduce the Learning Style Inventory here, we can discuss what others have gleaned from their work with it.

Environmental

Environmental preferences have to do with what kinds of study environments children prefer. Just as there is no one right way to learn, there is no one right or best environment to study in. Sounds, light, temperature, and formal or informal design in the environment all affect learning. Some children are distracted by any noise in the environment and need absolute silence; others are oblivious to sound. Others concentrate best when there is a radio or television playing. Children are affected by the amount of light in the room. Some learn better in brightly lit rooms; others prefer a dim classroom. You may need more light than your child. After all, he has youthful eyes. Some people can't do their best thinking when they are "too warm" or "too cold." I am a case in point. Anyone who's ever been in my office can attest to the fact that I like warm areas.

Many children learn best while sitting still at a desk and chair. Other people learn best in a more informal setup. For example, I am writing this section while sprawled on a floor with papers scattered around me. I have three desks in my home—none of which is located near a heating vent—and they are used mostly to hold stacks of papers.

Take a look at your child. Does she learn best in an informal setup? Does she squirm at her desk at school and get accused of fidgeting? Do teachers urge her to sit still, or do they let her fidget, knowing that she learns better that way? Encourage your child to find her own best listening or study position and her best learning environment.

Whenever possible, choose teachers who affirm and understand your child's learning style as well as the limits of that style. To do that you may have to spend some time at the school observing teachers or talking with the principal about your child's particular needs. This method worked well for Mimi's family.

■ ■ ■

"I now understand that Mimi has her own way of relating to a group," Mimi's teacher told the child's parents. "During reading, instead of sitting with her classmates, she lies down at the back of the group. Mimi and I have talked about her decision. I told her that as long as she stays in the back of the group and is careful not to touch or bump her classmates, I have no problem with that."

Emotional

The emotional elements of learning as identified by the Dunns include motivation, persistence, responsibility, and the need for either structure or choice.

Motivation •   Students who are taught in their preferred learning style seem to perform better and "try harder." According to Dr. Marie Carbo, the performance of unmotivated students improves when they are taught through their learning style, given learning material appropriate to their level, encouraged to succeed, and given immediate feedback and guidance during learning.

In an ideal world, all schools and teachers would address each student's learning style. In reality, with increasing class sizes and decreasing school budgets, this may not be possible. If you find that the discrepancy between the way your child learns and the way her teacher teaches is having a negative impact on your child's self-esteem or her ability to cope with schoolwork, however, you do need to consider your options.

What are those options? You could hire a tutor to address your child's learning style so that he does not fall behind the class. You could talk with your child's teachers and enlist their help. Tell them you understand how difficult it is to individualize instruction, but that your child's learning style demands a slightly different approach, then, work with the teachers to find specific ways to address your child's needs. In the final analysis, know that you may have to change teachers or even schools.

Persistence • Persistence is directly related to motivation. If children do not succeed they stop trying to learn. The traditionally gifted child is both motivated and persistent. Perhaps a teacher can increase other children's persistence by allowing them to take frequent "breaks" before returning to a task.

Responsibility and Choice • Consider other factors. Children who have academic difficulty often have trouble learning alone and are labeled irresponsible when it may simply be that they learn best in a small group of their peers or in the presence of teachers. Such learning is called cooperative or *interactive.*

Success perpetuates itself. Children who are successful become responsible; those who think they can't achieve become irresponsible.

■ ■ ■

Seven-year-old Justin began his tutoring sessions by race-walking around the desk. As he successfully completed some work, he began to sit down. At that point, his tutor stopped dispensing tokens for "time on seat." Which element helped Justin most—his success or the token system?

When classroom instruction does not involve a multisensory approach, it spells trouble for students who learn by doing. Kinesthetic learners need materials that approach them through their learning style. Sand trays help to teach reading and writing. Kinesthetic learners can write in sand and feel the letters. Blocks, dice, beads, and other manipulative objects help them to learn mathematics. When alternative materials are not available, kinesthetic learners find other ways to move. They are renowned for having the shortest pencils in class! They know teachers will seldom decline permission to sharpen pencils, and it is a way to move. Snacks or something to chew on also facilitate learning.

■ ■ ■

Eight-year-old Mary's tutor had a bowl of nutritious snacks for Mary to nibble on while she worked.

Choice of Structure • Finally, some children like to provide their own structure, while others prefer external direction. Active alerts have difficulty creating structure, but they need it: a sticky situation because they also want to be in charge. Too much structure may stifle their interest. Striking the right balance between the two dimensions is a challenge for teachers. Active alerts seem to need to know the patterns of their day. But when being given an assignment, it's helpful if they can either choose which assignment they do or some element of how to go about doing the assignment.

Sociological

Some children like to learn alone; others prefer learning in groups. Those who learn best with others may prefer a small group to a large one. Some children learn best from an authoritarian teacher who gives detailed assignments and has clear expectations. Others like teachers who are flexible, offer choices, and encourage self-starting.

Studies done by educators Elsie I. Cafferty (1980) and Michael K. Martin (1977) tell us that a mismatch between student preference and teacher style usually results in students who do not achieve well in school, often dislike it, and quickly experience decreased motivation.

Physical

Physical elements that affect learning include perceptual strengths, food intake, time of day or night, energy levels, and mobility. Let's take a look at each.

Perceptual Strengths • As defined by Carbo and the Dunns (1986), a child's perceptual strengths include auditory, visual, and kinesthetic preferences. But these researchers have refined Barbe and Swassing's definition of kinesthetic by distinguishing the kinesthetic learner, who learns by doing and experiencing, from the factual learner, who touches, manipulates, and handles. In the learning environment auditory students should be introduced to new information by hearing about it, visual students should read about it or see it, and kinesthetic or tactual learners should bake, sew, build, interview, or act out the new information, as appropriate.

Food Intake • When studying, children have different nourishment needs. Concentrating depletes energy in some children. It makes others nervous. For whatever reason, some children, such as Mary in the previous example, learn better if they can drink, eat, or chew on something as they learn. For active alerts, it is best to keep in mind possible food sensitivities and to be sure nutritional snacks are offered.

Time of Day • Consider the *time of day* when your child learns best. Carbo reports that at any time of the day, at least one-fourth of all children will be in an energy low.

Mobility • The last physical element is *mobility*. Some students learn better if they can move, squirm, fidget, or stand.

One teacher I observed understood this well. After lunch, she demonstrated her understanding of the kinesthetic learner by saying, "Some of you may need to stand up to listen."

Psychological

When assessing children's learning styles, you must also consider certain psychological elements, such as the global versus analytic learner, hemispheric preference, and impulsive versus reflective style. What does all this mean in English?

Global Learners • Most children are global learners up to approximately age eight. That means they strive to understand the big picture first; then they go back and fill in the details. In contrast, most teachers tested by the Dunns are analytic learners who piece together details to form some kind of understanding.

Our educational system has turned the global experience of learning to read into an analytic process. As a result, we see teachers who employ subskills, such as marking long and short vowels, dividing words into syllables, adding accent marks, or identifying "schwa" sounds. These intense subskill programs for six- or seven-year-olds discourage future readers who are global learners while they encourage children with other learning styles. Emphasizing the entire process of reading includes discussing not only phonics and sight reading but the joyful sounds words make and the lovely sight of the words on a page as well as the way in which stories are written. This approach is a far better way to teach some children.

Hemisphere Dominance • Hemisphere dominance theory refers to the possibility that the two sides of the brain process nformation differently. According to the Dunns, hemispheric dominance affects how children learn. Their research demonstrates that right-brain-dominant students are not as bothered by sounds, prefer dim lights, like an informal design, are less motivated by conventional schools, are less persistent, and prefer learning with peers and through tactual stimulation.

Impulsiveness versus Reflectivity • Some teachers fail to appreciate the student who calls out an answer, that is, the one who impulsively "answer grabs" for the word when he has only sounded out the first three letters. Students who are more reflective often seem more intelligent, perhaps, because they follow the rules more closely. But consider the big picture. The impulsive learner is a risk taker, whereas the reflective student may feel anxious or fearful. As adults, we need to use both reflective and risk-taking skills. Children need to develop both.

ACTIVE ALERT LEARNERS

The previous elements—environmental, emotional, sociological, physical, and psychological—are issues to consider when trying to facilitate your active alert child's learning. Although your child may not have distinct preferences in all of the above variables, he will have some. It's important to identify what those preferences are and to assess whether or not your child's school is meeting his needs.

Keep in mind that most schools address the needs of the child who is neat and orderly and can sit still in her seat—the visual learner. You and I know many children who do not learn in that fashion.

Active alerts are generally kinesthetic-auditory learners. A smaller percentage are kinesthetic-visual learners. Most seem to do fine in school. I think this is because most teachers strive hard to meet the majority of their students' needs. A combination of class size, required textbooks, and teachers' learning styles may result in a mismatch between child and learning environment, however. If your child is not doing well, consider ways to adapt the learning environment or choose a different school.

How do you do that?

I advocate that parents work with the principal to select teachers for their child before the school year begins. If your child is already into the school year and is having difficulties, you may have to intervene and advocate for him. Remember, approaching your child's teacher requires a delicate touch. Respect her expertise and try to enlist her help. Discuss what you find has worked well with your child at home. Remember, the term "active alert" is not important. What is important are the eleven traits and your child's learning style.

Ask the teacher whether what you know about your child is what he has observed within the classroom. By framing your child as a challenge—albeit a positive one—you invite the teacher to become part of a process that will benefit everyone involved.

Discuss how your child's characteristics might affect him in the classroom. Make your own suggestions, but also ask the teacher for specific ways that both of you can facilitate your child's learning at home and at school.

I see the process of learning as a particularly poignant issue for active alert children. Most of these children are gifted; however, many may appear almost learning disabled when tested. They exhibit what professionals refer to as "scatter patterns" in their test results—one area is above average and one is below average. Sometimes learning gaps develop when an area is not taught in accordance with the child's learning style. Addressing such deficits will not insure that all active alerts have above-average test scores, but it could help to close the gap.

MEETING THE NEEDS OF ACTIVE ALERTS IN SCHOOL

The following guidelines that I developed are helpful in educating all children. They make clear my biases about and hopes for schools.

The staff in a good school knows that:

1. Different children learn differently. The teachers approach the children in the various styles in which they learn. As lessons are presented, the teachers provide experiences in each learning style. By doing so, they broaden each child's access to different styles as well as help a child to learn using his strongest style.

2. Each child learns at her own rate. Chronological age does not automatically mean that a child is ready to learn certain material or skills; each child's own personal development determines readiness. Therefore, a range of ages within any given classroom is appropriate.

3. Most children—for that matter, most adults—can't sit still and listen to someone talk for four or five hours a day. The teachers create an environment that provides multiple ways—not just auditory—to learn the same material. They use learning centers that provide options suited to each learning style.

4. Learning is private. It is for the child only, not his parents, his classmates, or his teacher. The school emphasizes the love of learning for learning's sake. Active alerts are perfectionist and competitive. Making learning private diminishes arenas for competition and comparison. Teachers group children not on the basis of ability but on learning style or interest preferences.

   When learning is private, opportunity for humiliation or disgrace is lessened. Schools *must* be in the business of increasing self-esteem in children.

5. Children are talented or gifted in a variety of ways, not all of which are measured by our standardized testing procedures. Schools acknowledge and affirm each child's special gifts, recognizing ability in traditional areas like mathematics or music. They also recognize less traditional areas, such as creativity, world knowledge, interpersonal skills, or intuitive judging.

6. The child's learning process—not the content to be learned—is the school's focus. Good teachers are instructed in child development and are sensitive to children's issues. The child feels secure in the environment and knows she is valued there. The school is child-centered, not curriculum centered. Teachers do not consider children to be little robots who need to be programmed with correct knowledge. Instead, they recognize that learning is dynamic, not static. The school staff believes that the skills with which children gain knowledge and express thoughts are more important than the curriculum.

7. The young child learns in a more global fashion; therefore, the curriculum is presented in an integrated fashion. Teachers do not teach subjects as discrete, nonrelated topics. Instead, they teach reading, math, science, history, art, and music through projects that last several days or weeks.

8. Children need assistance in developing social and emotional as well as cognitive skills. Teachers instruct the whole child. They aid the child in learning to solve social as well as mathematical problems. Thus, children learn to handle anger, sadness, or feeling left out. Teachers help children develop positive interpersonal relationships. They frequently assign projects that are rich with opportunity to learn about belonging in groups.

9. Repetition of technical skills may not be the best way to teach reading and communicating. Indeed, it may deter lifelong enjoyment of these skills. When schools deny children access to the way in which they learn best, children feel incapable of meeting their goals. In that way, schools actually discourage learning. By giving each child a basal reader and testing each subskill in reading, the school discounts the child who does not learn to read through the methodology presented in the reading book manual. As a result, these children learn that they are incapable of reading and become terrified of tests. In schools that do not confuse the goal with the path, teachers use many methods for teaching reading and communication processes. In those schools, many

teachers do not teach reading as a specific subject; rather, they integrate it with projects on which the children are working. Those who do teach reading as a subject divide students according to learning styles and the skills they have yet to learn. Teachers use learning stations that make use of games. They match different assignments to the different needs of particular children.

10. Some children are overstimulated by a variety of things at school, such as the noise in the classroom or the number of morning activities. When that happens, teachers recognize the need to prevent, not to punish. They set the pace for the day and quietly deal with signs of overstimulation, such as silliness, getting carried away, inability to calm down, or fearfulness. Teachers provide ways in which children can calm themselves. Some of those ways are listed later in this chapter, such as the quiet space, aquarium, or hamster cage.

11. Observing is the best way to get information about children. Grades inadequately reflect the child's learning process and possibly contribute to competitiveness and diminished self-esteem. Observing, recording observations, and listening to the child's own self-evaluation help parents determine what is important to the teacher and the child. Such observations show the child what learning areas he needs to improve.

12. Class ratio of adults to children must remain low. In small classes, teachers are better able to facilitate and guide individual progress. They can use more whole-group learning and will not have to rely on ability grouping. Low student to teacher ratio means that teachers will have more contact with parents and other supportive staff—all of which benefit the child.

WHO SHOULD TEACH YOUR CHILD?

I know that meeting the above guidelines may not be 100 percent possible. Fulfilling them may depend on where you live and how comfortable you feel as an agent of change with your local school board.

If you cannot find a school that meets at least some of the above guidelines, find a teacher whose philosophy fits with them. In the end, I think that the teacher is the most important variable anyway: He or she is the most critical element in your child's education.

First and foremost, find a teacher who values your child, his energy, and his creativity. Not all teachers appreciate children who learn by doing and touching. Some believe this energy can and should be shaped out of the child. Seek the teacher who talks of "directing" or "focusing" your child's energy. Such teachers will be clear about your child's boundaries as well as the structure and procedures used within their classrooms.

Look for classroom environments that focus and direct movement. Are there learning stations—places to find materials and activities related to specific content? Does class time alternate between movement and focus? Are some people working individually or in pairs as the teacher presents a small group lesson?

Does each child clearly understand the order and agenda? Do students pace themselves as they complete their own work agenda? Do they know when the work is to be completed? Are the steps for completing the project outlined with guidelines that serve as deadlines for each step?

Is there a place in the classroom where a child can get away from stimulation, for example, a quiet reading corner, a magic carpet (that is, a rug in a quiet area where a child can read and be "transported" in his imagination on exotic adventures), a reading tent, or a rocking chair facing an aquarium or hamster cage or other quietly captivating item? Or carrels for older children?

Most important, is the teacher warm and accepting? Does he or she seem to enjoy and have a sense of humor about your child's learning style?

The active alert child's style makes some teachers nervous. It challenges others. Some teachers have difficulty outlining clear structure and expectations. Although these people may be superior teachers for other learners, pairing them with an active alert child will mean a difficult adjustment—for both child and teacher.

When you observe a teacher, make sure you stay in the class long enough to understand the tone, the agenda, and how the teacher handles kinesthetic energy and creative ideas. Watch the teacher deal with a child who is misbehaving. Note the tone with which the teacher handles the child. Does it make you uncomfortable? Many parents think they won't be able to discern differences between teachers, so I suggest that they observe two or three on the same day. In my experience, parents who follow the above guidelines and then trust their instincts are excellent observers who make good choices about their child's education.

A teacher of active alerts should be someone who:

- enjoys the energy and affirms the ideas of an active learner
- is clear in setting boundaries but believes children are more important than rules
- recognizes and identifies feelings—their own as well as the child's
- affirms a child's competence while clearly stating that the child must respect the group, the environment, and himself
- decreases arenas of competition within the classroom setting, that is, shuns ability grouping, blackboard contests, etc.
- provides choices of what to do within the classroom or how to do those tasks, but not both; for example, "You may choose an activity from the math center to work with, but you must follow the instructions for the one you choose."

The child-teacher connection is a vital relationship. When your child develops a rapport with a teacher, try to see that your young active alert spends most of his schooltime with that person. As a result, your child will feel more secure, will work harder, and will not have to make the transitions required when moving on to new teachers. He will not need to try to control new peers and new instructors hourly. When your child knows his teacher and what is expected of him, his anxiety diminishes.

The externally referenced active alert quickly learns to think of the teacher as a person she wants to please. She may work hard to do that—maybe too hard. If your active alert overdoes it and becomes too conscientious, step in and redirect the impulse. Remind her that she needs time to relax. Find ways to play with her.

When you find a teacher who connects with your child, check to see if the school setting coincides with the one described in the twelve school guidelines outlined earlier in this chapter. If it doesn't, ask the teacher to adjust some things for your active alert. Ask him or her to diminish emphasis on testing within the classroom. Externally referenced active alerts take tests too seriously. They tend to believe that tests tell something about how smart or how dumb they are, not how they are doing. Your child's teacher needs to counter this belief directly and affirm the child as well as his abilities.

Because the connection between teacher and child is so vital, I recommend working with the principal of your child's school to choose a teacher. When you do this, don't label your child "active alert." Instead, describe your child's traits and outline what works with those traits. Then ask the principal to help you to match your child to the teacher he or she believes will work best for your child and the way she learns.

Be your child's advocate. Staying in touch with your child's teachers will help you to know what is actually happening at school. Listen carefully to what your child tells you, but remember that children do not always perceive things as they actually are. When you hear things from your child that trouble you, call the school and check them out.

■ ■ ■

Stephen, his incredible sense of justice offended, was very hurt that his teacher "never gives me any rewards for behaving." He complained bitterly for three days in a row and then told his mother he would never go back to school and that he wanted to change teachers. His mom called the school. "I know that this is probably not the case," she told the teacher, "but Stephen feels that everyone else has had a reward but him. Is he having a problem behaving?"

The teacher was surprised and dismayed. "Oh, I give those rewards out at random. Stephen is behaving wonderfully. I'll be sure he gets a reward tomorrow. And thanks for drawing this to my attention."

Believe me, the time, energy, and worry that it takes to deal with a poor student-teacher match are far more troublesome than the effort needed to make a good match. The positive effects of your carefulness may ripple into the future. Often, the first teacher you select can recommend teachers who will help to insure your child's success in future years.

WHAT DOES YOUR CHILD'S LEARNING STYLE MEAN AT HOME?

Understanding your child's learning style will certainly help your child in school. But it has another welcome outcome! It may put an immediate stop to some of your conflicts with your child at home.

Do you understand, now, that your child prefers a poorly lit room? Great. You can stop nagging her to turn on the light in that dim corner. Now you know why your son can work with the radio on while your daughter is unable to accomplish a thing in the presence of background noise.

When you tell your child, "Sit down, be still, and look at me so I know you're listening," you are using the visual learner's listening tools. I agree that a kinesthetic learner needs to learn how to look at you—it increases interpersonal skills—but I also know that he may actually listen better if he stands up or fidgets while looking.

Clearly, if you are a visual learner and your child is kinesthetic, you have potential conflict areas. Visual learners need order and are distracted by movement. Kinesthetic learners move. Your reaction to living with such a mover and shaker may be a bit like that of an auditory learner listening to fingernails scraping on blackboard.

For someone who is deliberate and methodical, dealing with an impulsive child who attacks problems physically may be overwhelming. Emotionally reserved adults may find it a challenge to be with a child who expresses intense emotions. On some days, just being around a loud, talkative child may be too much for a quiet introvert.

Rest assured: You've taken the first step toward that peaceful coexistence we talked about earlier; you've identified your preferred learning style and that of your child. I hope you can use the information you've gleaned to help you to determine which conflicts with your child are due to your innate differences. It may even help you to understand how and where you get stuck with your child.

The next time you try to get your child to do something, ask yourself what learning-style approach you are using: yours or your child's. For example, do you call to your child to turn off the television and come to the table? If so, you are using the auditory approach, but you're competing with another sound: that of the television. Try turning off the television, touching your child's shoulder, and looking into her eyes. In this way you use all three modalities to contact her, and you increase the chance for a response.

Remember that when you ask your young active alert to perform a task, she needs more than verbal or written instructions: She may need to *do* something to grasp what you are saying. Encourage older children to write the steps down themselves in order to "feel" them. Assist your young child in *doing* what you want done. That way his body gets a chance to integrate the verbal instructions. Remember, however, that doing *with* is not the same as doing *for*. Doing for a child does not allow her to learn.

Be mindful of the differences in your styles when you assume the role of teacher, that is, when you help your child with his homework, music lessons, or art projects.

We already know that the active alert temperament makes this a potentially explosive situation; awareness of learning-style differences may make it less volatile.

■ ■ ■

*Jeremy always stood up to play the piano during piano
lessons. His fidgeting on the piano bench was more
than his visual-learner mom could bear. They struck a
compromise: She sat on the bench, he stood.*

Different approaches to learning become all too obvious when
you attempt to aid your child in math or writing. Remember, your
child's work belongs to him. If you reach an impasse, tell him
you'd like to help, but you don't seem to be able to explain in a
way he understands. Thus, neither of you is bad or wrong—you
just learn differently.

Talk with your child's teachers. Explain the difference in
learning styles to them so that they do not hold you, the parents,
responsible for your child's work. Be responsible for setting time
aside and providing a structure and environment in which the
child can study, but try not to take on responsibility for the work.

One final word: In chapter 4, I suggest how to make your home
a suitable place for a child who learns by doing. Needless to say,
both large motor toys (toys that are climbed on, jumped on or
with, etc.) and small motor toys (toys that you can draw with,
scissors, puzzles, etc.) are important. Consider blocks, scooters,
jump ropes, balls, small building sets, art materials, and craft
items. To a visual mom or dad, an array of these toys may look
like an incredible mess. Teaching your child to put away materials
is respectful of both of your learning styles. After all, in the final
analysis, that mutual respect is the key to learning.

9

Further Insights into Living with the Active Alert Child

For time will teach thee soon the truth.
—Henry W. Longfellow
"It is not always May"

Thirty years ago, I began observing and working with active alert children. Most of the active alerts I first worked with are now between the ages of 18 and 26. I consider myself fortunate to have been able to watch these families grow. As the children first identified as active alert moved into and through adolescence, and as I continue my work with the younger children, I have gleaned new insights which I'm pleased to be able to share in this chapter.

My, How They Grow!

Some developmental stages are easier than others. When active alerts are nine, for instance, life seems to get easier—not easy—but easier. Many nine-year-olds have now learned about friendships and school, and life feels less complicated and unsettled. However, even at their most calm, active alerts are still challenging. After all, we are talking about temperament.

Remember seven-year-old Lauren in chapter 4 who asked her mother about sex? Let me update you on her.

■ ■ ■

When Lauren was eleven years old, her mother and father were going on a romantic getaway. While her mom was packing, Lauren told her, "When you're gone, I assume you and Dad will be doing it." (Notice the eleven-year-old vernacular for sex.)

"Lauren, that's none of your business," said her mother.

"Well, I hope Dad uses a condom," she replied. "I really don't want any more brothers or sisters."

Some things change and some remain the same, but the active alert traits are a constant from infancy through adolescence.

TRAIT 1: MORE ABOUT BEING ACTIVE

The Gift in Your Hands

Active alerts have the gift of body wisdom. In fact, I tell the children with whom I work that their gift is in their hands; their hands make the great basketball shots, they put the legos together, they draw well. After all, being active means being active learners. It means you learn through touching and doing. However, their greatest gift can also be their biggest weakness.

When angry, the active alert child's tendency may be to strike out physically; they may even hit people. When making friends, extroverted active alerts often want to touch the other child, but the friend may be overwhelmed by touch. What do you do to help an active alert child learn appropriate use of touch? What do they need to learn about releasing their angry feelings without hitting?

If your child is eight or older, work with her. Talk with her directly about what she can do to resolve her feelings so that her need to touch and do—her hands—are indeed a gift and not a problem. A simple rule to give your child is to never physically enter another person's personal space (or bubble) when you are angry.

TRAIT 2: MORE ABOUT BEING ALERT

The 3R's: Routines, Rules, and Rituals

Active alert children are pattern-oriented children. Structure, pattern, and consistent rules are really important to them. Rituals make their lives easier. Recognizing that, I've developed some specific rules that have proven helpful to many families.

You can create rules for any situation. For example, your family may want to develop church rules, grocery store rules, grandparent house rules. Remember, before using any rules, explain them. Explicit instructions make it easier for the child to figure out the boundaries of any situation.

When developing rules, remember the following guidelines:

1. Keep them simple.
2. Clearly state what you expect the child to do.
3. Phrase the rules positively, such as, "Use quiet voices." Avoid negatives such as, "No yelling." "No hitting." (They don't work anyhow.)

When stating rules, use a teacher-like tone (i.e., calm and matter-of-fact). Rules are not intended to be used as control techniques. Rather they are skills and behaviors children need to learn.

Here is a sample of effective rules for a specific situation. Read it over, and then create some of your own.

Rules for going to sleep:

1. Lie down and be still.
2. Be quiet.
3. For children six and under, think gentle thoughts (i.e., leaves falling from a tree; a snowflake falling from the sky). For children seven and older, think boring thoughts (this does not include clouds as clouds can become dinosaurs that fight).

Keep in mind that active learners don't always know how to soothe and comfort themselves. Believe it or not, many active alerts do not know how to fall asleep. They get up and down repeatedly, they talk to themselves, never realizing they are keeping themselves awake. They seem to believe that sleep will simply come to them—no matter what they do. The more you can help them understand the skills involved in calming down, the better.

Morning Routines

Morning routines are often a problem in families with active alert children. However, they really need routines at that time of the day. Often, active alert children seem to think that they are getting up, dressing, and eating for their parents—not for themselves. In order to circumvent that assumption, my clients and I frequently develop customized routines.

Together we make audio tapes which the child records for himself. The child begins by saying, "Good morning, Nathan," using a voice like Robin Williams in *Good Morning, Vietnam.* He then instructs himself to get dressed; we dub in a dressing song of his choosing. He instructs himself to brush his teeth, eat his breakfast, and comb his hair. We record songs for each separate endeavor. His parents simply wake him up and start the tape, and in so doing, emphasize these things are for him!

TRAIT 3: MORE ABOUT SCHOOLS AND LEARNING

Active alert children are very bright but not in traditionally gifted ways; they have scatter patterns in their ability testing. However, academically they seem to do best in mathematical/spatial patterns. And that is related to their alertness. Indeed, they're the first ones to spot a bird's nest in the "P" of the local market's sign. Why? Because the bird's nest breaks the pattern. It is also why they respond so well to the three R's of parenting (rituals, routines, and rules). They are pattern kids.

Although the mathematical/spatial area may be their strong suit, it does not mean math in the elementary grades will always come easily for them. Some active alerts have difficulty retaining the rote memorization of multiplication tables—i.e., simple calculator math. Active alerts will be the strongest in junior high or high school mathematics unless early experiences with calculator math are so anxiety producing, the child develops a dislike of mathematics.

Another consistent trend among active alerts is the tendency to show some fine motor problems. This problem manifests itself as a death grip on their pencils, or it may be more pronounced and require occupational or physical therapy.

Remember, many talents of active alert children such as drawing, building, music, and physical adroitness cannot be tested. So, always be prepared to help your children see their own gifts.

Schools: Is There a Perfect Choice?

Each spring as parents anticipate the coming school year, a favorite topic in the letters I receive and among clients is, "Where should I send my active alert to school?"

After having read *Living with the Active Alert Child*, these parents understand the kinesthetic learner. Many ask about a Waldorf school; others wonder about a Montessori school setting. Those who ask such questions already realize that Rudolf Steiner's methodology, as exemplified in the Waldorf schools, is both kinesthetic and auditory. Others realize Maria Montessori created some wonderful kinesthetic learning tools. However, it is important to realize that although the philosophy and tools of a school may match the needs of an active alert learner, it may not work that way in each individual classroom. Remember, teachers have their own learning styles. Which school to choose, then, becomes a question of the match between teacher and child. I've found truly wonderful teachers for active learners in both public and private schools. I've seen matches and mismatches both in the Waldorf and Montessori schools. While there are no pat answers, you can look for teachers who understand your child's energy and who have a talent for directing that energy constructively.

You'll find those teachers in many different settings. Although, it never hurts to have the teacher's work philosophy matched in the school, working toward matching the teacher and child is the best course. Needless to say, an opportunity to stay with a teacher more than one year, smaller class size, and a noncompetitive environment in which learning social skills is considered equally as important as learning cognitive skills are ideal for an active alert. However, remember, since there are so many variables, a perfect match is a goal to work toward and is not always attainable.

In the end, active alerts are keen, intuitive people who decide relatively quickly if they are liked or unliked. If they feel they are liked, they work incredibly hard for their teacher. If they feel unliked, it will be a tough year for all concerned.

Trait 4: More About Being Controlling

Diffusing Double Binds

What is a double bind and how will you know if you're in one? Double binds are like being stuck in a pipe with both ends welded shut. A double bind is a no-win situation and it's one that four-year-old Timothy, in the next example, learned how to use at a very early age.

■ ■ ■

When angry, Timothy banged incessantly on the door of his bedroom until he got "Uproar" started in his family. His parents have asked him repeatedly to stop banging on the door. Recently, Timothy told them he will continue the behavior because they told him to stop. He says he will stop if they don't tell him to stop. In effect, Timothy set a trap for his parents. He won't stop if they ask him to; but, if they don't ask him to stop, how will he know his banging is bothering them?

Parents also use double binds.

■ ■ ■

When Margaret was eighteen and in nursing school, her mother left home on an extended trip. Margaret was expected to help her father with the younger children even though she already had a part-time job and was in school. Her father expected his daughter to do all the things Mom routinely did around the house in spite of Margaret's demanding schedule. When he became angry that she refused to bake cookies for her younger brother's school event, Margaret conceded. Eventually, after a number of concessions, she had to drop out of school as she had fallen behind in her assignments. Subsequently, her father called her a "dummy."

Faced with seemingly inescapable double binds, Timothy's parents and Margaret felt helpless; in truth, they are not.

To escape from their double binds, they need to take two steps. First, they must identify the dynamic of the bind (i.e., there is no way to please the person who has created the trap). Second, they must choose the path that honors the wishes and desires of their inner selves.

In Timothy's case, the parents can offer their son options for expressing his anger. He can punch pillows, throw bean bags in the basement, jump on a trampoline. If he refuses the options, they must then insist that he move to the middle of the steps where there is nothing to bang on. If necessary, they can take his hand and escort him there, gently.

As for Margaret, if her goal is to finish her school work, she needs to explain to her father that she cannot always comply with his requests. She will need to issue a firm "No," face her father's anger, and stick by her decision.

People who repeatedly experience double binds often feel helpless. And that helplessness becomes the predominant emotion in their lives, training them to act trapped. In order to change, they need to reclaim the power they have given away and, in doing so, may surprise the people they are closest to. While reclaiming power is no panacea, it will create a better balance of power in families. Although children who are used to using double binds will still fuss when asked to cooperate, the fussing will diminish as they become accustomed to the new structure.

For some parents who grew up in families that routinely used double binds, claiming power may take a long time. These parents are used to being responsible for other people's happiness. They may slip into the generational pattern of double binding their own children. As their children become older, it is important for people who come from such families to talk with their children about double binds. If they keep the lines of communication open, the child will eventually grasp the concept and recognize when her parents are putting her in a double bind. And that kind of discussion leads to good solutions for all concerned.

From Monkeys to Gorillas

Earlier in this book, I described an active alert's energy as monkey energy. I mentioned how I used the analogy to Curious George in the H. A. Rey books to teach active alert children where monkeys are appropriate and where they are inappropriate. As the children with whom I work grow, I expand the analogy from monkeys to gorillas. In gorilla society, there are certain leaders known as silverbacks. Nobody messes with the silverback unless it's another silverback trying to gain leadership of the group.

In the analogy, active alerts are junior silverbacks. They are potential leaders. The junior silverback is distinct from the senior silverback. In gorilla society, when a junior silverback approaches a senior silverback, the senior does not notice or brushes the junior aside knowing that he is no real threat. The only gorilla who can seriously challenge a senior silverback is another senior silverback. What does this mean for the active alerts?

■ ■ ■

Colin, a seventh grader at a small private school, decided to play basketball on the seventh-grade team. The school rule is that all players who attend practice will play. However, routinely the coach played the six or seven best players; the others sat on the bench. After a few games, Colin became upset at what he perceived to be an injustice. Clearly, the coach was not following the school's philosophy. Colin approached the coach in an angry manner and the coach almost kicked Colin off the team. That afternoon in my office, Colin and I discussed what had occurred. It became clear to me that Colin could not distinguish the senior silverbacks of the world. As a junior silverback he should not have approached the senior silverback, or coach, in a threatening manner. He could have asked questions, but he should not have threatened. Only another senior silverback (mother or father) can threaten a senior silverback. It was a useful analogy for Colin, one that he learned to apply in other situations including boundary issues.

TRAIT 5: MORE ABOUT BEING FEARFUL

■ ■ ■

When Johnny wants to make a friend he marches right into the middle of the group. Heedless of others already playing there, he bumps and pushes his way in. He then tells the child he wants to befriend that he can play the game better or build a better lego car. Johnny, unaware that he's interrupted the play of the other children, is oblivious to the nonverbal cues from them. Sound familiar? Johnny sits right on the border of aggressiveness. Some teachers think he crossed it, others think he's simply immature. His parents describe him as socially inept but fearless.

Every fall, Susie is anxiety ridden as she worries about school. She worries about which teachers she'll get and who'll be in her class. She's scared the first time she visits new friends at their homes. In fact, she fears a variety of things, including thunderstorms. In the classroom she sits back and waits until someone asks her to play. Seldom, if ever, does Susie walk into a group of children already playing. Once engaged in play, however, you hear Susie, above the voices of children who have joined her, offering instructions and ideas about play. What does Susie have in common with Johnny? How are they the same? How are they different? Does fearless Johnny bear anything in common with fearful active alerts? Yes, he does.

Susie and Johnny may both be active alert children, although Susie is much more introverted than Johnny. Johnny, in his love of others and his rush to join them, is awkward. Because he does not learn visually, he is unable to learn by watching other people enter groups. Susie, who also loves people, does not place herself in a difficult situation by entering an existing group. Instead, because her fears and introversion combine to prevent her pushing into groups, she attracts others to her with her ideas.

Although it appears otherwise, Susie and Johnny are both fearful in exactly the same ways. They fear being out of control and they fear being abandoned.

The fear of being out of control is very important to understand as it is linked to the fourth active alert trait of being controlling. How so? Remember, as infants, active alert children cannot block stimulus. Everything—light, sound, temperature, texture— stimulates them and overwhelms them. Combine that inability to block with their tendency to feel intensely (Trait 6), and you begin to understand how much active alerts fear being out of control. They are afraid that if they start crying, they will never stop; that if they really get angry, they will be angry forever. In a nutshell, their fear of losing control is why they attempt to line up or control everything and everyone around them.

Their second core fear is the fear of abandonment. Because children who are active alert are kinesthetic learners, they are busy, messy kids. Messy kids who try to be controlling get lots of negative feedback—much more so than visual learners. This feedback cycle reinforces the awareness that they are different. All the active alert children I've met have one common denominator— they know they are different. Some tell me that's because they're weird, others believe the difference is the result of something about them—their nose, their religion, their ears. Given the negative feedback they so often receive, it's easy to understand how they might conclude their difference is bad. Their awareness may lead to the fear that they will be abandoned. Whether they have parents who took a two-week maternity leave and then returned to work, a stay-at-home mom or dad, or a birth plan that allowed them to live with their loving, adoptive parents immediately after birth, the fear is still there. Partly because of this, I urge parents to read such affirming books as *Love You Forever* by Robert Munsch, or the *Runaway Bunny* by Margaret Wise Brown, or *On the Day You Were Born* by Debra Frasier. I also urge parents to tell their children how important they are and how much they love them by using key phrases like "I love you more than there are stars in the sky."

Needles, Shots, and Other Moments of Panic

It's your worst nightmare. Your child needs a measles shot, and you are dreading the doctor's appointment. You're afraid your child will panic at the thought of having blood drawn, getting an immunization, or having a throat culture. That is not an uncommon reaction for active alerts. Given their intensity, their super alertness, and/or the idea of being forced to participate in anything unpleasant, many active alerts can frustrate both their parents and physicians.

So how do parents get through these experiences? First, help your child understand the limits of his choice in this matter. It is important that he knows he does not have a choice in whether or not the procedure is performed. The doctor orders the procedure to help him get well or to keep him well. He needs to learn that he is competent and can handle the discomfort. The choices your child does have are whether or not he sits on your lap, where the blood is taken from, and when the technician performs the procedure. In this way you honor your child's need to be in charge while you set the limits on that power (he cannot choose to forego the procedure). It is also very important for your child's sense of control that he not be physically restrained.

Prior to clinic visits, you can teach your child how to relax using a breathing technique (for instance, the technique you learned for childbirth). Coach your child to breathe so it tickles his belly button. Tell him that as he lets the air go, he can also let his fear go. It's almost as if you can teach him that the fear and the air can't be in his tummy at the same time. Through your voice, gentleness, and belief in your child, you help him to relax. In the simple process of relaxation, he learns that discomfort is less intense when muscles are relaxed.

TRAIT 6: MORE ABOUT BEING INTENSE

Diffusing anger is a recurring desire for parents of active alerts. Active alert children challenge their parents from the moment of birth. They challenge their moms and dads to come up with ways to help them sleep, to help them entertain themselves. Is it any wonder parents get used to thinking that keeping their child calm is their job? Somehow with an infant it became their job to figure out what was bothering the baby when she cried and to resolve the discomfort. Is it surprising that parents believe that if they could anticipate what will upset their child, the tantrums will subside?

As the child moved out of infancy, many parents retained that expectation. Parents are responsible for teaching their children; however, if they are going to teach about anger, they must first understand it.

The first question to consider: Is it the parents' job to make the world perfectly peaceful or happy for their child? If a child wants to remain angry, she will do so despite all heroic efforts on the part of her parents. Even when parents are aware of and respect their child's basic temperament, there will be times when tantrums are unpredictable and unpreventable. And that's okay. Parents of infants have to assume most of the responsibility for their child's emotions, but in life we all know it's impossible to be responsible for someone else's happiness, anger, or feelings. The person must come to know and understand her own emotional makeup. The job of parents is not to solve all their child's problems, but to help her understand her feelings and learn skills to resolve her own anger. Between the ages of three and nine, children need to make that all-important switch. That is a difficult transition for active alerts, and it is one that parents must nurture if their children are to become happy, healthy adults.

Consider the alternative. Parents who continue to assume responsibility will end up angry at their child, and no parent wants that to occur. Interestingly, feeling helpless and out of control is exactly what children feel until they learn that control lies inside of them and not with their parent.

TRAIT 7: MORE ABOUT BEING ATTENTION-HUNGRY AND ITS AFFECT UPON SIBLINGS

An active alert's boundless and insatiable need for attention has an impact on the relationship between him and his sibling. One suggestion for dealing with this situation is the victim's reparation fund, a quick intervention technique which immediately decreases physical and/or verbal aggression.

Victim's Reparation Fund

This system is based upon a victim's fund concept and is currently being used in many courts. The victim's fund requires lawbreakers to compensate their victims by paying for what was stolen or by working through community service projects. A version of this same system can work in your home.

First, specify the rule. No hitting or name calling, for example. Choose the issue which is most disconcerting for you. Establish a fine and method of payment in advance. It can be a quarter, a dollar, or a task (i.e., making the sibling's bed). Then if a child breaks the law, she must repay her victim. The fine is assessed immediately upon the violation. If the children do not cooperate, you can keep separate jars for each child with some of their past allowance in coins. Let both the victim and the perpetrator see the transfer of funds. This system is quite successful in attaining an immediate decrease in aggression.

Although one child is hitting, the other may be baiting the other one to hit. Therefore, it's important to point out that although both are playing a role in the aggression, in real life only the one who assaults will be charged. This technique is best used with school-aged and older children.

TRAIT 8: MORE ABOUT GETTING ALONG AND SOCIAL SKILLS

The Ultimate Dilemma

The more experience I have with active alerts, the more I believe one of the greatest parental tasks is to show and teach children about the impact they have upon the people they love the most. Often, active alerts tread lightly around their friends or other relatives but seem oblivious to the ways their behavior affects their siblings or parents. Parents must somehow teach their children about the impact they have on others without shaming them.

Approach the child in the most respectful way possible and try to frame comments in ways which do not diminish his self-esteem, or, in other words, cause shame. Be aware that, as the active alert's awareness of the negative impact of his behavior is heightened, he may feel guilt. That's not all bad. Small doses of guilt, as distinguished from shame, help teach morality and social skills. In the end, then, the parental task is not to prevent the child from feeling guilt, but instead to help him learn to work through the guilt and discover the impact of his behavior on others.

Without such self-knowledge, children can only continue on their current course, and as they mature, that course may prove unhealthy.

Building a Sense of Others

One thing seems certain, active alerts have a large sense of self. This is true in part because all children are egocentric. But because active alerts feel intensely about life and are bombarded by the sensations of existence, they demonstrate a lot of awareness about life events in reference to themselves. Interestingly, if an incident occurs between two other people, active alerts can relate how those two people must feel and what they might have done differently in the situation. However, if the active alert is one of the two people involved, her insight and empathy disappear. Her perspective is the only one that matters.

As parents of active alerts, a major goal must be to help build in their child what I call a sense of "other." It is that sense which allows us to know what the people with whom we are interacting think or feel.

There are two ways to help build a sense of "other." The first is for parents to encourage awareness of others' feelings. That encouragement can be posed speculatively, such as, "I wonder how Molly felt when you said that?" There are other times when you may need to be more direct and instructive, such as, "Michael, when you ran up to Charlie to hug him and say hi, he pulled back and looked scared. I believe he was frightened when your hug was so big. I know you don't want him to feel afraid of you."

The second and equally important way is to insist on being shown respect. Your child must ask for what he wants rather than scream. Ignore his imperious demands. When parents do not ask the child to respect them, they do two things: 1) they teach that his manner isn't really important, and 2) they inadvertently role model low self-esteem. Most parents do not wish to do either of the above, but in their haste to do anything to "calm the child" or "shut him up," parents actually teach unintended lessons.

In my clinical work, I have become aware that some parents were not allowed to have a sense of self as a child; therefore, many have grown up with a large sense of "other" but only a small sense of self. These parents, who are just gaining in self-awareness, find teaching their active alert child the above lesson very difficult. Their child's demands may overwhelm their own growing self-awareness needs. For the child, in such situations, the parent's role model may give rise to an ambivalence about his own large sense of self. Sadly, he may never know how he affects his parent.

Trait 9: More About Self-Esteem

The Difference between "Oh, Well," and "Oh, My Gosh!"

Do you know the difference between "Oh, my gosh!" and "Oh, well"? Many families have never stopped to think about it. Because active learners are into many things, have many ideas, and take many risks, it is an important difference to consider. When you or your child make a mistake, how do you respond? "Oh, my gosh!" (i.e., this is terrible) or "Oh, well," (i.e., mistakes can happen to anyone). The difference is subtle, but important.

Many good families do not mean to be shaming but still have a tendency to scapegoat. Family members act as if someone has to be at fault for everything that happens. That changes the tone in the family from "Oh, well," to "Oh, my gosh!" It's a subtle game played in even the best of families.

Is it possible to have an accident in your family and still be okay? Is it possible to make a mistake and not be blamed, or are mistakes something which must be eliminated? Are people always subtly or directly being told how they are at fault or to blame for a mistake? Even when this is done in an attempt to make sure the same mistake doesn't happen again, the effect is devastating. The intended learning can be achieved instead by having the child help "clean up" the mistake and by assuring her that she will learn from the mistake.

Obviously this is not an either/or phenomenon. At various times different family members are more capable of letting things go with more grace than others. What is the balance in your family between "Oh my gosh!" and "Oh well"? It's a question to ponder.

The Struggle Within

A few years ago one of the children I was working with drew me two pictures. One was of "good." Good is a pretty, normal-looking girl. On her right shoulder sits a little character which has wings and wears a halo; on her left shoulder sits a little character with a pitchfork. Her second drawing was of "evil." Evil is a girl with wild fiery hair and on each of her shoulders is one of the pitchfork characters—only one is colored slightly lighter than the other. These drawings interested me and I have the one of "good" prominently displayed in my office.

Often when working with a child I point out the "good" drawing and ask that child to tell me about the picture. The child almost always smiles knowingly and explains. The last child, seven-year-old John, simply stated, "Oh, that's me!" Questioning him further I asked him about the two little characters on his shoulders, "When does the little angel come out?" John said, "Oh, I take him to school." "Well," I asked, "when does the little devil come out?" John quipped, "I only let him out at home."

Children, like many adults, believe the best way out of the internal struggle is to force the bad guy out—make him go away. However, I have to explain that inside this "bad" guy are also many things to love. "Anyway," I always say, "I don't think anyone can be good all the time. I know I can't." The question becomes not one of denial and trying to make the "bad" go away, but of acceptance. The part that gets children into trouble may be the curious part. Curiosity can be a wonderful trait; however, without boundaries, curiosity can be a problem. Boundaries may be something the "good angel" can provide. When we accept our whole self, every part of our being can then work to benefit the whole. And that's ever so much better than denying a part of our humanity.

As we talk about the struggle between good and evil, some children decide to give their parts a name. The part they struggle with may have a different name than their own. They may both have different names. In doing this, I am trying to make concrete their own internal struggle so they can learn to deal with it. In the process, some children become really good at recognizing that their parents may need a little more of the good character at home or that the part which acts out does so because they believe no one loves them for the moment. All of these kinds of realizations are easier to reach once the discussion between these characters becomes open.

TRAIT 10: MORE ABOUT PERFORMERS

■ ■ ■

At six-and-a-half years old Raymond is an extroverted active alert child who uses "bathroom talk" at school to entertain his friends. His parents have enlisted his teacher as an important team member to help Raymond learn the boundaries for his behavior. Raymond has simply made a bad choice in using "bathroom talk" to get his friends' attention and approval. At this point he doesn't quite understand why it's a bad choice, but his parents and teacher will help him understand the consequences. Raymond will learn. It may help him to know the rules about cursing or "bathroom talk."

Rules about cursing:

1. Grownups can't use those words around and toward children. Why? It is not condoned by other grownups.
2. Children can't use those words in front of grownups. They will be disciplined for doing so.
3. Children who use curse words with other children need to realize those children may tell their parents. As a result, parents may restrict their children from playing with the child who uses the swear words.

*The above rules are adapted from the work of Richard Gardner, M.D.

TRAIT 11: MORE ABOUT EMPATHIC ABILITY

Many of the parents I meet grew up in families which did not allow expression of feelings. In such families, "bad" feelings were never acknowledged. Adults from those families learned that it is wrong to feel anger or sadness, fear or frustration. More than likely their parents had the same beliefs about feelings; those who acted on such feelings probably did so inappropriately (i.e., by raging verbally, hitting, or through passive-aggressive behavior, depression, or alcoholism). Adults who grew up in such families received no direction or models for discussing or appropriately displaying anger or frustration, joy or love. In order to deal with their childrens' emotions, parents need to deal with their own.

Indeed, families who live with an active alert child are well aware that she has feelings in abundance, many of which are freely shared with all members of the household. While it is vitally important for parents and children alike to acknowledge and accept their feelings, for active alerts, whose feelings are so intense, that acceptance is critical.

First acknowledge that feelings exist. Tell your child that it is okay to have feelings. Name feelings with your child. "You're feeling sad." "Are you feeling angry or frustrated?" "I am so happy today."

Teach your child that her feelings are inside of her. Remind her that feelings simply are. They are not bad or good—they simply exist.

Help your child be accountable for her feelings: Tell her it is okay to be angry (or proud, or frustrated, or fearful), but that it's not okay to act on feelings in a way that hurts others. That is, it is not okay to hit when angry or to belittle when proud. A child must learn she is the only person who can ease or express her own anger. Parents, when faced with their inability to change the child's emotions, must learn to deal with their own feelings of helplessness.

As your child learns she is competent to deal with her own emotions, she will begin to make good choices in expressing them, and you will learn that choosing to ease emotions is your child's responsibility. Seeing you accept and express your feelings will give your child permission to begin her own self-discovery process.

In summary, there are three key points to keep in mind as you deal with active alert children and their feelings:

1. Model appropriate expression of feelings.
2. Name the feelings your child is experiencing.
3. Hold your child accountable for how she expresses feelings.

TEMPERAMENT VS. CLINICAL ISSUES

During my travels and lectures people repeatedly ask me to clarify the distinction between active alert children and children who really have clinical problems. Following a recent speech, one teacher described a "busy" child who attacked his mother with a knife. "Isn't that child active alert?" she asked.

Active alert children function fairly well in society, although they don't always feel that they fit in. When a child cannot function, when he is violent, it is not a matter of temperament (active alert), but a clinical issue. The child needs professional help. Whether or not the child has an active alert temperament, there are other factors which need to be addressed to help the child become a successful member of society. In seeking to understand children, we need to consider many variables. Temperament is only one. Learning style is another. Family system and history are also important.

When deciding if a child may be active alert, I consider the following questions:

What kind of family is the child growing up in? What kind of family did the parents grow up in? What kind of patterns and rules got passed down from generation to generation in the family system? Is there a history of chemical dependency or mental illness? Has there been physical or sexual abuse or neglect of the child? If there are two parents, what is the marriage like? Is it competitive, cooperative, hostile, friendly?

Keep in mind that a child who is being or has been sexually abused may look active alert. However, in some instances, the appearance of hypervigilence (extreme alertness) is the result of having his boundaries violated and not due to temperament. The child's keen alertness is an attempt to anticipate and ward off future abuse.

From a physiological perspective, the family history of allergies should also be considered. Does the child have any vision or hearing difficulties? Is she completely overwhelmed by stimulus? For instance, can she even be held? She may have a problem with tactile defensiveness. Can the child attend school and complete her work? Remember children are like puzzles. When trying to comprehend them, parents need to consider all the pieces or, in other words, the whole child and her family as well.

If you really want to understand a child, I offer the following suggestion. Draw a timeline of her life. Include significant events such as births of siblings, changes in day-care providers and schools, death of a relative. Then try to understand how those events fit with the developmental stages of the child at the age they occurred and how the events appeared in the eyes of the child.

CHEMICAL DEPENDENCY AND MENTAL ILLNESS

Many people ask me if there are clinical concerns for active alert children born into families with a history of mental illness or chemical dependency. Most of the children I see from such families are not chemically dependent or mentally ill.

Most active alert children already have intense mood swings and worst-possible-scenario thinking which are indicative of depressed thinking. At an early age—seven, eight, nine—they need help understanding this type of thinking and their choices. Such self-knowledge will aid them as they journey through the turbulent puberty years. One of my chief concerns is that they be monitored in those years for development of depression.

As for chemical dependency, remember that active alerts are risk-takers. The introverted ones have fears which dampen the risk-taking, but they too are daring. We know from Suomi's monkey research (see page 267) that under stress uptight monkeys have a tendency to "hit the sauce." For active alert risk-taking children, the idea of experimenting with drugs may be especially alluring.

For children who are attracted to the forbidden, "Just Say No!" won't cut it. However, newer drug education based on themes such as, "There are more ways than one to get high," may be effective.

When to Choose Therapy

Faced with parenting an active alert child, people who believe counseling is a useful way to learn about themselves may decide to receive therapy as a way to gain understanding about their children and the parenting process. They seek a therapist for enrichment, to learn new coping skills, or to gain support. Some want to know if the behavior they see in their child is normal. In such instances, checking with a trustworthy therapist is not unlike checking with an early childhood specialist, a pediatrician, or a pediatric nurse practitioner.

Some adults use their concerns about their child as an entry point to therapy so they can begin work on some individual concerns (e.g., their own lack of nurturing or the uneven parenting they received as a child) or marital issues (needless to say, even if you began with a healthy marriage, parenting an active alert child can be hazardous to your love life!).

Regardless of the individual or family issues, there are five situations for which therapy is definitely indicated:

1. A dramatic change in the nature (temperament) or behavior of your child which continues for several weeks. If a child looks either angry or sad most of the time, or if a normally even-tempered child begins acting out and is angry most of the time, therapy is indicated. If a child is sad most of the time, even in happy situations, therapy is indicated.
2. If your child is experiencing difficulties in her school setting that continue for several weeks, it might be a time to seek outside help. Those difficulties at school may be learning problems and/or behavioral problems. In either case, an outside person will be useful in assessing the child and the child's learning environment to determine what action may be taken to aid both the child and the teacher.
3. If the parents feel stuck in constant, angry interactions with their child, intervention is usually advisable. Remember, negative spirals are destructive not only for mom, dad, and child concerned, but also for siblings observing constant angry interactions.

4. When a dramatic stressor occurs within the family (i.e., death of a family member or divorce) therapy might be needed. However, if the child has experienced abuse, therapy is always advisable. Although many families handle these stressors well, sometimes parents, because of their own grieving, may not be as strong a resource as they would like or need to be for their child.

5. Finally, a time to consider therapy is when the child asks to speak to someone else or indicates she has a problem she doesn't want to talk about with her parents. This does not occur often, but when it does, it's important to listen and respect the needs of that child.

Keep in mind that the professional you choose should be someone with whom you can comfortably entrust your child.

Part IV

BEYOND CHILDHOOD

Meghan [see page one] is away at college now. The transition from high school to college was an enormous struggle for her, since she is such an introvert. She attends a college three hours from home, which means most weekends she remains on campus. This is her junior year, but it is really the first year in which she identifies with her campus community and truly enjoys being there. We have begun to see signs of true maturity. She is more responsible when home and most of the time speaks with less anger in her voice. Meghan seems to be more genuinely empathetic towards us as parents these days. During her adolescence, we remained calm in the face of her efforts to control everything around her, but strong in our values. It truly seemed as if she could devour the weak.

Let me go back a few years. The difficulty with transitions is not new. She struggled a long time to adjust to her junior high after she finished elementary school, and then to her high school after junior high. Any time there is a change she still gets anxious. Her anxiety seems to come out as anger towards us—her parents. The good news is she pushes herself to make the change. She even spent a semester abroad last year. She is hardest on the ones who love her during times of transition.

Meghan's teen years were tumultuous from age 14 when she began eighth grade. Many of her friends were boy crazy and giving their parents a hard time earlier than she did. Meghan seemed to want to continue to play with her friends and be a child a while longer. She actually hung up on the only boy brave enough to telephone her in seventh grade.

When Meghan finally moved into adolescence, she needed me to shop with her to buy each prom dress, which often took hours and several trips because of her indecisiveness. While acting dependent, at the same time she made her independence clear. For example, her father and I were not to volunteer to chaperone any dances. She was independent, but, oh, so dependent! There were times Meghan's father and I wished we had not taught her to express her own opinions in our home. It has taken her a long time to understand and accept that we don't have to agree with her. She decided to give up meat in ninth grade and still wonders where she went wrong with us (we still eat meat!).

Meghan has grown into a lovely young woman. She is an honor roll student. She works hard at her summer jobs. I cannot be prouder and happier. Her father and I do wonder if she will always have trouble with anxiety. Will those who love her always get blamed and mistreated at each new transition in life or will life one day become easier for her?

■ ■ ■

Our extroverted son Colin [see page 35] graduated magna cum laude from a large Midwestern university last spring. Given his level of activity and risk taking, his survival to adulthood was our greatest worry.

Colin had the entire campus buzzing for a while in his sophomore year when he published an article about how rich Jewish students all seemed to live in the same plushly furnished building. He referred to the women in the building as "Jewish princesses." After the article was published, Colin received death threats for being anti-Semitic—and he comes from a devout Jewish family!

As Colin entered adolescence, it seemed the number of explosions went up in our house. Getting him to believe we meant business when it came to the family rules was no small feat. It helped that as our younger child, we could always remind him the rules had not changed from the ones we used with his older brother. We still valued the same structure. Colin experimented in junior high with not doing or handing in homework at times. We had to develop a structure with his teachers so that they would understand him and his work (or lack of it) would not go unnoticed.

During high school Colin became a DJ for dances, bar and bat mitzvahs, and other birthday parties. He liked being in front of a group and controlling the "vibes" of the room. He got good grades but was not the star of the class. In fact, he often reported he was stupid.

Colin loved climbing and took classes in rock climbing at our local sports club. He was also an avid snowboarder. He was always attracted to high-risk stunts. One time Colin was riding on the hood of a car when his friend who was driving decided to speed up and then suddenly jam on the brakes. Colin ended that adventure spending time his junior year in high school in an intensive care unit at our local hospital. I was always aware that Colin had no fears and liked what are referred to as "adrenaline rushes." As his parent I was terrified he would not make it to adulthood. He has at least made it twenty-two years.

Next year, Colin plans to go to China to teach English. I will miss him, but I know he has many adventures ahead of him. He is still intense, passionate, and busy, but at least for now he seems to be directed and positive.

10

Living with the Active
Alert Adolescent

It takes a village to raise a child.
—African proverb

In a native Guatemalan village a pre-teenage boy no longer lives with his parent, but with his adolescent peers. Male adults, uncle figures, oversee that hut. Similarly, girls live with other women of the village who oversee the transition from child to adult. In Europe years ago, there were apprenticeships during the adolescent years to move the child out of the home and into adulthood. Now we live with our children in a family unit during some of their most turbulent years, both physiologically and psychologically, and try to aid them in their transition to adult responsibilities. This transition is a time of letting go while still keeping safety boundaries and coaching or prompting adult competencies. Daniel Goleman, a *New York Times* writer and author of *Emotional Intelligence,* once said that all adolescents seem to suffer from "humanophobia"—the fear of being human. They fear being different, being imperfect, and having feelings. Yet they are confronted with their own differences, imperfections, and feelings on an almost hourly basis.

GROWTH COMES IN SPURTS: WHEN BODIES GROW, SOMETIMES BRAINS DOZE

During the adolescent years, the human body goes through enormous changes.

■ ■ ■

Ryan came to me in August, before his eighth grade year. I was amazed. I'd just seen him at the end of seventh grade. Over the summer he had grown six inches. He now spoke in a deep voice. He came to talk about his concerns for the coming year and how his legs ache at night.

Of course, his legs ache at night! Growth is obvious; more difficult to understand is how your child suddenly forgets what he has learned in the past, such as his need to sleep and eat nutritional meals, and sometimes even to do his homework. Parents complain most about the ages of 12 to 14 years.

Herman Epstein in his work on brain growth has found the brain grows in a set of five discrete periods, approximately in the age intervals of 3 to 10 months; 2 to 4 years; 6 to 8 years; 10 to 12 years; and 14 to 16 years. At 13 you will notice that your child forgets previous learning. It is frustrating to have to reteach the basics.

Teens feel invulnerable, too. Needs of mere mortals are beyond your adolescent. This kind of thinking may also take your child onto paths such as drinking, smoking, and having sex without contraception or without thinking of the emotional consequences. He appears to have forgotten all you taught him or simply does not apply what you have taught him to his daily life. He is invulnerable and often cannot think "beyond the nose on his face." What that means is, he cannot "hold in his brains" the consequences of his actions.

■ ■ ■

Cody starts his ninth grade year boasting that he plans to attend Duke University when he goes to college. Clearly, he is bright enough. However, his first report card shows numerous missing assignments in subjects that require daily work. As an extroverted active alert, he has found his first girlfriend this semester. He is completely caught up in the world of present time.

Cody and I must have a discussion about how Cody can hold onto his future goals while he lives his daily life. His goal of attending Duke will require more commitment to studies. Constantly "connecting the dots" becomes one of your roles as an adolescent's parent. In other words, if your teen's goal is "b," then today you must remind him or her to do "a." Coaching or prompting becomes the first step in letting go of direct control.

Somehow you have to communicate respect for your teen's intelligence while gently reminding her of the connection between present behavior "a" and subsequent consequence "b." There is an art to doing this and you may wonder if you will ever be completely successful. You and your teen live in a world of double binds. Anthony Wolf describes this world and captures its essence even in the title of one of his books, *Get Out of My Life but First Could You Drive Me and Cheryl to the Mall?* Your teen wants you to leave him alone and at the same time, help him get where he wants to go.

If this is true of all teens, what is different for the active alert teen? Remember, the active alert is more of everything that is normal developmentally. She is both more dependent and more independent. She is all or nothing. She has a high need to control her environment in a developmental period where there is little control over her body growth, little control over the transitions to junior high school, high school, and college and/or leaving home. Therefore, this period of life is very painful from moment to moment as these challenges are faced. However, keep in mind as parents that there are also moments of great pride and joy as you see how competent, creative, and persistent these young people become as they grow.

During these years your adolescent often seems to forget *how* to clean his room. Active alerts who live in an internal world of bombardment need some external order to maintain sanity, but they become disabled and overwhelmed by the prospect of room cleaning. You may need to decide how often you want to disagree about this chore. Can you let this go? If not, how frequently does the room need to be cleaned? Once a week, a month, a semester? I have suggested to some families that once in the beginning of the semester is a good place to start. That seems to diminish family conflict. It also helps the active alert start each semester in an orderly environment, which will help with his studies. This may take outside help from a parent in organizing the chore.

Teens need structure. The very lesson of adolescence is for a young person to be able to recognize her needs and begin to set guidelines for herself. The transition from your structuring role as parent to a teen structuring herself is a long and arduous journey, often with a parent having to set limits when the teen can't do it for herself.

You may often wonder what happened to everything your teen previously knew. During the teen years your adolescent must redo all his previous psychosocial learning. As an infant he asked, are you and the world trustworthy? As a teen he asks, are you worth my trust and can I trust myself in all these new arenas? As a toddler, he clearly tested if he was separate or autonomous from you by walking away and saying, "No." As a teen, he clearly tests these same limits again. As a preschooler he had "good ideas" and initiated them. As a teen, he checks out lifestyle choices you may not appreciate, like hair dye, piercing, strange clothing, new religion. As a school age child, he asks, "Can I learn what I need to learn? Can I accomplish or finish my work?" He questions the same abilities as he applies for college or tries out for a team or dramatic play.

■ ■ ■

Serena told her mother she needed the family car on Saturday. When her mother reiterated the curfew for returning that evening, Serena blew up. She yelled, "I am not going to be responsible like you. You are not accepting me for who I am. Responsibility is not my thing." Her mother just looked at me perplexed, questioning, "How could the same person expect to have the family car and yet at the same time reiterate her need to be irresponsible?"

Serena is clearly stating her need to be different from her mother. However, that difference, irresponsibility, is not one of her family's values. She may have yet to discover that she really values having responsible people in her life and being responsible to the people she loves. At the current moment, that value of responsibility seems to be in conflict with her values of being her own autonomous self. Unfortunately, she is only beginning to sort through this conflict and to her mother, she just sounds like she has lost her mind.

Another issue that arises when your child faces her teen years is a lack of perspective. Because she is so "now" focused, she will beg to be allowed to do something that is clearly against family rules, such as attend an unchaperoned party, miss a major family event to be with a friend, etc. She truly appears to believe the lack of this privilege to do as she wishes will be the end of her life. She begs and pleads her case, stating she will lose all her friends if she does not participate in their lives. Having confidence that her real friends will still be there even if she does not attend a party hasn't come yet. Remember, adolescents do not have the ability to take a long-term perspective.

■ ■ ■

Fourteen-year-old Sydney wanted to go out on a boat with two teen boys one afternoon. Her mother relayed to me that she thought she had found the perfect way around "no" by insisting she, Sydney's mother, talk to the boys' mother first. Of course, given the last minute nature of teenagers' plans, the two mothers could not reach each other. Sydney's mother stated with pleasure that this technique had prevented many fights with her active alert daughter. Sydney also had to learn to take responsibility in connecting her own mother with the other teens' mothers, a family rule before yes or no could be given.

The Power of Hormones

Hormones are big. Hormones are powerful. As hormones—estrogen and testosterone—begin to course through the sensitive body of a sensitive child, you will know it. Active alert children who have begun to develop some ability in emotional regulation lose it once again. Given sensitivity and intensity, gaining a sense of emotional regulation is important to a self-definition of sanity for these children. I began my work thirty years ago with a group of 12- to 13-year-old boys who were brought to me because their parents thought they needed help. The boys vacillated from shouting at their parents in rage, to crying, to being okay, all within a few minutes. Both the parents and the boys were alarmed by the teens' emotional intensity. They needed to know that hormones act as fuel to the already existent fires within active alert children.

This is a time when I watch closely to see that the emotional lows do not move into the realm of a clinical depression. Some parents worry about the possibility of bipolar disorder. The evidence for this disorder comes from the family's mental health history and whether the child has ever reached emotional regulation before adolescence began.

Remember, hormones do not suddenly arrive at this point of the life cycle, or disappear later. They begin and regulate over a period of years. Because surging hormones add to a sense of disregulation or feeling out of control and because teens as a whole are so "now" focused, hormones become the perfect foil for your parenting. When your teen pleads that it is really okay to leave him home alone in the house with a member of the opposite sex or that it is okay for him to rent a hotel room with someone, you have a foil. If your family does not value those behavior choices, you can simply reassure your son you trust him, but not hormones. He may need more time in a safe environment to learn to make responsible choices despite the way his hormones make him feel.

Is It Narcissism or Egocentrism?

According to Jean Piaget all children are egocentric, but learn to become empathetic during their development through interaction with their environment. The last portion of becoming empathetic comes when your young adult learns to think from another person's perspective to understand how his actions impact those around him. Narcissism, however, is a clinical issue which involves placing your needs or the love of self above other people's needs. The narcissist is an adult who does not know how to take into account his impact and his own needs. Active alert teens may take a little longer to learn to be empathetic, but do not have to have a lifelong pattern of narcissism.

Teens by nature can be very self-involved. You may wonder why your child works hard on a project at someone else's house, but at your house, he seems to have forgotten how to take his dishes to the sink, do his chores, or clean his room. You ask him to shovel the snow, and it is still there when you return from work. What's going on? Most teens are involved in their own social, academic, and extracurricular worlds, which may include wonderful community service through the church or school but not the same effort at home. Remember that as a 3.8 GPA student who plays sports, he is really demonstrating responsibility even when he accomplishes little at home. Help your teen stay connected at home and help him learn the impact his behavior has on the people who love him during these years. Many parents completely withdraw, considering this a losing battle. I do not encourage such an "all or nothing" approach in families because of the risk of overwhelming your teen, or of severing ties altogether through disconnection. There is a middle road when he needs to try out independent behavior and you need to be present.

■ ■ ■

Evan is a 4.0 student. He does all the lighting for theater productions including designing and hanging the lights. He plays violin in the orchestra and stays late at school to help the faculty with their computer problems. At home his mother complains he stays up at night making noise that keeps his parents awake. He never does any chores to help them with daily tasks. She's at her wit's end and worries about her son's ability to be responsible with the people he lives among.

Adolescents believe they are unique, special even to the point of not being subject to the natural laws of the universe. A pregnant teen told me that she only had sex once and did not think she could get pregnant the first time. This same teen had a sex education class her eighth grade year, yet she had no awareness that biology does not stop to count the number of times people have intercourse.

Adolescents believe in an imaginary audience. For most adolescent girls a first-hour gym class is a fate worse than death. Clearly, five minutes after gym is not enough time to recreate the look she had worked 30-45 minutes on in front of the mirror at home. Every adolescent believes he or she is the complete focus of everyone's attention at school. To them, it seems they are performing in front of an audience all day long and are continually up for review. This is why they spends hours on the telephone trying to figure out what people think, what to wear, and how to belong. When windswept hair-dos were in fashion, one mother once told me she could always tell which way the wind was blowing by the direction her daughter's head tilted as she walked to school that day.

Needless to say, these forms of egocentrism lead to a painful time of life. Part of growing up is learning each of us is special, but not unique. There are others who have walked these paths and had these feelings before. No one is the center of the universe. Not all the people are watching us every minute. We can make a mistake and others may not have noticed or may even be forgiving if they did notice. Unfortunately, we all know adults who have yet to gain these perspectives. They are truly narcissistic and, no matter their age, still see the world only as it is connected to them; they expect daily to be the center of the universe. The good news is many people grow beyond this and do gain a more realistic perspective. Most teens only act narcissistic for a time, but are not that way as they grow up. Part of parenting the adolescent is to help her learn by asking her to be responsible for her impact on others. At the same time, you need to have great compassion for the strange lenses of egocentrism your teenager wears.

Independent and Dependent

Active alerts assert their independence from you almost at birth. They have their own ideas, and they are stubborn and persistent about them. Remember the baby who only wanted to nurse on one side? Keep in mind that overstimulation and a child's inability to self-soothe make him very dependent upon you, however. This contradiction still exists in adolescence when a teen can be threatening to defy you at one moment and cuddling with his feet or head on your lap at the next moment.

During adolescence the introverted active alerts experience this double bind most acutely and are almost hostile about their dependence. She may need you to assist her at the beginning of each new step into adulthood—how do I call the doctor's office, where do I go to get this, where do I find out about that? She may seem almost angry that you give her the steps even though she did not know them. Her anger is mostly at herself for needing help, although it seems directed at you. The extroverted active alert is still dependent upon you to recognize social cues or boundaries. He may become confused over whether these boundaries are yours or society's. He certainly does not believe he should have to follow *your* rules.

■ ■ ■

Sean had experimented with tagging (spray painting public property) in the suburb in which he lived. There, if kids were caught, they were slapped across the hand and made to serve time doing community service. One night while visiting a friend in the inner city he decided at 1 A.M. to go out and do his "artwork." However, in the inner city tagging was considered a gang activity; therefore when he was caught, the police "threw the book" at him. Suddenly Sean was a criminal facing jail time, lawyers and court. Sean was shocked and confused by the difference in approach to the law depending upon the site of the crime. He complained to me that it was unfair. I had to help him understand that once he broke the law he had handed over his fate to the legal system. The legal system handles issues differently in different parts of the city, state, or country.

At this age teens feel like they are ready to take on the world. However, there is still much they have to learn.

Active Alert Adolescents Need to Stay Active

Active alerts are still both active and alert as adolescents. By this time their activity frequently has found a direction, be it sports, acting, dancing, or something else. To help her focus and direct herself well, she will need to play her sports, dance, or whatever.

She needs a constant outlet for the creativity and activity. My experience both clinically and personally is that an active alert does better academically if she does her activity. However, balancing both extracurricular activities and academics may at times yield a grumpy person with whom to live. Her social focus will remain with her friends, which means she has little kindness left when she comes home.

Grumpiness seems to be associated not only with the stress of both activity and academics but also with the alert trait. There are a lot of new stimuli bombarding your teen during these years, both socially and sexually. Another aspect of being alert is her tendency not to recognize boundaries. An extroverted active alert can also be a dangerous risk taker.

■ ■ ■

Cory, age 15, was racing a friend on his bike to get to another friend's house. He was so focused on getting ahead that as he turned the corner he did not notice the parked car. He ran right into it. His body flew from the bike onto the car windshield. He spent the next three days in intensive care at the hospital.

Directing such risk taking to sports such as snowboarding or mountain climbing seems to provide an appropriate outlet without a high level of danger.

CRUELTY, BULLIES, AND POPULARITY

One of the cruelest periods of your child's development in my experience is middle school or junior high. By this time hormones are beginning to flow. The rules about who is popular and who is not become clear. Groups divide. The rules of popularity seem to have changed very little since my peer group was young. The most popular boys are those who grow taller faster, play sports, and are sometimes good at being clowns. The most popular girls are those who develop early, wear the right clothes, act dumb, and laugh at boy's comments. All kids want to be popular. Often the ones who are, are the cruelest, pointing out how other kids are not popular in order to make themselves seem more popular.

■ ■ ■

Laurel, a ninth grader, once told me, "I was looking down at the floor at school one day and I realized every girl had on the same Dr. Martin brown leather shoes. I realized then and there that to be popular, I had to dress like everyone else. But I liked my sense of style. I had an opinion. I didn't want to wear what everyone else did. I also realized that everyone had to laugh at the boys even though what they said was dumb. Nope, it just wasn't important enough to me to be popular."

Unfortunately, most teens are not yet strong enough in their middle school years to take Laurel's stance. During the middle school years I see child after child being abused by this process of establishing a hierarchy of popularity within the school.

■ ■ ■

In Liam's first session, he and I began to discuss Harry Potter. As he played in the sand, designing a sand world, he discovered my black gargoyle figures. He placed them in the sand, stating they were dementors like those in Harry Potter. Dementors are creatures who suck the happiness from your soul. As he created his world, he stated that his dementors were the seventh grade boys at his school. Liam was very bright, small in stature, and socially awkward, and was subjected to bullying.

It is important for the extroverted and the introverted active alert teens to learn about bullies, how they impact others, and how to deal with them. The extrovert will keep bumping into them as his ability in sports may even gain him entry into the popular crowd. The introvert may become overwhelmed and may develop a school phobia as a result of being bullied. To deal with a bully, teens must know one thing. A bully wins when their victims either get angry or hurt. If they respond with anger or sadness, a bully will come after them again. The best way to deal with a bully is to get him or her off balance by doing something they do not expect. My karate teacher once told us this story.

■ ■ ■

A woman was in bed alone one night and woke up to a
strange man standing over her. She assessed her danger
and replied, "George, you know you can't be here tonight.
This is Fred's night and he will be here any minute." The
intruder ran away.

Schools are beginning to initiate more programs to help young
adolescents learn their impact upon each other and how to
include versus exclude each of their peers. I applaud these efforts
and believe them to be as important as the academic curriculum
of middle school or junior high.

TALKING WITH YOUR ACTIVE ALERT TEEN

When your active alert teen starts talking, never act more invested
or interested in her topic than she is. If she is speaking in an
everyday, casual manner, then respond with the same
nonchalance. If she is very excited, it's okay for you to be excited.
Never be more worried, sad, happy, or excited than she is.
Remember, your active alert teen is in some ways too emotionally
connected to you. She will react against that connection by
pushing her independence. Due to that struggle within herself, if
you're too excited about something of hers, she will then turn
around and downplay or reject it.

If you want her to talk to you, ask her action questions like
who was doing what, what happened when, etc. If you can, ask
questions that help her tell the story of the evening, the event, or
the school day that can grease the wheels of speech. The
questions need to be concrete and specific. Open ended questions
like "Did you have a good day?" won't get you much information.
Also, be careful about asking her how she feels. It will come out
as part of the story, but to ask her directly may be too nosey.
Some children think parents are trying to "analyze" them at that
point (especially if Mom's a psychologist!).

The third suggestion is to not ask about personal relationships. You can ask how's so-and-so doing but don't ask if she has

broken up with him. That's none of your business unless your teen volunteers. Then, somehow, you're supposed to know.

The best time to talk is when the two of you are doing other things. Car time, when you're driving her somewhere, is excellent. While cooking together, doing the dishes, or playing cards are other great times. Usually the most important information comes out while other things are happening.

When you are with your teen, try to talk about something interesting to her, even if her music seems outrageous or you have no interest in horror films. See if you can begin to gather bits and pieces of information about those interests. That way you can at least ask semi-intelligent questions.

If you need to ask her to change a behavior, be direct and short; don't lecture. Start with "I want," as in, "I want you to stop calling your brother names." "I want you to take responsibility for your part in this problem." Many times, in dealing with your adolescent, you will want something but will have no real control over the outcome of the conversation.

Have patience. A discussion with your active alert may seem to have gone nowhere. He may have had an immediate negative response to your request and justifications. He may verbally have absolutely refused to consider what you said. Have patience. He will walk away. He will chew on the conversation for a while. Your words may gradually seep into his consciousness and you may be surprised later that he may have heeded your words and followed your advice. Don't feel you have to gain agreement from your active alert *during* a conversation. That may come later.

State your own awareness of your limitations about what you can and cannot control. That way the child does not have to do it just to prove to you that you did not have that kind of control. For instance, "I do not want you to smoke. But I recognize that I am not around you, and smoking is your choice. However, if you are smoking and I find out, I will reduce your allowance because I will not pay for cigarettes." If you are going to recognize your own limits, have clear enforceable consequences for what will happen if your teen doesn't follow through.

Most of all, as you live through these interesting times with your adolescent, I wish you luck.

SUMMARY OF RECOMMENDATIONS

- Never act more invested or interested than they are.
- Ask action questions where they can tell the story. Do not ask how they feel.
- Don't ask about personal relationships.
- Talk while doing things together, such as dishes, driving, cooking.
- Talk about what they're interested in (baseball, soccer, rap music, horror films) even if you're not interested.
- Be direct and short when saying how you wish them to behave. Start your comment with "I want" and provide clear, enforceable consequences for what will happen if they don't follow through. Recognize when the "I want" is not within your control.
- Have patience to see the results of your discussions.
- State your own awareness of your limitations about what you can and cannot control.

SOLUTIONS FOR POWER STRUGGLES

When the surge of hormones combines with active alert temperament, you are in dangerous territory. Truly you are in the middle of a hurricane.

■ ■ ■

Shelby's dad called the office. He told my assistant they needed an appointment and fast. Dad said, "Shelby turned thirteen and we need some coping mechanisms. If you don't get us in, someone in the family is going to jail. I'm not sure who—Shelby for killing us or us for killing her."

Remember, your active alert is intense, which means he does every developmental stage with more intensity. Being a parent of a teenager is difficult enough without this added element of temperament. Not that you have any choice.

The first piece we as parents must relearn or learn to a new level is how to disengage from power struggles. Jan Faull defines a power struggle in her book *Unplugging Power Struggles* as an emotional battle between parent and child over who is in control. She states you know you are in a power struggle when 1) your child does not accept your discipline; 2) the conflict comes up over and over; 3) emotions run high; 4) the parent–child relationship is slowly deteriorating; and 5) the issue never seems resolved. The first step to resolving a power struggle is to disengage emotionally. You cannot solve a problem with an active alert by out shouting her. Remember, these children have extraordinarily high needs for control. If you up the ante, your active alert will simply one up you.

To disengage emotionally you must decide first if you have to deal with the issue right away or if you can step back for a few minutes or a few hours.

■ ■ ■

Tasha broke her curfew and came in at 3 A.M. Her father and mother were frantic. They called all the places she was supposed to be, and she was not there. When she walked in the door and saw both parents waiting, she became frantic. She started screaming, "You have to tell me what my punishment is." Her mother looked at her and quietly stated, "We have been waiting several hours to see if you were safe. Now it is your turn to wait. We will talk about this in the morning."

When you or your active alert are in a power struggle you have three choices; to hold on to your stance and not negotiate, to use choices or compromise, or to let go of the issue. Ross Greene in his book *The Explosive Child* refers to prioritizing your fights. He says there are three baskets in which to place possible conflicts with your child. Basket A contains issues of safety, worth the fight. Basket B contains all the conflicts that you can use to teach your child the art of negotiation and compromise. Basket C are the conflicts that are just not worth the explosion or fight. They are meant to be let go. Parents are reticent to put many things in Basket C because they feel as if they have lost or failed. However, remember if you let go, your child has the opportunity to come forward and demonstrate your family value with his own unique flair. An active alert often will not do that until you let go. Letting go does not have to be an all or nothing phenomenon. You can let go most of the way but not completely.

■ ■ ■

Caitlin's parents were upset with the way she dressed. Every morning they fought. The school clearly had rules about display of belly buttons and spaghetti strap shirts, but this was not enough for Caitlin's mom. Finally Caitlin's mom decided to let go and let the school do its job. She told Caitlin, "You know I am concerned that the way you dress is not appropriate, but I have reconsidered. As long as you follow the dress code of your school, I will let you choose the way you dress. However, when we get together with relatives, I still get a voice in what is appropriate."

Basket B involves all the ways you can move your child from childhood to adulthood by negotiating and coming up with options that work for both the parent and child.

■ ■ ■

Skye knew that if for some reason he was going to be late for curfew, it would meet his parents needs and therefore his needs if he called before his curfew deadline, not after. He knew to tell them what was wrong and when he would arrive home. They had reached this agreement when he was late a few times after having dropped some friends home after a movie. He had explained that he had not realized the movie would go that late.

Conflict-Deadening Responses

Remember that in learning how to negotiate with an active alert, you must remain emotionally disengaged. To that end you must develop a number of conflict-deadening responses. My favorite is to simply state, "That won't work for me." Your intention is not to try to get your child to understand your position, but simply to state your position, seemingly indifferent.

Ray Levy in his book *Try and Make Me* refers to "zip it and clip it" responses. These responses are not used in negotiation, but are simply to deflect the power struggle before you move on to state the consequence of your teen's behavior. The following are examples Levy uses: "good try," "could be so," "thank you for letting me know how you are thinking (feeling) about that," "sorry you feel that way," or "I see." For instance, if your child disputes the facts in a situation you could use "good try" to indicate you don't agree. If your child challenges a rule by stating it is stupid, you could state "could be so" to agree but not change the rule. If a child blames you for his/her behavior, state "Thanks for letting me know how you are feeling about that," and administer the consequence anyway. If your child attacks your love, state that you are "sorry you feel that way." If your child accuses you of being cheap for not buying him something, agree with him by saying "it could be so." Remember, in any of these circumstances you cannot be sarcastic, but instead are agreeing with indifference or sadness so you can move on to applying the consequence.

■ ■ ■

Sadie told her mother that after the prom she and her friend would be driving to another friend's cabin to spend the night. The cabin was an hour and a half drive from the prom. It was clear to her mother that there was to be a party with no adults present, so she replied quietly, "Thanks for letting me know what you're thinking about, but I'll need to discuss this with the parents who own the cabin. Please get me their name and number."

Book of Contracts

Given that the purpose of adolescence is to move people from childhood to adulthood, it is an excellent time to help your child learn about contracts in our society. Therefore, once your child reaches adolescence, I suggest you keep an ongoing book of contracts. These contracts involve the rules of the household, curfews, responsibilities, etc. Each rule is clearly written out. The penalty or consequence for breaking the rule is clearly stated. Both parties (parent and adolescent) sign the contract. It can be in the book if it belongs to Basket A or Basket B. However, one of the rules must be that the rules are only up for negotiation once per week. This is vital for active alert teens who believe rules are constantly open for negotiation. The family can choose what day and time is most convenient for them, say, Sunday night. The reason for this structure is to prevent your active alert from trying to renegotiate the contract every time it does not fit her needs. By restricting renegotiation, you allow breathing space for parents. At the same time you give yourself time to reconsider your stance. If a rule is violated, you only refer back to the book without emotionally engaging or fighting. She agreed to the contract. It is in writing.

■ ■ ■

Alex's mother became very adept at just holding up the book of contracts when he came in late. She refused to talk, just opened up the book to the appropriate page. They both knew at that point what choice he had made.

ATTITUDES AND RESPONSIBILITIES

There are many things that are not under your control as a parent. For instance, you cannot make a toddler use the toilet, you cannot force your child to go to sleep, you cannot force your child to eat a particular food she dislikes, and finally you cannot force someone to be happy who is unhappy or mad. As you know, throughout life active alerts have negative moods. The idea is to ask them to express a modicum of respect through neutrality, yours and theirs, but you cannot ask them to have a happy attitude. In order to get your adolescent to neutrality he may need to relearn emotional regulation—not blowing up in your face, not calling out any expletive that comes to his mind, not throwing things, etc. In order to get there, you may even want to set up periodic charts for reinforcing a good attitude. Again this does not mean you require a happy, cheerful attitude, although that certainly needs encouraging. It simply means anything that is disrespectful is not allowed. Remaining respectful certainly includes the choice to separate herself from the rest of the family by going for a walk or going to her room after stating she needs to be alone for a while.

Attitude and emotions are among the many things your adolescent is learning to self-regulate or control. It is one of his ways of demonstrating how he is growing and becoming responsible. There will be ups and downs, three steps forward and two steps back. Always keep in mind that the privileges of life must be balanced with the responsibilities. If you wish your teen to become a healthy functioning adult, you must balance privilege with the level of responsibility he is demonstrating and taking upon himself. An example of this might be that obtaining his driving license is based upon keeping honor roll grades if that is within his grasp.

In America today, there is a problem with parents working hard to make sure their children have certain privileges—the wrong person is working. This often sets up an attitude of entitlement where the child thinks he deserves something, such as a car when he turns sixteen, without any awareness or concept of the responsibility that goes with such a privilege. The wrong people worked for it or paid for it.

■ ■ ■

Brady, a senior, came into my office in late April and was complaining that his parents wanted him to miss school to visit colleges so he could choose which one to attend. He was angry. Brady had not completed the college applications. His parents had submitted the applications after pleading with him to write an essay. They had spent hours doing the work. Brady insisted he was too busy to choose a college then. I explained that the deadline for the decision was May 1, and that deadline was a national deadline, not his parents' deadline. Brady was acting incredibly entitled because he had not taken on enough of the responsibility for his college selection.

On the opposite side of the continuum are the teens I get to see clinically who are asked to take on far too many responsibilities. A young girl may be asked to do all the housework and babysit her younger sibling. Although this teen is not entitled, she is being asked to grow up too fast without the support and nurturing that will lead to a healthy adult. She may quit attending school, believing she is already a grown-up without completing what she needs to finish at this stage of development.

The entitlement concern leads me to a larger issue of our society. America is a litigious society where we sue and claim others are responsible for our own choices. We take our children to the park and sue the city when they fall off the climbing apparatus. This societal modality further feeds an adolescent's belief system that someone else is responsible for their choices. We are not perfect; we all make mistakes. It is important for your active alert teen to move from an oppositional position of "Well, don't tell me what to do because then you'd better know I won't do it simply because you said so . . ." to accepting responsibility for his own choice. A teen can choose to simply react to his own parents or he can chart his own course. I have learned through the years that active alerts like to be in control. If you point out he is giving up control by simply reacting, he will work to regain his own choice. You will see it when he says, "I did my homework because I want the grade, not because you told me to."

Shame and Parenting the "Conformably Challenged"

One active alert teen recently told his mother that he thought he was "conformably challenged." I love the expression; it sums up the spirit of an active alert throughout life, but especially as a teen. To be "conformably challenged" means being disabled, having a "weak muscle" in the area of conforming. More formally stated it means having trouble conforming to the rules, procedures, or expectations of society. Another active alert teen recently told her mother the singer Ani DeFranco expressed her reality in a song where she states if you're a lion why try to be a mouse. It's wonderful to have pride in your difference, but what happens to the lion living in a mouse's world?

If an active alert is conformably challenged, where does that leave the parents? If a parent's job is to socialize, to help teach a child the social expectations of life or the social rules, and the child is challenged in this same arena, where does this leave us? The parent may be seen as constantly giving social instruction to the child. The active alert child may come to believe the parent is not understanding or is not listening. Is it that the parent is really not listening, or is it that they are trying to teach them that when lions live in society they cannot bite or roar in people's ears?

Parents of active alerts are constantly trying to teach their children they can have their emotions but they need to express them respectfully. To a concrete operational child, which all young children are, the world is black or white. "If I cannot bite or roar at you, that means I cannot have my emotions. If I cannot have my emotions, then you do not accept me." It takes a very long time to learn the idea that you can have emotions, just express them respectfully. In the meantime, no matter how hard you try, shame is inevitable. When you try to talk to your child and set boundaries for her, she believes you are saying something is not okay about her. Therefore shame, although not intended, is a by-product. We as parents can make it worse or better by our presentation, by our tone, by balancing the socialization with huge doses of appreciation, but shame is still there.

The cycle looks something like this:

A child is born whose purpose is to move independently (active alert).
In needing to move independently the child constantly challenges rules, expectations.
Parents correct child, teach her the expectations of the situation, ask her to conform.
Child feels bad, feels shame, or feels unaccepted.

Let me be clear; *parents must teach their children the rules of social interaction and basic respect.* The active alert is challenged in this area. This is clearly a weak muscle for him. His emotions are so big, the respect part is a weak muscle that needs to be strengthened. In your teaching, most of all you need to be respectful; a child cannot learn respect if he does not receive respectful treatment in return. That respectful treatment is often taught when a parent sets a boundary and walks away from a child who is yelling, cursing, or calling names. The very act of asking that you be treated respectfully, however, may be interpreted by your child as rejection or shaming.

Shame is the feeling that arises when a child believes he is being asked to abandon his "self." The child may feel as if he is being asked to abandon his self when he is being asked to express his passion respectfully. However, it is also interesting to note that the parent of the active alert child is asked by the intense needs of an active alert infant to abandon his/her self. I have already mentioned that an active alert infant catnaps, may be fussy, and in general has "high needs." To meet those needs in infancy the parent, to a more or less extent, abandons her self. So where does this leave us?

I see no way in preventing this dilemma. It seems inevitable with the cast of characters and the nature of the task. It is my hope that in teaching respect when you walk away you claim yourself, you make a statement that you will not abandon yourself. Simultaneously, you role model to your child a way for him to claim his self that is respectful. Another piece to your role modeling is your ability to choose your fights. Conformably challenged or not, it is necessary to learn to pick your fights: what is worth challenging? what is simply not worth the energy? when it would be easier to conform? An important skill to be learned by an active alert is to choose her fights—where and when is it important to claim yourself and your uniqueness. If you have to fight every battle, you are simply reacting to the world around you, letting it control you. There is a constant decision to be made about what fights are worth the energy, where can you have the impact you choose to have.

What are the signs of hope to look for in this battle? As your child grows, her thinking will become less "all or nothing." Things will not simply be as good or bad, right or wrong, for him or against him. When the active alert child begins to understand the both/ands or the continuum in the world, rejoice. This is a developmental process. The brain and ways of thinking develop as we grow and mature. Robert Kegan in his book *In Over Our Heads* talks about a third order of consciousness which involves the ability to make cross-categorical meanings and occurs in the late teens and early adulthood. A cross-categorical meaning occurs when a child can hold not only his own perspective but other people's perspectives simultaneously and has the ability to set his own perspective aside for the other's perspective. Translated, that means your teenager is no longer coming in on time simply because he knows he will be punished for being late. Instead he comes in or calls because he genuinely understands his parents would be worried if he is late. Therefore, he calls or comes in on time.

■ ■ ■

Lindsey called home from college to chastise her parents. They had gone on a trip the previous weekend. Upon returning, life became very busy and they did not call to tell her they had returned safely. The next day her message on the telephone said: "It works both ways, guys. How am I supposed to know you got back safely? You could be dead or something!"

Until your child has attained this ability, the issues of shaming and how to help her learn about the world go round and round. "I'll die my hair blue and society needs to accept me for who I am." It seems active alerts like to find ways to challenge parents or society and complain at the same time that they are not accepted. Development and maturation allow those active alerts who have been loved and respected to evolve. It gives them the opportunity to learn to not abandon themselves, to not challenge all conformity, to recognize the relief certain boundaries and structure provide, and to appreciate the heroic deeds their parents performed.

MARKS OF DIFFERENCE

Most active alerts have a sense of their difference. They may not be able to name it but they feel it. I am surprised at how many active alert boys come in with a pierced ear, even before age 10. Others wear their hair long in a school where they are the only one doing so. A certain proportion during their teen years feel the need to make that different feeling more visual. Some do this by the clothes they wear—all black, or loose jeans when tight jeans are popular. Others may need to be more shocking—blue hair, tongue piercing, lip piercing, tattoos. They seem to be challenging us all to accept them for who they are. Then they become morally outraged when they cannot find a job or get pulled aside to be frisked at the airport. An extroverted active alert likes to push these societal boundaries. "After all," they explain, "it is unjust for someone to judge me by what I wear. I could sue. I'm sure it is illegal."

The introverts will be less showy and are more likely to be too scared of needles to pierce or tattoo. The role of the parent again becomes pointing out the boundary and the consequences of their choices. When you choose to be different in a society which is struggling with difference, you need to be aware of the consequence of your choice. They can continue to be morally outraged or accept that some things are bigger than they are and they cannot control the outcome. Is it (hair, piercing . . .) worth the struggle? Learning to choose what is worth the fight is an important part of growing up.

"YOU DON'T UNDERSTAND ME"

Who has not heard this statement coming out of the mouth of their adolescent? The teens may say it when they want to do something and you say no. They may also use it when you want them to do something and they are too busy. So what does "You don't understand me" mean?

Do you take time to listen and find out what it's like to live in your teen's world? Remember that the challenges they face daily are far more than you may have confronted at the same age. When I was an adolescent growing up in a small town in the South, kids who wanted to push the edge might smoke cigarettes in the bathroom or put some Jack Daniels bourbon in their coke bottles as they drove around town. Today, children in elementary schools have access not just to alcohol and tobacco, but also to marijuana, cocaine, heroin, and acid. We know the earlier they start drug usage, the higher the likelihood teens will be addicted to a hard core drug by high school.

■ ■ ■

A young person in his first year of college was not doing well in school and asked me to help him focus. I was surprised that he was completely oblivious to how nightly pot smoking interfered with his academics. He had smoked pot all the way through high school and had still received good grades! Obviously, he was smart, however, he failed to see what skills he had missed developing while buzzing through adolescence.

Even if you do talk to your child and you think you do understand what his life is like, you still will hear the words, "You don't understand me." What does it mean? Remember that all adolescents are to a more or less extent egocentric. At this age they have a limited world-view and most do not have the ability to take a future perspective. Developing a future perspective is the ability to think about where you want to be a month from now or a year from now. What actions need to occur in the present so the future can come true? These are skills most adolescents are working on developing. Many times the clash is caused by an adult's ability to connect a path between present and future and an adolescent's inability to make that connection. Your adolescent may be overwhelmed by the present. Overwhelmed, she may be lying on the couch when you know that right now is probably the only time for her to accomplish certain family tasks. She may even need to get them done in order to receive a necessary allowance. When you suggest she get up and get to work, you hear, "You don't understand me!"

Your teen uses "You don't understand me" when the two of you disagree about an issue. He quips, "You don't understand me" as a manipulative way to try to get you to agree with him. You may simply not agree that it is all right for him to attend an unchaperoned party. He says, "You don't understand me" as a way to state he wants you to understand he is trustworthy and makes good decisions. However, as much as you may agree with him you are simply trying to say it's not his trustworthiness, but instead the mob phenomenon you do not trust.

Is There Hope?

My husband asked me as I wrote this, "Would you say there is any hope for parents?" My answer was, "Of course—active alerts develop into absolutely wonderful human beings by the time they are 20." However, I will not diminish the fact that the adolescent years are difficult. As I have always said, "Active alerts are not difficult, but parenting them is." This is even more true during their adolescence.

Over the past thirty years one piece has become clear. Active alerts are strong people with strong opinions and great passions. They need someone to love and nurture them as well as hold their "feet to the fire." No, I do not mean this in a physical way. They need parents who are secure in their strength, who do not need to yell or hit to demonstrate their strength, but who clearly say, "This is the lay of the land. You are accountable and responsible for your time here."

The field of child psychology and the many books that are currently available have yielded parents who are insecure, indecisive, and unclear how to approach their children. The parents often end up vacillating between trying to be their child's friend and yelling at their child out of fear or shame. Clearly, for these children who already have incredible emotional sensitivity and volatility, this path will not teach them how to self-regulate. Active alerts are begging for the security you provide. This is especially true of the adolescent who once again asks you to show the way with confidence, strength, and neutrality (containment of emotions). The adolescent active alerts ask you to stand toe to toe with them, love them and help them through their graduation to adulthood. It is a daunting task, but one you must be up to.

11

Active Alerts as Adults

Life can only be understood backwards;
but it must be lived forwards.

—Søren Kierkegaard
Life

When I began giving speeches about active alert children, tearful adults approached me, saying, "I thought I came here to learn about my kids. I had no idea I'd learn about myself as a child."

My clients said, "You're not only talking about my child; you're describing my wife [or husband, aunt, brother, father . . .]."

Then they asked me what I knew about active alerts as adults.

To tell you the truth, I hadn't given it much thought. Granted, I 1ad spent many years watching active alert children, but the oldest one with whom I had worked was only fourteen. I had been so engrossed watching these little people grow and helping strengthen families that I had thought only vaguely about what they would be like as adults. My curiosity was piqued.

It seems to me that many grown-ups are in a process of reclaiming who they were as children. Often this process culminates in middle age—just as people begin the second part of their life's journey.

In Murray Stein's *In Midlife,* he talks of this phenomenon:

> When the unconscious erupts at midlife, what first come most strongly to the fore are rejected pieces of personality that were left undeveloped and cast aside sometime in the past, for one reason or another. . . . Life still clings strongly to them. And actually the seeds of the future lie in these neglected figures which now return and call for restoration and attention.

I began to observe those adults who identified themselves as active alert and who claimed to have had the characteristic traits as children. I collected a pool of such individuals and began the interview process.

The interviews taught me fascinating things about active alerts as adults. Their lives have not been without pain. But given boundaries and acceptance—either as children or as adults—most of them now live rich and energetic lives.

I learned that those who were dealt negative messages throughout childhood may spend years undoing the effects of such messages. For active alert adults who grew up in a family that labeled them difficult or a problem, reclaiming—even recognizing—their undeveloped or repressed gifts may be a long, stressful process. As children, they learned to discount their wonderful energy, incredible perseverance, intuitive insights, and enormous zest for life—all of which are attributes we value in adults. On the upside, many can and do reclaim those attributes.

Other adults who grew up in an atmosphere of love, affirmation, and acceptance entered adulthood with their active alert gifts more fully intact and accessible to them.

But don't take my word for it. Read for yourself what these eloquent adults say about their lives. You may gain a window through which you can view what your child may face as an adult. Beyond that, I think these insights will affirm that what you do now as a parent will have an enormous impact on your active alert—long after he stops being a child.

WHO ARE ACTIVE ALERT ADULTS?

The insights I'd like to share with you are the results of interviews I have done with adults who might claim the descriptors active and alert. The men and women I have interviewed are a voluntary sample and they do not represent any particular group, although they include lawyers; professional athletes; people who own design, communications, real estate, or insurance companies; all kinds of teachers, including those of the learning disabled and gifted; conductors; artists and art educators; social workers; psychologists; writers; and managers in computer firms. The interviews provide glimpses of the rich variety of lives active alert adults lead.

I frequently joke with frustrated parents that their argumentative active alerts who negotiate endlessly would make great lawyers. As it turned out, that has actually happened in two instances.

In another man's case, the kinesthetic, physical energy that kept him from sitting still in grade school earned him millions of dollars as an athlete. One woman's ability to observe and to be empathic—both of which were discredited when she was a child—yielded a wonderfully talented therapist.

To accommodate their urge to control, many of these active alert adults assumed their natural leadership roles either by working on their own or as managers. They are also leaders in their communities (for example, presidents of parent-teacher organizations, committee chairs at church, or directors of community boards).

THE IMPORTANCE OF CARING

As I talked to adults about their childhood, two issues related to caring for active alert children emerged:

1. Parents of active alerts need to be accepting.
2. Parents of active alerts need to help their children see boundaries in the world around them. I call it "revealing the stoplights."

Acceptance

The adults whom I interviewed said that acceptance was the single most important quality in the caretaking they received. Simply put, accepting the child in all his positive and negative glory and understanding the multifaceted nature of this mercurial person allows him to unfold and fulfill his potential.

Adults with a parent or grandparent who understood their energy and who "believed" in them experienced less pain than those who did not receive such nurturing. They "successfully" followed occupational or career paths and felt accomplished in their work life. Because they were accepted as children, they didn't seem to have the same problems with low self-esteem as the other active alerts who had lacked acceptance throughout childhood.

By emphasizing acceptance, I in no way intend to "shame" anyone. I am simply trying to point out that in some families a pattern of dealing with children in a certain way gets handed down from great-grandparents to grandparents to parents. Overcoming these age-old patterns is no small feat. No one needs to feel shame that they did not figure out how to overcome this generational pattern.

The adults I interviewed confirmed by observations that active alerts are externally referenced when it comes to self-esteem. Many of these adults remember doing better—working hard and subsequently getting better grades—for certain teachers. When asked why they liked a certain teacher, many replied, "She knew how to relate to me better." Some described teachers who were consistent in what they asked of children and consistent in their classroom structure and teaching style. "I knew what to expect," said James. Stephanie recalled teachers who "were warm and liked me." Clearly, the connection between teacher and child was valuable. In some cases, it determined whether the school year was good or bad, interesting or boring.

Lanny did not realize the extent of the influence of her fifth- and sixth-grade teacher until she realized she had attended and graduated from the same small Eastern college as her teacher. Quite a coincidence, given that Lanny was raised in the Midwest.

Active alert adults who grew up in families where they did not feel accepted by a parent or grandparent said that the acceptance process began with a person or group other than the parents: a mentor, therapist, sibling, friend, spouse, Alcoholics Anonymous, or the Peace Corps. The accepting person was someone or some group that repeatedly affirmed the child within the adult by saying, "You are a wonderful person," "You have incredible energy," or "You are so creative." Acceptance, even late in life, meant that these adults could at last nurture themselves. Once they felt such unconditional acceptance, they began their own incredible "reparenting" journey.

The Second Path

What do I mean by "reparenting"? For active alerts, developing self-trust is the process of learning to believe in their own assessments of situations and to trust their innate intuitive abilities. Initiative is the ability to envision a course of action and follow through with it. Opposing is knowing how to recognize the need for change within a system and advocate for that change.

Self-trust • When it comes to trusting themselves, active alert adults whose special traits were not affirmed in childhood had difficult journeys. As children, they had intense feelings that their families either did not allow or were unable to validate.

These were youngsters who desperately needed to touch and examine their world. Their exploring was messy, and often people around them discounted and disparaged their learning method. As a result, they began to question their ability to assess their environments and what was happening around them. They developed self-doubt rather than self-trust.

Initiating • Because they were messy, busy (kinesthetic) learners who made a lot of noise (auditory), people often told these children directly or indirectly that they were bad, difficult, dumb, or otherwise worthless and undeserving. Active alerts learned not to initiate behaviors that would be reprimanded, which was just about everything.

Two active alert adults who grew up in shame-based families said they coped by "shutting down" their risk-taking behavior. They did not trust themselves to risk. Both women remembered spending hours daydreaming—a passive endeavor that requires no movement, initiative, or risk of disapproval.

Many who grew up in an unaccepting family still feel unworthy. These active alert adults have great difficulty initiating action to do anything nice for themselves. This became clear when I interviewed Joan, who had made major strides in recovering from a childhood of both physical and sexual abuse. As an adult she used her creativity to give magnanimously to those around her, but she was terrified at the thought of doing something for herself.

Initiation involves movement. Since these adults were criticized for their movement as children, their very being, their way of learning, was shut down. Some grew up with lots of questions and ideas about the world, but whenever they proffered problem-solving ideas, they were either punished or their ideas were disregarded. They learned not to initiate. As a result, some have had arduous career paths. They often took jobs that did not fit their being. One father had worked for many years as a laborer. He shared with me ideas he had for inventions. Sadly, he had never tried to build any of them; his dreams are trapped inside his head. With his vast knowledge of machinery, I have no doubt that some of his inventions would have worked. Now, however, he lacks the confidence needed to pursue his dreams.

Opposing • Since their movements or ideas were blocked, many active alert adults became excellent opposers, constantly blocking the ideas and actions of others. However, those who learned to block movement failed to make wise choices about when and where to oppose. As young adults, such indiscriminate opposing got them in trouble at work with fellow employees and employers.

■ ■ ■

Marty had been fired from his factory job after a decade of opposing in which he repeatedly told the company how it should operate. Luckily for him, bolstered by the loving acceptance of his spouse, he learned to initiate, risked going back to school, and became a teacher.

Within certain family systems, people could not oppose for fear of abusive retaliation. In those homes, some active alerts learned to block out their unhappy daily lives by numbing themselves with alcohol or drugs or by creating a fantasy world peopled with playmates and a loving family. When I asked them where their kinesthetic energy went, some told me that it went into fighting with their siblings—the one place where they could oppose!

Revealing the Stoplights

Teaching children to see the boundaries in the world around them is the second part of caring for an active alert child. Keep in mind that active alerts are born red light/green light color-blind. They do not see the stoplights of the world and therefore rush headlong through intersections.

As children, they may look as if they want no boundaries, structure, or order. Interestingly enough, however, the adults who described less pain-filled lives said that their parents taught them manners and how to act respectfully and appropriately. Of course, different families had different boundaries, but those families that bothered to teach about the stoplights gave their children a wonderful gift: a sense of social respect and order.

Adults who were not offered boundaries in childhood grew up rejecting limits. Susan said, "It chafed me to have boundaries." She added, "In the last year and a half I began to learn how they make me feel safe. When I heard the word 'boundary,' I used to think 'I'm outside those rules.'" Susan has learned that boundaries protect her from feedback that she doesn't have to take in. They keep her out of problems and issues in which she really has no stake. She is now using the idea of boundaries to help her to organize and order her life. "I didn't think they were necessary before, but boundaries are the very things that have helped my life move forward."

Two other things suffered when parents did not help children set boundaries: friendship and focus. Active alert children from such families were overpowering and intrusive friends. As for problems related to focus, these people tended to tackle so many projects, activities, and occupations that they had trouble satisfactorily following through on any of them.

THE ACTIVE ALERT TRAITS
IN ADULTS

As part of my interview process, I asked each adult to recall memories related to each active alert trait. I asked them whether they exhibited these traits as children, and how the traits manifest themselves now that they are adults.

Active

When asked about their activity, many laughed and told great stories. John said that his mom often tells the escalator story.

■ ■ ■

Often, when I went shopping with Mom, I'd take off in the store. I was known for touching everything. If there was a door I opened it; if there was a drawer I pulled it out. One time I went exploring behind the clerk's counter. I saw a button and pushed it. The escalator in the store stopped. It took the store manager quite a while to figure out what had happened.

Many people only remember that they were physically busy. They biked, skated, swam, ran, played, and built things. Those who had televisions remember the "draw" of the television.

Some still show their kinesthetic learning styles, saying that they stand or get up and down several times during the course of an evening meal. They describe themselves as busy both in mind and body. One is involved in four different businesses. Most report having sleep trouble: They have trouble settling into sleep and many experience insomnia.

Many active alert adults stressed the importance of learning to focus or to organize their energy. They describe how they force themselves into a discipline that keeps them from jumping from idea to idea. Most need a certain amount of downtime or time spent alone. Some provide a structure for their energy by stretching, exercising, walking, biking, building, or meditating (it's interesting to note, how, even as adults, active alerts seem to relax best by using their physical energy).

Their intense activity level has its downside. Some adults feel their lives are too diffuse in purpose. Those whose busy minds have led them on many different paths see this more as a liability than as an asset. They express a desire to be more purposeful or focused.

Anne said that her energy's greatest liability is that she moves too fast. "I always go for efficiency instead of effectiveness." She lamented this tendency and sensed that because she did not stay long with one activity or interest she lost out on something.

Alert

Mary said, "My mother says that when I was a baby, she never saw me with my eyes closed."

Tim's friends tell him he is the "most aware person" they've ever met. "No detail is too small to escape my eyes."

No detail, that is, except those related to boundaries. Active alert adults frequently described red light/green light color blindness. As Stephanie put it, "I tell people I don't understand subtle. Give me a sign, but make it neon."

As for the benefits of this trait, Mary says that her keen observations heighten her appreciation of the world. "I believe that sensitivity makes me appreciate beauty better. And food—I'm a great gourmet cook!"

Adults who are aware of their boundary issues know that they are sometimes intrusive. They tend to ask questions of friends and strangers that other people might consider too intimate or nosy.

Sometimes this is as much an advantage as a disadvantage; after all, it gets them the information they need or want. Certainly no one can accuse them of being indirect or passive manipulators. These adults use directness in their approach to others and they value others who use the same approach with them. Active alerts find small talk difficult, however. They tend to move right to the heart of the topic—often with no segue or context for their discourse. They just plunge in.

"I am a question asker," Katie told me. As a child she used to think that meant she was not as smart as her peers. Now she knows that others either don't think fast enough to create the questions or are not brazen enough to ask them.

Some active alert adults are still working on boundary issues, such as learning to let a telephone ring so that it does not intrude upon time with their children. "I even get off the toilet to answer the phone," said Jenny, rolling her eyes.

Learning to screen out some of the tension or frustration they pick up in groups at work, at home, or in voluntary committees is an important boundary. Because these adults have no boundaries, most have had to learn not to take on emotional situations at work that do not involve them.

Many report situations in which they were the scapegoat at work. These situations evolved when they picked up on group stress, vocalized it, and then became the target of it. The situation was particularly poignant for a father who offered his fellow office workers' complaints to management and was eventually fired. Such scapegoating occurs at home as well.

Some active alert adults who are parents have had to learn not to intervene when the other parent in the family is working out a problem with their child. They have a difficult time learning to back off from such situations; however, if they don't back off, their interference irritates the other parent and makes that parent appear incompetent to the child.

Children can learn this skill from parents who remind them not to intervene in situations that do not concern them. These early reminders heighten awareness about when and where to get involved. Furthermore, it is far less painful to learn this skill as a child than as an adult.

Bright

During the interviews, I realized I was talking with some extremely bright people, although one theme came through consistently: None of these people considered themselves smart. Mary graduated sixth in her class and did not realize it until graduation. Dan, an accomplished professional with graduate degrees, said, "I never thought of myself as smart because I lived next door to a 'certifiable genius.'"

This did not surprise me. The active alert children I know and love express the same sentiment. They are keenly aware of who is best in math, reading, science, or any other subject. Then they compare themselves to the excellence they observe, they come away thinking that they are not smart. Their assessment may depend, however, on what happened moments ago. Additionally, they have difficulty giving themselves credit for what they do. Even though many of them are quite accomplished, they focus on the negative—what they haven't done.

There is another way to view this negative self-perception. It was painful and shocking for many of these adults to realize that other people were not red light/green light color-blind but seemed to see a full array of colors. When struck with such a realization, they felt foolish and embarrassed about some of their past behavior. Not having the skills with which to undo their color blindness, they felt helpless to change.

Some active alert adults discover that they get caught up in "analysis paralysis" as a result of their high intelligence. They can see all the angles and options. This awareness of all the possibilities sometimes leads active alert adults to feel wishy-washy.

At the same time, these adults are keenly aware that some fights are important and, as a result, they can be passionate fighters. They have distinct opinions about what is just or fair. The same is true of the active alert children I work with. For years I have heard stories about how they entangle adults in words when they feel they have been treated "unfairly" or "unjustly."

When I address this issue with a child, we talk about how "fair" and "unfair" are sometimes related more to the child's own feelings about what is going on than to any sense of global justice. To illustrate this, we talk about the rights and wrongs of particular situations in which the child was involved. Did she need to fight or could she have accepted the situation? Was someone getting hurt? Was something stolen, or did someone simply take her favorite seat on the bus? As part of the discussion, we talk about the ethics of injustices and how to know when to stand up for what one believes in.

In the children's book *That's Not Fair*, Jane Sarnoff and Reynold Ruffins discuss justice by pointing out the difference between elephants' knees and chocolate cake. Elephants, by a quirk of nature, have four knees; other animals have only two. It is not fair or unfair. It just is. But if someone gets a huge piece of chocolate cake and another person gets a tiny sliver, well, that's injustice! And such a situation may demand protest.

Controlling

Dealing with a sense of helplessness is difficult for active alerts at any age. Many adults I interviewed remember battling with a significant other who elicited helplessness in them—a mother, a father, a sibling, a lover, an employer. Many choose fairly independent professions or find flexible roles within their profession. Others work for firms that grant them independence.

Gwen, a therapist who is known as a great group leader, said, "I'm good with a group, but I have difficulty when I have to co-lead."

Most active alerts are quite adept at pushing their agenda in groups. Being a leader and being in control can often be lonely, though.

The active alert adults I talked with discussed knowing they were different as children and feeling they didn't belong. They often blamed an external force for the loneliness or isolation they felt. One thought her family was too wealthy, one too poor; another said his family was too religious. One man had a physical disability. I think, in truth, that it was just plain too scary to attribute differentness to themselves. Children who admit they are different might relinquish any hope of ever fitting in.

Here's a fascinating observation: Those who said that they felt they didn't belong had been student council and club presidents, members of honorary societies, and student representatives. In spite of their ability to adapt well to situations, these active alert adults were always keenly aware that they were somehow different. It was almost as if they were playing roles on a stage while they stood in the distance, watching themselves perform.

Fearful

Although not all of the active alert adults recalled having fears or trouble making transitions as children, some shared poignant memories of their fears. Gerald remembers hiding under his teacher's desk in the second week of first grade. "I sat there thinking, 'What's happening in this room is not connected to what is happening outside of it, and I have no power to change what is happening here.'"

Jessi's fearfulness led her to try to be perfect and invisible to adults, especially those outside the family.

Some adults describe being fearless as children. This was especially true of the men. To a person, however, they all agreed on one thing: All were afraid of rejection—not being accepted in groups or by friends, at church and at school. Some still struggle with that issue.

Intensity

"Intensity—that's my whole thing," said Gwen. Intensity accounts for her passion, anger, and loyalty. As James said, "My intensity allows me to get the job done bigger and better." This trait contributes to active alerts' competitive sense that they must always do things better than others. Some of the adults I talked to have moved beyond competition with others, but many remain fiercely competitive with themselves.

Intensity has led these adults to develop some interesting coping mechanisms. Some are aware that they learned to use their anger to give them space. Some adults—just like the children I see in my office—had to learn not to snap and be grumpy to make someone else go away. These people now recognize that they need to take time for themselves. They have, in essence, learned to be responsible for their own emotions rather than try to place them on their loved ones or fellow employees.

Many of these adults have also spent time trying to deal with their extremist "all-or-nothing" thinking. Jenny has worked on her "urge to merge" as she calls her tendency to be either all in or all out of friendships. She has learned to disengage. She still has some very intense friendships, but she also values those that are less intimate.

All-or-nothing thinking correlates with the pull some active alerts feel toward food, alcohol, chemical, and spending addictions. They have had to work through these urgings and develop new coping strategies.

James said that he learned his sense of balance in the Peace Corps. There he was finally able to construct his own personal, ethical boundaries and get some perspective on what is and is not important.

These active alert adults seem well aware that their all-or-nothing mentality leads to perfectionism. As a group, they have high standards. Most have dealt with their perfectionist tendencies and are more gracious to themselves. Some are still in pain over this issue. To help children deal with this issue, I ask parents to look closely at their ability to admit mistakes. Often I encourage parents to give children rewards for showing them words they don't know when they read. This is a way to reinforce that it's okay to admit that you don't know something.

Attention-Hungry

"My mother summed it up," said Ann. "She wrote in my baby book that I seemed to need to be the center of attention." Other active alerts wince at the recollections that teachers constantly made remarks like "Johnny's really smart, but he seems to need a lot of attention."

Active alert adults remember how they made themselves the center of attention, be it as the president of a club in school or, in Mary's case, the only woman on a state board. At work and in the community, they assume leadership roles. As a result, many are still in the center of attention.

Trouble Getting Along with Others

Bob told me, "The great paradox of active alert adults is that they are the most gentle, loving people you'll ever meet and at the same time they are the most stubborn, hardheaded, and judgmental." This certainly has implications for getting along with others— another area of extremes.

Most active alerts either are your greatest friend or could not care less about you. When it comes to friendships, active alerts seem to have trouble striking a balance. They don't seem to know how to be an acquaintance. A friend to them is only someone who they "really know." And that knowing implies a depth of certainty that insures their friendships will endure—in spite of anything that comes along—forever. (Once again, the need for attention and approval surfaces.)

Many active alerts who grew up in families where someone accepted them do not remember difficulties in making friends; however, even those people still feel alone or different somehow. Those who lacked that early acceptance remember how painful it was learning to be a friend. Susan, who has worked hard at becoming a good friend, remembered her high school years as a time when "people thought I was loud and obnoxious." Mostly, these people recall not having friends at all. Some say that it's still difficult to keep friends.

"Most people just pass through in my life," said Tim. Tellingly, those who came from dysfunctional families said they never felt they deserved a friend.

"Friendship problems in my early years as an adult were related to my 'diarrhea of the mouth.'" said Jessi. "Not only did I ask inappropriate questions, but I shared inappropriate experiences about my life or family." Jessi went too fast too soon in friendships. After she shared her experiences, she felt ashamed, sometimes because of the way others reacted, sometimes because she felt so exposed. She's learned through the years to make choices about where, when and with whom she shares her most intimate insights and experiences.

Fluctuating Self-Esteem

Sara, who grew up without an accepting family, said "My self-esteem was terrible until I turned thirty-seven, went to therapy, and discovered I was a competent person." I listened, awestruck. During her first thirty-seven years, Sara had accomplished so many wonderful things. She'd even earned a graduate degree.

James, who described a more nurturing path, said that when he was younger he experienced many more doubts about himself. "The older I become, the more I'm able to do and the better I am able to feel about myself." (Could there be any better testimony to describe what happens when you let a kinesthetic mover move?)

Martha, troubled by the peaks and valleys of her self-esteem, worked hard to level them out. She thinks the valleys resulted from her tendency to take on responsibility and blame in situations. "Often, I did this when it was not even appropriate for me to assume such responsibility." Not until recently did she begin to check out her assumptions with others to see if her feelings of involvement and blame were valid or exaggerated.

Performer

Stephanie admitted, "Adults just loved me as a child. I knew how to please them by being polite and cute."

Mary, who is a speaker, said, "My presence is large enough to reach out to a whole group, but it is too big one-to-one."

James attributed his ability to perform to his tendency to "mask his real feelings." He said others in his corporate environment "marvel at my ability to appear calm and relaxed." Laughing, he said, "Sometimes I actually am." It appears that active alert adults have, at their disposal, a chameleon ability. If they so choose, they can adapt to many different environments. Sandra, who is in incredible personal pain and who has begun to re-parent herself, explained, "No one knows this in my office. There I play the role of a clown. I delight all those who work with me." But she has paid a high price for using her ability.

Others, who have learned that being a chameleon only makes them feel more isolated, use the ability in more congruent ways. Samantha said that singing in the choir is the onstage outlet she needs. James is well known as a knowledgeable and entertaining speaker. Clearly, his success as a presenter is related to his "stage" presence.

Empathic Ability

Stephanie's mother told her, "I used to be afraid to think things when you were young because you'd tell me what my thoughts were."

Jenny's father called her his "counselor for the defense." She remembered, "If the family had a fight going I leaped right in." Over the years, she has paid a price for this ability to tune in. She tends to pick up on and assume responsibility for all emotions around her both at home and on the job. It's almost as though empathic active alerts plug into an invisible "electrical" current of emotions. "I had to learn boundaries so I wouldn't direct all the negative attention at myself," said Jenny.

James uses his empathic ability to "go inside someone or a system." Many times he's been asked, "How do you know that?" In his view he frequently jumps from one to five and has to back up to figure out what two, three, and four are so that he can explain his conclusion to other people.

It has taken a long time for these adults to learn that other people do not always grasp what is happening as quickly as they do. Many have come to appreciate and use their intuitive abilities while recognizing the margin for error and the need to check out their leap.

"After coming to trust my intuitive sense, I have learned that it is quite accurate in an uncanny way," Mary explained. "I know when something is wrong in my business. But I often have to wait alertly until the concrete data finally comes in. That can take as long as three to six months."

The major problem with empathic ability is that it can generate a type of reactiveness in active alerts. Samantha believes that because she picks up on others' needs, she tends to "just respond" to those needs, sometimes forgetting to wait for people to ask for what they need. She thinks that this is a dysfunctional use of her skills—a perceptive insight. Samantha risks a lot with her responsiveness. She interferes in other people's issues, attempts to control situations that do not concern her, and sets herself up for scapegoating.

FAMILY MEMORIES

I asked my interviewees to describe how their families had helped and/or hurt them as children.

In many cases, these active alerts felt that their parents derived pleasure from their energy. Others felt proud that their parents cherished their ideas. Some said one or both of their parents had given them leeway to express and explore. Many believed that their families had given them a strong sense of love and said that their parents were always there when they needed help. Often, parents recognized talents in art or singing, for example, and encouraged their children to use them. Mary said that her parents always allowed her to be independent. For her, that was both a blessing and a problem. Stephen believed the active alert traits did not have as negative an impact on him as on others because his mother had been extremely clear about "good manners." He thinks her emphasis taught him boundaries and a sense of appropriate behavior.

How Families Can Hurt Active Alerts

Jenny believes that her family allowed her too much control and did not give her enough guidance about rules or boundaries. "They let me be in control of my family," she said. Others remember a parent who was too intrusive; for them, memories of the parent who opened mail or went through dresser drawers still sting.

Children also were hurt when parents did not provide a role model for handling emotions within interpersonal relationships. Many active alert adults remember feeling shamed by their parents. They report they never felt they were good enough. They trace these feelings to a variety of messages—some subtle, some direct. Sara recalled hearing, "If you loved me you wouldn't do that."

There is a twist to this issue. Adults reported feeling shame sometimes because of their parents' competence. Some adults said that their parents had been too skilled and did not let children do things for themselves. The inadvertent message to the child is either "You can't do this" or "You can't do this well enough." Others said simply that parents had seemed too perfect, too competent, and had never made mistakes.

Growing up as an active alert is never easy; however, two cornerstones—acceptance and boundaries—seem to create a stable and steady foundation on which active alerts build their lives. Those cornerstones, as we will see in chapter 12, become critically important when active alerts become parents.

12

Active Alert Adults
as Parents

Familiar acts are beautiful through love.
—Percy Bysshe Shelley
Prometheus Unbound

What happens when an active alert adult becomes a parent? It depends. Those adults who have claimed their wonderful attributes say that they are (what else?) active, alert, bright, intense, and passionate parents! As such, they delight in their own children—especially their active alerts, who are so much like themselves. These same parents are wary, however, of the pitfalls and pains of childhood. They are also keenly aware of their own traits and how those characteristics affect their parenting. In general, active alert parents work hard to create an atmosphere in which their own children can thrive.

Clearly, active alert adults who received early acceptance seem to have less difficulty in providing nurture and structure for their own children than those who are still struggling with an early lack of acceptance. Active alert adults who grew up without acceptance lived their childhood in a world of shame. From those whom I interviewed, I surmised that parenting from such a shame base worked like this: Those parents who as children were criticized for their own active alert behavior grew up to criticize their own active alert child for that same energy. The child, like his active alert parent, is "sensitive" to his environment and lacks a layer of protection. He takes on his parents' shame. As a result, he feels blamed and demeaned for being curious and energetic. That legacy gets passed along from one generation to the next.

One day in my office an active alert parent asked me how I might handle a certain behavior in her son. We discussed several options to help him move his behavior and make him responsible for his own choices. She looked at me in surprise and said, "When I do things like that there's still a disbelieving voice inside me. I wonder if he'll really get the point if I'm not yelling at him."

A voice of doubt—sometimes soft, sometimes vociferous—remains even after parents recognize that shaming did not help them as children.

I believe with all my heart that parents need to learn to nurture their children in the same way they have learned to nurture the child within themselves. How fortunate active alert adults are. They have a wonderful opportunity to undo a generational process when parenting their own active alert children.

WHEN ACTIVE ALERTS PARENT ACTIVE ALERTS

What happens when active alerts parent active alerts? First, parent and child, each unaware of their own personal boundaries, may collide. They may get too close to the other, and at some point the parent will unexpectedly say, "No" or "Stop." This can be confusing to the child, who doesn't understand what he has done.

What can parents do? They can learn about their own needs for personal space. By understanding those needs, they can teach their child how he violates boundaries, whether it be by climbing all over adults or by being too loud in the family room.

When adults refuse to be climbed on and talk about appropriate "inside" noises, they are teaching their children about boundaries. Commanding respect for their own body or physical space plants the seeds of interpersonal reciprocity.

Sometimes active alert parents find themselves teaching their child something they are just beginning to grasp themselves. Some of the parents I see in my office are still learning about the appropriate expression of anger. As children, they learned to suppress and deny anger. As parents, they find they are no longer able to "stuff" their anger, but because they have never had a chance to practice expressing anger, they find their reactions are explosive, unpredictable, and frightening. Some are just beginning to make choices about when and how to oppose and to find a constructive use of their independent spirit. Others are starting to learn how to keep their energy focused. Still others are wondering how they will teach their children to be good friends when they are only now understanding what that means themselves.

One thing is a struggle for all parents who are active alerts: allowing their children to move at their own pace and to interrupt busy adult agendas. Sara, an active alert mom, said, "Making space for the busyness of a child in my own orbit has been a challenge," or, as her six-year-old active alert son Tim once said to her, "My busy is bugging your busy." As we all know, the fine art of parenting is to some extent the art of handling interruptions. Many active alert adults who have active alert children tell me, "Now I begin to understand how difficult I was for my own mother."

Susan summed up her parenting issues in the following way: "Besides the obvious boundary issues we run into, there's the issue that we're both alert and kinesthetic. That means I become overstimulated from being touched by my son and by having his noise around me. Faced with his constant stimulus bombardment, I sometimes just get deadened—I can't respond. I use my intensity to hold a focus when confronted with my son's constant inter- ruptions. But sometimes I get scattered and then my need for control gets going." In this way, competition and power struggles accelerated over whose needs were most important.

Pam said that parenting was "the most influential thing that's ever happened to me." She had her active alert child at thirty-five and said, "I always told everyone I was afraid to have a child for fear he would be like me." She now believes that her traits provided her with wonderful coping skills. Among the most beneficial are her energy, her ability to organize, and her openness to ideas. She is still working on trusting herself and feeling that she is making the right choices in her parenting.

I think this lack of trust is related to the fact that active alerts grow up knowing that they are different. It's the old adage about disliking in others what we perceive is the negative about ourselves.

13

Questions, Please

We're near the end—an end that I hope will be a beginning for you and your family. In this chapter I've answered the questions I am most frequently asked after I give speeches.

- When do you first know your child is active alert?

By the time their infants are six months old, most parents suspect their child is more active and alert than other babies. Because I do not like to label children, however, I tend to avoid calling them active alert until they are at least three years old. Partly that is because *all* two-year-olds look active alert!

Always remember that in using the term "active alert," I am not telling children who they are, who they must be, or who they will continue to be throughout their lives. Rather, the term provides a loving description of behavior that both perplexes and frustrates many parents. The name is a positive way for parents to frame or think about their child and her unique gifts.

- How can I tell whether my child is an active alert or has an attention deficit disorder?

Some of the behaviors that active alerts exhibit are the same indicators used to diagnose an attention deficit hyperactivity disorder (ADHD). But there is a difference. What distinguishes active alert behavior from attention deficit behavior is the duration and level of that behavior. A child who has an attention deficit exhibits behavior so extreme that it can only derive from a physiological problem or deficit. Intensity of and inability to control behavior in school and at home are good ways to distinguish deficit from nondeficit behavior.

How long the behavior lasts is another telling factor. Active alertness is noticeable in infancy and continues throughout one's life. As an active alert child grows older, he may develop coping methods to help him to fit into the world, but his basic temperament remains the same. Because of his temperament, stresses such as divorce or death of a loved one may intensify the traits. If the stresses are attended to, however, functioning improves. Thus, an active alert's behavior does not remain extreme indefinitely.

To qualify for clinical diagnosis as having ADHD, a child must first exhibit dysfunctional behavior for at least twelve months. Additionally, these behavior problems must place her in the *top 3 to 5 percent* of her age group and sex on child behavior rating scales. The onset of an attention deficit disorder occurs by age five years, eleven months, with the average diagnosis at about age eight, or the third grade. The behavior problems must occur at least 50 percent of the time in both home and school settings.

Since attention deficit means that a child has trouble with inattention, impulsivity, hyperactivity, disorganization, and low stress tolerance, I understand how it can be confused with being active alert and why parents are uncertain about assessing intensity on their own. Remember, active alerts can pay attention within developmentally appropriate norms for children their age.

A final key indicator is that many active alerts do not have problems at school. More often, they become the anxious kids in the corner, struggling to quietly overcome fears. Some children, however, do develop behavior problems when their learning style is poorly matched to the environment. In the end, you may not know if your child has attention deficit without testing by a team that includes professionals—psychologists, neurologists, teachers, and you—all working together. The testing process should consist of evaluations from home and school, a clinical interview with both the child and the parents, and performance tests for the child.

- Are there parenting techniques that are used more often by the parent of an introverted active alert versus an extroverted active alert?

Your child's nature depends on the level of her worry and whether that is internalized or externalized. For each type child different parenting techniques are useful.

Coyote Man

"Coyote Man" is particularly useful with introverted active alert children. This is a fictitious character in Native American mythology, in which the coyote is a trickster.

The introverted active alert is fearful. Sometimes she is afraid you will not pick her up after school even though you have never missed a pick-up. Sometimes she has other fears. I tell such a child that Coyote Man often visits and whispers in her ears, saying, "Your mother is going to leave you at school today. You will have to spend the night there." I tell the child how important it is to recognize the voice of Coyote Man, to know he is trying to play tricks on her. She has to learn to say, "I know your voice. You are Coyote Man. You are a liar. I will not believe you."

Children have to learn the difference between a real fear, which is prompting them to think and act safely, and the voice of Coyote Man, who is lying. A child about to cross the street must look both ways first because accidents do happen. However, there is no history that a mother will not pick up her child, so the fear is unrealistic.

Red, Yellow, and Green Lights

Red, yellow, and green stoplights made of colored construction paper work well for extroverted active alert children. These concrete symbols can let an active alert know when his energy level is appropriate or moving out of control.

Place two black circles over the colors not relevant at the moment. For example, expose the green circle if the child's (or children's) energy is reasonable, children are getting along, and the noise level is acceptable. Expose the yellow if children are starting to get out of hand. Expose the red when everyone needs to stop and calm down. As you drive around, you can emphasize the importance of the stoplights and their role in keeping people safe. Tell your active alert that the paper symbols used at home have the same purpose.

- Is being active alert genetically or physiologically based?

Once again, I would like to preface my answer: I am neither a geneticist nor a physiologist. As I took family histories over the years, however, parents often described others in their family of origin who could have been active alert. Besides my intuitive response, I think we see the best data to support an inter-generational transfer pattern in Stephen Suomi's work with rhesus monkeys.

Suomi is a psychologist and the director of an outdoor laboratory funded by the National Institute of Child Health and Human Development (NICHD) and the National Institute of Mental Health (NIMH). According to Suomi, in his article in *Perinatal Development: A Psychobiological Perspective*, about 20 percent of his 200 monkeys are genetically predisposed to separation difficulties and stress when faced with new stimuli. Suomi has developed neonatal tests for early detection of these tendencies in the monkeys he calls "uptight monkeys."

Uptight monkeys are seldom born to "non-uptight" parents. However, Suomi does not believe that being uptight is learned behavior, since the monkeys he studies are reared away from their birth parents, yet continue to exhibit anxieties.

When they are in stable, familiar environments, uptight monkeys are not much different from non-uptight monkeys, although Suomi describes them as having difficult temperaments. Additionally, they have different sleep patterns and spend more of their sleep time in irritated sleep.

When faced either with separation from their parents or with new stimuli, these monkeys have higher levels of ACTH (adrenocorticotropic hormone) and cortisol and reduced levels of CSF (cerebral spiral fluid) norepinephrine in their blood. These differences indicate a clear physiological disparity between uptight monkeys and non-uptight monkeys. Moreover, the heart rate in uptight monkeys remains elevated longer than that of non-uptight monkeys after the stressor is first introduced.

Suomi has used imipramine, an antidepressant, as well as environmental changes to lower the high-stress response in his monkeys; however, environmental changes seem to be the most effective way to handle their stress. Environmental restructuring includes surrounding uptight monkeys with friendly, outgoing peers and nurturing foster grandparent or parent. The foster parent aids these monkeys in learning coping strategies. The effects of such changes are longer lasting than those achieved with drugs, although Suomi believes a combination of the two treatments works best with his monkeys.

It seems to me that Suomi is doing with monkeys what I've been suggesting parents do with their human "monkeys"—and to good effect! Suomi says that when these monkeys grow up with nurturing mothers, they often respond even better than their non-uptight peers and become leaders in their group.

- Do active alert children exhibit all eleven characteristics?

The children I first began working with exhibited all of the characteristics. Subsequently, many parents have approached me saying, "My child is everything but . . ."

I note a real difference between active alert children and other children—the "sure and steadies." The latter are more forgiving and offer parents more latitude. Thus, you don't have to parent all children in the manner I've suggested for active alerts. With sure and steadies, you have many more parenting options because they have good internal coping resources. The active alert requires the thoughtful, consistent, and intentional parenting I describe in this book. The suggestions in the preceding chapters reflect much of what I believe works well with them.

- You mention that active alert children are externally referenced. Does this affect how they feel shame?

Shame is a specific, clinical term in my field. Shame-filled people feel they are inherently bad. For them, that feeling goes far beyond thinking they have made a mistake. They feel exposed. They know their behavior is bad and they believe they are bad people. Furthermore, they are certain everyone knows it.

Because active alerts are painfully aware of the external world, they derive most of their self-evaluation from others. They are, in essence, always conscious of their mistakes and frequently feel they are being judged. They have few internal resources and little knowledge of their wonderful aspects with which to balance the sense of external judgments.

Over the years, I have been privileged to work with incredible, positive, nonshaming parents. And still, their children are affected by shame. I have watched their children make one mistake, overgeneralize its importance, and before my eyes, decide they are worthless.

What is the challenge for parents of such children? Help the child see her incredible competence and wonderful gifts. Assist the child in developing internal coping resources so that when she makes mistakes or doesn't know all the answers, she will still feel okay about herself.

I lovingly joke that active alerts are born shame-based. They are autonomy masters who want to do things on their own, in their own way. They frequently make mistakes. As a result, they deal with doubt and shame more often than many of us. They must learn to balance autonomy and shame. Erik Erikson, a renowned Harvard developmentalist, suggests that finding this balance is the core issue of a two-year-old. For the active alert, it is the issue of his life!

- We'd like to get a puppy. How do active alert children respond to them?

In my office, the subject of puppies comes up a lot! Puppies and active alert children seem to have the same endless energy. Picture your child's wonderfully active energy. Picture a puppy. Do they look the same rolling around the living room or running across the backyard?

Whether the dog excites the child or the child excites the dog, introducing puppies into your family life may create extra demands that no one in your family needs.

The presence of a puppy is not a good arena in which a child can learn about boundaries. In fact, the dog's wild behavior rewards the active alert child's lack of boundary awareness. In the presence of a wagging, jumping puppy, the child may never learn how to treat animals with gentle consistency. In the midst of all the confusion, your child may not understand when the dog is distressed and might get nipped in retaliation.

In general, active alert children love animals, but it may be best to wait until your child has established a sense of boundaries before bringing a puppy into the family. I offer one other caution: Be alert to changes in behavior in older pets who were part of the family before the child arrived. If those animals are gentle, they will set their own limits or, when necessary, remove themselves from the child. Jealous dogs may retaliate against the child who has invaded their territory.

- You noted that swimming is a good individual sport for the active alert child. Why? What should I consider when choosing a sport?

Swimming is one of many individual sports that work well for active alerts. I like it because it teaches a life skill involving safety while providing an outlet for energy. You can start swimming with your baby before she is a year old. Swimming provides positive structured time for both you and your active alert infant.

What is the key to success? Eliminate some of the overly stimulating variables. If possible, check out area hospitals or clubs to determine how warm the pool is. Many hospitals offer lessons in their therapeutic warm pools. By eliminating the factor of cold water, you increase the chances that your child will relax in a new environment.

Try to find a teacher who understands children. Many summer lessons are taught by college-age water safety instructors who may know a lot about swimming but little about differences among children. If you find an instructor with whom your child feels comfortable, see if he or she will teach your child for several sessions. You will not only get an understanding teacher but also eliminate transitions between terms.

Swimming is only one way to focus your child's physical energy. Giving physical energy a purpose and release helps to prevent a frenzied child. In the elementary-school years gymnastics, skiing, skating, karate, and dance are all good choices. You can extend the benefits of these focused activities at home by helping your child practice skills learned in class. Or you can provide other less formal activities, such as digging a garden, mopping a floor, or building a doghouse or fort. The possibilities are endless—and who knows, you might get some work done for you. I know one child who loves to scrub the bathroom sink and tub!

- Are active alert children more likely to be abused than other children?

Research about child abuse indicates that abused children are often viewed as "different." Clearly, active alerts are different. They feel different. They act different. As one adult who was an abused child put it, "I was always being told I was too everything— too noisy, too active, too sensitive . . ."

That tendency to be "too everything" combined with active alerts' lack of boundary awareness makes them ideal targets in a dysfunctional or disabled family.

Active alerts explore and get into things they are not supposed to touch. They don't accept rules. They persist, coming back again and again, trying to change their parents' minds. Even for a nonabusive parent, on some days such behavior is, at best, difficult.

Abusive parents may use active alerts as a release for their rage. They may think that their child's behavior justifies such treatment. I believe that in some instances, the empathic active alert may believe it's his job to release the parents' rage or anger. What a dangerous role to assume!

The only data I have to support my assumptions are clinical observation. But it has been my experience that the active alert child's temperament can render him a natural scapegoat for families.

- Are most active alerts oldest or only children?

This question assumes that active alert children are somehow created by anxious first-time mothers. As a psychologist, I could never deny that environment has an impact on the child. My work with active alerts focuses on temperament that is present at birth, however. Being active alert is a temperament-based phenomenon. I have met active alerts who are only children, firstborns, second, third, fourth, fifth, or sixth children. My caseloads do not reflect a prevalence of any one birth-order position.

Certainly, some children do form anxious attachments to their mothers. These children may sleep poorly and overstimulate easily. But given the active alert temperament, I am unclear where the anxious attachment begins—with the mother or the child.

From a therapeutic standpoint, assessing who or what is at fault would only add to the shame and distress of the parents who come to my office. My clients and I do not discuss blame, therefore, we discuss the phenomenon of temperament. That frees us to get on with the business of strengthening families.

- Can a family have more than one active alert child?

If you believe, as I do, that this phenomenon has a genetic basis, asking this question is a bit like wondering if there can be more than one redhead in a family.

I have seen some families with two active alert children. These families need a lot of support from our culture. As much as I love active alerts, I know that they demand high-energy parenting.

Unfortunately, when a family has two children who are active alerts, friends, relatives, and neighbors are more likely to assume—and to communicate their assumptions—that the parents are to blame for the traits. As a result, the families who could use the most support are caught up even more in the shame-blame cycle and may not receive the help they need.

Let me conclude on an optimistic note. Most families with active alerts have only one. The other children in those families tend to be "sure and steady." (That does not mean, however, that families can't have more than one redhead!)

- Wouldn't active alerts obey better if they just had a good spanking?

Ah, yes—the perennial question. Since this is the one question that parents of active alerts hear most often, I would like to address it.

I do not believe that spanking is an effective way to teach an active alert child anything. A father of four who came to see me put it quite succinctly: "I believe in spanking. It works with my other three. Somehow, it doesn't work with my second child. She never seems to learn. So I'm here to figure out what else we can do with her." I know of two reasons why spanking is an ineffective discipline tool for active alert children.

First, active alerts have no boundary awareness. One of the most important aspects of boundaries deals with how people touch one another. If you spank a child, you violate his physical boundary. Thus, you make it impossible to teach him to respect other people's physical boundaries.

Children learn far more from what we do than from what we say. Some active alerts tend to have social problems with bossiness and aggression. Those who have been spanked have much greater trouble learning to use power in nonphysical ways. They don't seem to understand that they can use verbal power rather than physical assault with people who are doing something they don't like.

Second, I do not like spanking because of the two ways active alerts respond to it. They yell and scream as if they've been spanked seventy times harder than they actually were. The performance they put on makes parents feel worse than they ever did about the child's misbehavior. They therefore often succeed in changing the focus from their own to their parents' behavior. By doing so, they don't learn what you wanted to teach them. Instead, they increase their ability to shift responsibility away from themselves.

Active alerts may react in a different way when the yelling and screaming strategy is not effective. They fix their parents with an "I don't care" or "You won't hurt me" look. In effect, they say, "I am not in this relationship with you. I will not let you touch me," and the touch they are alluding to is not physical but relational.

You have violated the connection that allows you to teach your child. Do not break that connection, for if you do, you lose the essence of parenting—what it's all about.

Rather than risk such a tremendous loss, I encourage parents to look at options. At your disposal are a million and one tricks and methods that have evolved over time. Each is an effective tool to use in teaching the lessons your child needs to learn.

- Are there other learning disabilities or differences that I should evaluate when considering an active alert temperament?

Being active and alert is a particular temperament. Some children who have this temperament also have learning differences, or learning disabilities as our society has come to label them. These differences may be an unusual pencil grip, an auditory processing disorder (often along with chronic ear infections), nonverbal learning disorder, or attention deficit disorder. You may learn more about learning differences in Mel Levine, M.D., *A Mind at a Time.* Keep in mind that active alerts may have none of these problems, or they may need help with something, just as any other child, active alert or not, might.

Some active alerts (and other children) suffer from a sensory integration dysfunction. They seem unable to analyze, organize, and connect—or integrate—sensory messages. Sensory integration therapy can be very useful for these children. To read more about this problem, look at Carol Stock Kranowitz's *The Out-of-Sync Child.*

- Are active alerts more prone to chemical dependency?

I have always thought they were. Partly because they are so externally referenced and partly because they have no boundaries, I believe that the wrong peer group could quickly move them from experimentation to abuse.

There is another aspect to this question: pain. Active alerts are sensitive and might choose drugs to numb their pain—the pain of negative feedback, of feeling different.

What I thought was true about active alerts and chemical dependency was just a hunch until I reviewed my caseload. I noted many families with histories of addiction. Even though the parents I see are not abusing chemicals, most come from families with backgrounds that reflect addiction to, first and foremost chemicals, and to a lesser degree, work, sex, and religion.

My assumption was further validated when I interviewed adult active alerts. (See chapter 12; however, let me remind you that not everyone I interviewed had been chemically dependent.) One of the adults I talked with was a recovering alcoholic. When I showed him the active alert traits, he said, "I don't know if I'm active alert. Those traits sure fit me, but I always thought that's what an alcoholic was." I explained that the list was based on observations of how certain children grow, not on studies of alcoholics.

Further evidence came to light when I read John Madden's *Adaptation, Learning and Affect,* in which Stephen Suomi's work with rhesus monkeys is discussed (see the question on page 267). Suomi's findings support my conclusions. Based on his research, he states that "uptight monkeys" are more prone to anxiety and panic attacks and have a higher potential for substance abuse. Suomi has tested this supposition in the following way: He placed a container of alcohol and NutraSweet in the cages with his "uptight" and "non-uptight" monkeys. There seemed to be no difference in consumption during stable times, but when there was a challenge or change, the uptight monkeys "hit the sauce."

14

Conclusion

In Beverly Cleary's book Ramona and Her Mother, *Ramona Quimby is distressed by neighbors who say that toddler Willa Jean is Ramona all over again. How insulting to be compared to that messy show-off Willa Jean—the same Willa Jean who attended the Quimbys' New Year's brunch and commanded center stage, running around the room, pulling tissues from the tissue box. Ramona pensively wonders why her mother proudly said she couldn't get along without Beezus, Ramona's older sister, but never says she couldn't get along without Ramona.*

A ctive alerts are different, but they do not look different. They want to be movers, but their movement is often at cross-purposes with society. Except for labels that no one would care to claim, active alerts have gone unnamed until now. I think it is time to give them a name that lifts up the gifts they bring to the world and allows them—indeed, all of us—to value the music of their souls.

I was awestruck by the talent and character of the adults who consented to be interviewed for this book. Clearly, given acceptance and boundaries, these people do fulfill their enormous potential.

I hope that the suggestions in this book help to begin a more constructive process for parenting these wonderful youngsters, so that active alert children growing up today can proudly own their gifts and talents throughout their lives.

Resources and Readings

Adults

Amen, Daniel G. *Images into the Mind: A Radical New Look at Understanding and Changing Behavior.* Newport Beach, California: Mindworks Press, 1997.

Ames, Louise B. *He Hit Me First: When Brothers and Sisters Fight.* New York: Warner Books, 1989.

Armstrong, Thomas. *Awakening Your Child's Natural Genius.* New York: Jeremy Tarcher, Inc., 1991.

———. *In Their Own Way.* Rev. ed. New York: Jeremy Tarcher, Inc., 2000.

———. *The Myth of the ADD Child: 50 Ways to Improve Your Child's Behavior and Attention Span Without Drugs, Labels or Coercion.* New York: Plume, 1997.

Attwood, Tony. *Asperger's Syndrome: A Guide for Parents and Professionals.* London, England: Jessica Kingsley Pub., 1998.

Balter, Lawrence. *Dr. Balter's Child Sense.* New York: Poseiden Press, 1985. OP*

———. *Who's in Control?* New York: Poseiden Press, 1989. OP

Barbe, Walter B. *Growing Up Learning.* Washington, D.C.: Acropolis Books Ltd., 1985. OP

Barbe, Walter, and Raymond Swassing. *Teaching Through Modality Strength Concepts and Practices.* Columbus, Ohio: Zaner-Bloser, 1979. OP

Brazelton, T. Berry. *Infants and Mothers.* Rev. ed. New York: Delacorte Press, 1994.

Calladine, Carole and Andrew Calladine. *Raising Brothers and Sisters Without Raising the Roof.* Minneapolis: Winston, 1979.

Carbo, Marie, Rita Dunn, and Kenneth Dunn. *Teaching Students to Read Through Their Individual Learning Styles.* Needham Heights, Massachusetts: Allyn & Bacon, 1986.

Carey, William and Sean McDevitt. *Coping with Children's Temperament: A Guide for Professionals.* New York: Basic Books, 1995.

Chess, Stella and Alexander Thomas. *Know Your Child: An Authoritative Guide for Today's Parents.* 1987. Reprint, New York: Basic Books, 1989. OP

———. *Temperament in Clinical Practice.* 1986. Reprint, New York: Guilford Press, 1995.

Clarke, Jean Illsley and Connie Dawson. *Growing Up Again.* 2nd ed. Center City, Minnesota: Hazelden Information Education, 1998.

———. *Self-Esteem: A Family-Affair.* Rev. ed. Center City, Minnesota: Hazelden Information Education, 1998.

Clarke, Jean Illsley. *Time In: When Time Out Doesn't Work.* Seattle, Washington: Parenting Press, Inc., 1999.

Constantine, Larry L. *Family Paradigms.* New York: Guilford Press, 1986.

Doherty, William. *Take Back Your Kids: Confident Parenting in Turbulant Times.* Notre Dame, Indiana: Sorin Books, 2000.

Dunn, Rita and Kenneth Dunn. *Teaching Students Through Their Individual Learning Styles: A Practical Approach.* Upper Saddle River, New Jersey: Prentice Hall, 1978. OP

Dunn, Rita, Kenneth Dunn, and Gary E. Price. *The Learning Style Inventory.* Price Systems, Box 1818, Lawrence, Kansas 66044 (a service).

Elkind, David and R. Bowen. "Imaginary Audience Behavior in Children and Adolescents." *Developmental Psychology,* 1979, 15:38-44.

OP* = out of print

Erikson, Erik. *Childhood and Society.* 1950. Reissue, New York: W. W. Norton & Co., 1993.

Faber, Adele and Elaine Mazlish. *How to Talk So Kids Will Listen and Listen So Kids Will Talk.* 1982. Reprint, New York: Avon Books, 1995.

———. *Siblings Without Rivalry.* Expanded ed. New York: Avon Books, 1998.

Faull, Jan. *Unplugging Power Struggles: Resolving Emotional Battles with Your Kids, Ages 2 to 10.* Seattle, Washington: Parenting Press, Inc., 2000.

Greene, Ross. *The Explosive Child: A New Approach for Understanding and Parenting Easily Frustrated, Chronically Inflexible Children.* 2nd ed. New York: HarperCollins, 2001.

Greenspan, Stanley and Jacqueline Simon. *The Challenging Child: Understanding, Raising, and Enjoying the Five "Difficult" Types of Children.* Massachusetts: Perseus Publishing, 1996.

Gurian, Michael. *Boys and Girls Learn Differently.* San Francisco: Jossey-Bass, 2001.

Haerle, Tracy. *Children with Tourette's Syndrome: A Parent's Guide.* Bethesda, Maryland: Woodbine House, 1992.

Harris, Scott O. and Edward N. Reynolds. *When Growing Up Hurts Too Much: A Parent's Guide to Knowing When and How to Choose a Therapist for Your Teenager.* 1990. Reprint, Maryland: Lexington Books, 1992.

Hartmann, Thom. *Attention Deficit Disorder: A Different Perception.* Rev. ed. Grass Valley, California: Underwood Books, 1997.

Kagan, Jerome. *Galen's Prophecy: Temperament in Human Nature.* 1994. Reprint, New York: Basic Books, 1997.

Kantor, David and William Lehr. *Inside the Family: Toward a Theory of Family Process.* San Francisco: Jossey-Bass, 1975. OP

Kegan, Robert. *In Over Our Heads: The Mental Demands of Modern Life.* Boston, Massachusetts: Belknap Press, 1995.

Kranowitz, Carol Stock. *The Out-of-Sync Child: Recognizing and Coping with Sensory Integration Dysfunction.* New York: Perigee, 1998.

Kurcinka, Mary Sheedy. *Kids, Parents, and Power Struggles: Winning for a Lifetime.* New York: Quill, 2001.

———. *Raising Your Spirited Child: A Guide for Parents Whose Child Is More Intense, Sensitive, Perceptive, Persistent, Energetic.* 1991. Reprint, New York: Perennial, 1992.

Lerner, Harriet Goldhor. *The Dance of Anger.* 1989. Reissued, New York: HarperCollins, 1997.

Levine, Mel. *A Mind at a Time.* New York: Simon & Schuster, 2002.

Levy, Ray and Bill O'Hanlon. *Try and Make Me!* Emmaus, Pennsylvania: Rodale Press, 2002.

Mason, Paul and Randi Kreger. *Stop Walking on Eggshells: Coping When Someone You Care About Has Borderline Personality Disorder.* Oakland, California: New Harbinger Publications, 1998

Masters, M. Gay, Nancy Stecker, and Jacke Kate. *Central Auditory Processing Disorders: Mostly Management.* Needham Heights, Massachusetts: Allyn & Bacon, 1998.

Papolos, Demitri and Janice Papolos. *The Bipolar Child.* New York: Broadway Books, 2002.

Pearson, Carol. *The Hero Within.* 3rd ed. San Francisco: Harper San Francisco, 1998.

Rapp, Doris J. *Is This Your Child? Discovering and Treating Unrecognized Allergies.* New York: William Morrow, 1992.

Reit, Seymour. *Sibling Rivalry.* New York: Ballantine, 1988.

Satir, Virginia. *New Peoplemaking.* 2nd ed. Palo Alto, California: Science and Behavior Books, 1988.

Schaub, Janette. *Your Kid Has ADHD, Now What?* Minneapolis: Beaver's Pond Press, 1998.

Simmons, Rachel. *Odd Girl Out: The Hidden Culture of Aggression in Girls.* New York: Harcourt Brace, 2002.

Suomi, Stephen. "Genetic and Material Contributions to Individual Differences in Rhesus Monkey Biobehavioral Development." In *Perinatal Development: A Psychobiological Perspective,* edited by N. Krasegor, E. Blass, M. Hofer, and W. Smotherman. San Diego, California: Academic Press, 1987.

———. "Primate Separation Models of Affective Disorders." In *Adaptation, Learning and Affect,* edited by John Madden. Athens, Ohio: Raven Press, 1990.

Swift, Madelyn. *Discipline for Life: Getting it Right with Children.* 3rd ed. South Lake, Texas: Childright, 1999.

Taffel, Ron. *Getting Through to Difficult Kids and Parents.* New York: Guilford, 2000.

Whitney, Rondalyn Varney. *Bridging the Gap: Raising a Child with Nonverbal Learning Disorder.* New York: Perigee, 2002.

Wold, Anthony. *Get Out of My Life but First Could You Drive Me and Cheryl to the Mall?* Revised. New York: Farrer Straus & Giroux, 2002.

Children

Brett, Doris. *Annie Stories.* New York: Workman Publishing, 1988.

Brown, Margaret Wise. *The Runaway Bunny.* 1942. Reissue, New York: HarperCollins Juvenile Books, 1974.

Blume, Judy. *The Pain and the Great One.* 1974. Reprint, New York: Yearling, 1985.

Cleary, Beverly. *Ramona and Her Mother.* 1979. Reprint. New York: HarperCollins Publishers, 2002.

Crary, Elizabeth. *Children's Problem Solving Series.* Seattle, Washington: Parenting Press, Inc., 1996.

Doleski, Teddi. *The Hurt.* New Jersey: Paulist Press, 1988.

Duncan, Riana. *When Emily Woke Up Angry.* New York: Barron's, 1989.

Jousse, Barbara M. *Mama, Do You Love Me?* California: Chronicle Books, 1991.

Levine, Mel. *All Kinds of Minds.* Cambridge, Massachusetts: Educator's Publishing Service, 1992.

Mayer, Mercer. *What Do You Do with a Kangaroo?* 1973. Reissue, New York: Scholastic Trade, 1987.

Montgomery, Lucy Maud. *Anne of Green Gables.* Reprint. New York: Bantam Doubleday Dell Publishers, 1997.

Munsch, Robert. *Paper Bag Princess.* Toronto, Canada: Annick Press Ltd., 1988.

Osofsky, Audrey. *Dreamcatcher.* New York: Orchard Books, 1992.

Palmer, Pat. *Liking Myself.* California: Impact Publishers, 1978. OP

Rey, H. A. *Curious George* books. Boston, Massachusetts: Houghton Mifflin Co., 1973.

Seuss, Dr., and Roy McKie. *My Book About Me.* New York: Random House, 1969.

Wilder, Laura Ingalls. *Little House on the Prairie* books. New York: Harper and Row, 1973.

Index

For a complete catalogue of books
published by Parenting Press,
please contact:

Parenting Press, Inc.
P.O. Box 75267
Seattle, Washington 98175
Toll free 1-800-992-6657

In Canada, contact:
Raincoast Books Distribution Company
Vancouver, B.C.
www.Raincoast.com

For weekly parenting tips,
book descriptions, author information,
and more, please visit:

www.ParentingPress.com